For Dorothy

Published by HarperCollins Publishers Ltd

First edition

HarperCollins Publishers Ltd
2 Bloor Street East, 20th Floor
Toronto, Ontario, Canada
M4W 1A8

www.harpercollins.ca

Caption text: Hayley Caldwell, Steve Ducharme, Elizabeth Fraser, Kristy Hoffman, Danelle Cloutier, Jessica Knapp, Mark Collin Reid, Mark Schram.
Copyediting and proofing: Stacey Cameron, Phil Koch, Nelle Oosterom, Danelle Cloutier, Barbara Kamienski.

Library and Archives Canada Cataloguing in Publication
information is available upon request

www.canadashistory.ca

ISBN 978-1-44342-015-0

Printed and bound in Canada
FR 9 8 7 6 5 4 3 2 1

Contents

Cavalry and Tanks at Arras, 1918,
by Alfred Theodore Joseph Bastien.

Foreword

DON NEWMAN

It's a question that continues to challenge historians, writers, and students: What is real history? Is it the grand, sweeping narratives that chronicle the major events that shaped our world? Or is it the multitude of personal tales that together weave the fabric of humanity's story?

This ongoing debate was on my mind as I approached *Canada's Great War Album*, published by Canada's History Society and HarperCollins Canada to commemorate the one hundredth anniversary of the beginning of the First World War. I wondered: Will *Canada's Great War Album* settle this age-old argument, or exacerbate it?

On one hand, *Canada's Great War Album* offers wonderful accounts, by some of the country's best and most respected historians, of Canada's contributions to the First World War, describing on the macro scale how the fighting unfolded and Canada's role in the conflict.

But *Canada's Great War Album* tells us so much more: it brings us personal accounts of the lives of the Canadians who fought in the trenches, at sea, and in the air, as well as those who served in nursing stations tending the wounded. It puts a human face on the wives and children who kept the home fires burning back in Canada—the family members who constantly feared receiving news from the front that their loved one had been wounded or killed in action. Their stories are made all the more poignant by the inclusion of never-before-seen photos and mementoes from the war.

In 1987, I became the national Remembrance Day broadcaster for CBC Television. Each November 11, for the next twenty-one years, we broadcast Remembrance Day ceremonies to the nation. Canadians everywhere were able to witness the National Act of Remembrance wreath-laying ceremony at the National War Memorial in Ottawa. And for the first few years of our broadcast, there were still First World War veterans in attendance. They were elderly, often frail, and many were in wheelchairs. But despite their advanced years, they came out, year after year, to honour their fallen comrades.

During those early Remembrance Day broadcasts, I would look at the faces of those Great War veterans and wonder what memories they were recalling.

Often, my mind would turn to the members of my own family who had served in the Great War, had survived, but whose service had taken a terrible toll. I would think of my grandfather Percy Newman, a British Army veteran who immigrated to Canada after serving in the Boer War. In Winnipeg, he started a family and ran a successful business until the collapse of the real estate market with the outbreak of war. At the age of forty-one, he again answered the call of "King and country" and enlisted in the Great War. He returned from the conflict wounded both physically and emotionally, ending his days in hospital and eventually dying without ever knowing any of his grandchildren, or they him.

Alan Arnett McLeod was my mother's first cousin. A native of Stonewall, Manitoba, he was only eighteen when he joined his Royal Flying Corps squadron in France in November

1917. The 2nd lieutenant quickly developed a reputation as a skilled and fearless pilot and, on March 27, 1918, he needed to be all of that and more. On that day, he got involved in a dogfight with eight German planes. During the fight, Alan's plane was hit and caught fire. Pulling the plane into a glide, he climbed onto the left wing and managed to guide the burning aircraft into a crash landing.

Alan was thrown clear of the wreck, but his gunner, Lieutenant A.W. Hammond, was trapped in the burning cockpit. Despite his injuries, Alan ran back and pulled Hammond free, dragging him to safety before both men passed out. For his bravery, Alan was called to Buckingham Palace, where King George V presented him with the Victoria Cross; Alan Arnett McLeod remains the youngest Canadian ever to receive the VC.

Alan received a hero's welcome in Winnipeg after he was sent home to recover from his injuries. Sadly, because of his weakened condition, in September 1918 he contracted Spanish flu. He died in Winnipeg on November 6, 1918, five days before the armistice that ended the war.

Reading *Canada's Great War Album* triggered these personal memories for me, and I'm sure the book will have the same effect on others. The book is a testament to the courage, the pride, the sacrifice, and even the humour that our relatives—just two or three generations back—displayed when the world seemed to go mad and dissolve into carnage.

Once you start reading *Canada's Great War Album*, it is difficult to put it down. And it proves that real history is not an either-or proposition. It's not grand narratives or personal stories alone. It's both, woven together—context and compassion, events and emotions—that put a human face on world-changing moments.

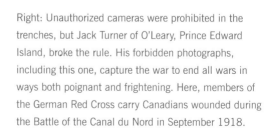

Right: Unauthorized cameras were prohibited in the trenches, but Jack Turner of O'Leary, Prince Edward Island, broke the rule. His forbidden photographs, including this one, capture the war to end all wars in ways both poignant and frightening. Here, members of the German Red Cross carry Canadians wounded during the Battle of the Canal du Nord in September 1918.

Introduction

MARK COLLIN REID

Martin O'Connell's attestation paper tells us many things. He had blue eyes and light brown hair, and, despite his missing two toes from his left foot, he was deemed medically fit for service. Standing five feet six inches tall and weighing 153 pounds, he was graced with a "florid" complexion. By all appearances, O'Connell looked every inch an Irishman. But O'Connell was actually a proud first-generation Nova Scotian, ready to "do his bit" when the call came for volunteers.

On March 4, 1916, O'Connell appeared before a recruiter in Truro, Nova Scotia, and read through a gauntlet of enlistment questions: Are you willing to be vaccinated? Have you ever served in any military force? Do you understand the nature and terms of your engagement?

I wonder: Did the latter question give him pause? Did anyone on the home front really "understand the nature" of the savagery unfolding in Europe?

By the time O'Connell stepped forward to volunteer, Canada had already suffered thousands of casualties. The patriotic fervour that had marked the early days of the First World War had cooled, and the torrent of volunteers had slowed to a trickle. The military tried new tactics to encourage enlistment; one was to create battalions tied to specific regions, so that friends and kinsmen would sign up in the belief that they would train and fight together.

Such was the case for the 193rd Battalion (Nova Scotia Highlanders). Formed in early 1916, the battalion drew its strength from the fishing and farming communities of northeastern Nova Scotia.

O'Connell, a labourer and a farmer's son, was the sixty-ninth man to volunteer with the Highlanders. But soon after his enlistment, life grew complicated. O'Connell met a woman, Viola Madill, and fell in love. In June 1916, as the couple's relationship deepened, O'Connell appeared before a Halifax medical board. Citing the soldier's two missing toes, the board declared O'Connell medically unfit and sent him home. Less than two weeks later, that decision was overturned and O'Connell was ordered to return to duty.

By this time, Viola was expecting, and in August, the couple married. O'Connell suddenly faced a difficult choice: head overseas with his battalion, or stay home to care for his family.

In the end, he remained behind. His daughter, Dorothy—my grandmother—was born a few months later, in March 1917.

Sadly, the O'Connell family shared only a few short years together; Viola died in 1922, and just seven years later, Martin also died, leaving my grandmother orphaned. And that is my family's Great War story.

Canada's Great War Album is being published at a time when few Canadians have strong views—much less memories—about the conflict. A century is a long time, and one hundred years after the start of the war, most of us have a vague understanding of how it started—something to do with an assassination of an archduke in the Balkans in 1914 and a series of alliances that toppled nations, like dominoes, toward war. But the numbers associated with the Great War—65 million combatants worldwide, 37 million wounded and injured, 8 million dead—remain almost incomprehensible.

When the war ended in November 1918, communities across Canada erected cenotaphs in tribute to their "glorious dead." They tried to make sense of their loss by fixing it in marble and limestone. We're grateful for their efforts—otherwise, we would not have breathtaking monuments such as those found in France at Vimy Ridge, or near Parliament Hill in Ottawa.

However, the story of the war goes so much deeper than the trenches. The war's impacts were felt throughout society and have echoed down the generations to today. From the soldiers who volunteered, to the women who worked in the factories, to the children who lost parents, to the "enemy aliens" who were imprisoned simply for their ethnicity—all of their stories are strands in the larger and ongoing narrative of the Great War.

In 2012, *Canada's History* began the process of searching out these stories. We sent out a call for submissions, asking readers to send us their family photos, letters, artifacts, and mementoes relating to the Great War. Our goal was to showcase these stories in a book that also featured essays from some of our nation's greatest historians.

We wanted to know what it was like to endure an artillery barrage—and also, how the soldiers endured it. How did the war affect women on the home front? What was it like to lose a loved one? And what happened to the men who returned?

In *Canada's Great War Album*, you'll learn what it was like to be shot down behind enemy lines; to be gassed in the trenches; or to be a war widow struggling to provide for your children. You'll meet couples torn apart by distance and loneliness, and others brought together by fate and circumstance.

Why did we make *Canada's Great War Album*? Certainly, to honour all those who lived, loved, fought, served, and sacrificed during the First World War. But we also created it for the generations to come. Someday, our generation will fade—like the Great War veterans—from memory to history. When that day arrives, we'll want our children to know that, when called upon to honour the legacy of the Great War generation, we remembered. And, most importantly, we cared.

Top right: Benjamin Hayes Carey was one of four brothers who served in the First World War. He was killed in action on October 26, 1917, the opening day of the Second Battle of Passchendaele in Belgium. Carey was the son of George and Elizabeth Carey of Shawville, Quebec. He enlisted in 1915 with the 44th Battalion and was transferred to the 10th Canadian Machine Gun Company after arriving overseas. His brothers William, George, and Linden survived the war. (Submitted by Barbara Anderson. The Carey brothers were her distant cousins.)

Right: George Henry Harrington was paralyzed from the waist down after a bullet entered his left hip and lodged in his spine during the Battle of St. Julien in April 1915. A year later, the bullet miraculously moved and he regained full movement. Harrington served in the 23rd Battalion and later as a sergeant in the No. 4 Detachment of the Canadian Military Police Corps. (Submitted by Philip Authier, George's grandson.)

Left: The Great War experience of Stephen Sullivan and Lillian Hawkins is a love story with a twist. It began on November 6, 1917, when Sullivan was wounded in the leg during the Battle of Passchendaele and sent to England for medical treatment. While there, the Saint John, New Brunswick, native fell in love with a local woman, Mame Hawkins—or so he thought.

Sullivan's grandson Bud Sullivan explained: "Aunt Mame was dating Grampie, and things were going great. One night Grampie came over to visit, and Aunt Mame was working, so she suggested that Gram (Mame's sister, Lillian) go out with Grampie. They did, and, as Aunt Mame put it, that was it—Gram stole Stephen from her. I told Grammie that story . . . and that was the first time that I ever saw her blush, so I guess it was true!"

Granted permission to marry, Stephen and Lillian tied the knot on July 15, 1918. After the armistice, the couple went to Canada. For Lillian (shown here on her wedding day), the move from England to a life of farming in rural New Brunswick came as quite a shock.

"She was scared of large farm animals, including horses and cows," said great-granddaughter Jen Barlow. "She once got trapped in the outhouse by a draft horse called Duke, who leaned on the door. She would never go out into the barn unless she was escorted by Grandpa Sullivan. If she wanted one of the children who were in the barn, she'd stand in the doorway and yell, 'Yoo-hoo!'"

The couple lived in Four Falls, in northwestern New Brunswick, and had nine children. Lillian never saw her family in England again. Stephen died in June 1968, at the age of seventy-four. Lillian died ten years later, aged eighty-three.

(Submitted by Karen Renaud. Stephen and Lillian were the grandparents of her husband, Jerry Sullivan.)

Above: Laura Elizabeth McCully, seated, worked in a munitions factory during the Great War and later held a career as a poet. McCully was also the great-niece of Nova Scotia Father of Confederation John McCully. She had this 1905 studio photo taken in Toronto with her friend Grace Gurnett, who also had a notable great-uncle—George Gurnett, mayor of Toronto during the rebellions of 1837. (Submitted by Margaret Gibson, Grace's daughter.)

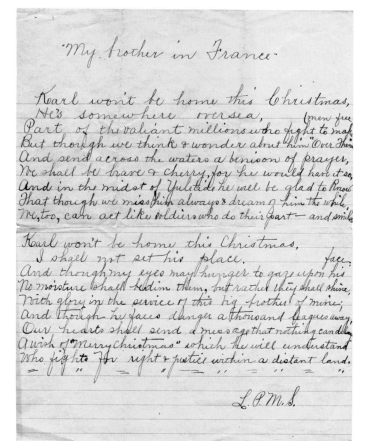

Left: Lillie Mizener wrote this poem for her brother Karl, and sent it at Christmas 1917. (Submitted by Keith Mizener, Karl's nephew.)

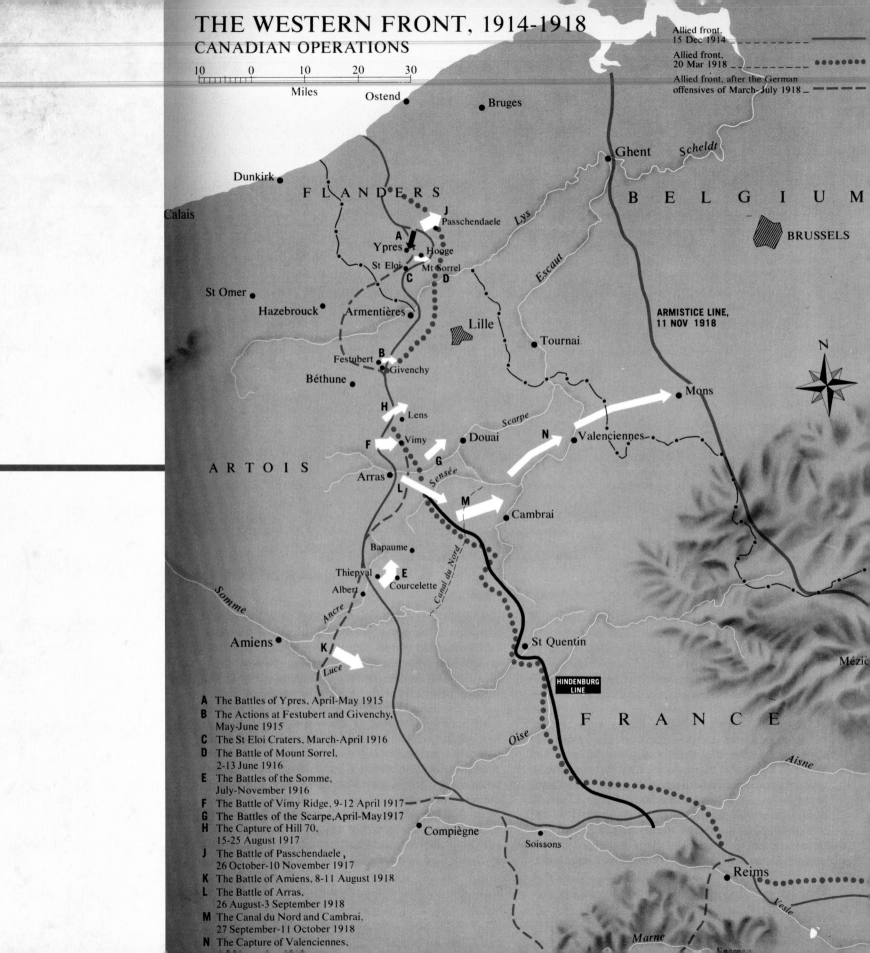

THE WESTERN FRONT, 1914-1918
CANADIAN OPERATIONS

Allied front,
15 Dec 1914
Allied front,
20 Mar 1918
Allied front, after the German
offensives of March-July 1918

10   0   10   20   30
Miles

Ostend
Bruges
Dunkirk
FLANDERS
Ghent   Scheldt
Calais
BELGIUM
J   Passchendaele   Lys
A
Ypres   Hooge
St Eloi   Mt Sorrel
C   D
BRUSSELS
St Omer
Hazebrouck
Armentières
Lille   Escaut
ARMISTICE LINE,
11 NOV 1918
Tournai
Festubert   B
Béthune   Givenchy
H   Lens   Scarpe
F   Vimy   Douai
ARTOIS   Sensée   N   Valenciennes   Mons
Arras   G
L
Bapaume   M   Cambrai
Thiepval   E
Albert   Courcelette   Canal du Nord
Somme
Ancre   St Quentin
Amiens
K
Luce   HINDENBURG
LINE   FRANCE
Oise
Mézi
Aisne
Compiègne
Soissons
Marne   Reims
Vesle

A   The Battles of Ypres, April-May 1915
B   The Actions at Festubert and Givenchy,
    May-June 1915
C   The St Eloi Craters, March-April 1916
D   The Battle of Mount Sorrel,
    2-13 June 1916
E   The Battles of the Somme,
    July-November 1916
F   The Battle of Vimy Ridge, 9-12 April 1917
G   The Battles of the Scarpe, April-May 1917
H   The Capture of Hill 70,
    15-25 August 1917
J   The Battle of Passchendaele,
    26 October-10 November 1917
K   The Battle of Amiens, 8-11 August 1918
L   The Battle of Arras,
    26 August-3 September 1918
M   The Canal du Nord and Cambrai,
    27 September-11 October 1918
N   The Capture of Valenciennes,

Timeline

June 28, 1914
Austrian Archduke Franz Ferdinand is assassinated during a visit to Sarajevo, sparking a chain of diplomatic and political events that leads to the declaration of the First World War.

August 22, 1914
Canada enacts the War Measures Act, giving the government far-reaching powers to control the media and detain citizens.

December 21, 1914
Members of Princess Patricia's Canadian Light Infantry land in France.

April 22, 1915
Canadian troops see their first action of the war, at Ypres, Belgium. The Germans attack the Allies with chlorine gas. The Canadians hold their ground, but suffer 6,000 casualties.

May 1915
Lieutenant Colonel John McCrae writes "In Flanders Fields."

1914

1915

August 4, 1914
Germany invades neutral Belgium a day after declaring war on France. Britain declares war, and Canada, as part of the British Empire, is automatically at war as well.

October 3, 1914
The first contingent of the Canadian Expeditionary Force—32,000 volunteers—ships out for England, arriving safely after an eleven-day voyage. Newfoundland, still a British colony, sends five hundred men.

September 20, 1915
The Newfoundland Regiment arrives in modern-day Turkey and joins the ongoing Gallipoli Campaign.

Far left: A Canadian soldier places rocks on the grave of a comrade who fell during the Battle of Vimy Ridge, which raged from April 9 to 12, 1917.

Left: Canadian troops cool their feet, shave, and freshen up in a flooded shell crater prior to launching an attack on German trenches, circa June 1917.

Left: This handmade poppy belonged to First World War veteran James Stanley Taylor, who served with the 14th and 174th Battalions. For years after the war, veterans organizations urged the public to buy poppies made by former soldiers rather than pay for commercially made copies.

April 9–12, 1917

All four Canadian divisions fight side by side for the first time during an assault on German-held Vimy Ridge. The Canadians suffer more than 10,000 casualties over four days of fighting before finally capturing the ridge.

July 1, 1916

The Newfoundland Regiment is almost wiped out at Beaumont Hamel, France. Of the 801 soldiers who went over the top, 710 were killed or wounded.

June 1917

Major General Arthur Currie, a Canadian, is knighted by King George V for his role in planning the attack at Vimy Ridge and promoted to command the Canadian Corps.

May 28, 1916

Lieutenant General Julian Byng—a future Governor General of Canada— assumes responsibility for the Canadian Corps.

September 15, 1916

Tanks are used for the first time in modern warfare, at the Battle of Courcelette.

1916

1917

May 2, 1917

Canada establishes a series of training bases for the Royal Flying Corps., producing several thousand pilots, air observers, and other airmen for the Allied cause.

September 20, 1917

The Conservative government of Robert Borden passes an act to permit women to vote for the first time in a federal election.

Left: Alexander Wright McSeveny in Sarnia, Ontario, circa 1915, shortly after enlisting. McSeveny served in the 58th Battalion and saw action in France. (Submitted by Scott Birdsall, Alexander's grandson.)

Middle: Bruce Anderson Smith, left, from the 2nd Canadian Railway Troops and friend George Tarbat from the 203rd Battalion in 1916. (Submitted by Richard Krehbiel, Bruce's grandson.)

Right: Joe Tillman of Hooper, Nebraska, sailed on the RMS *Carpathia* with the 2nd Division of the American Expeditionary Forces the year before the vessel was torpedoed and sunk. On its way over to Scotland in 1917, the ship stopped in Nova Scotia for nine days. Tillman's grandson believes his mother was named Nova after the location of the nine-day stopover. (Submitted by Kevin Boatright, Joe's grandson.)

December 17, 1917
Borden wins the federal election by creating a "Union" government made up of pro-conscription Conservatives and Liberals. Soon, thousands of Canadian men begin receiving draft notices.

December 6, 1917
Two ships collide in Halifax Harbour, causing the world's largest man-made explosion to date, killing up to 2,000 people.

Left: Wilfred Dingley joined the Canadian Expeditionary Force in early 1918. After a period of training, he sailed out of Halifax for England, arriving in August. The war ended before he could be sent to the front. Dingley returned to Calgary after the war. He married in 1923, and he and his wife, Leah, lived in Calgary the rest of their lives. (Submitted by Marjorie Robinson, Wilfred's daughter.)

Right: William James Proctor enlisted with the 119th Battalion at Massey, Ontario, in December 1915, twelve days before his twenty-second birthday. The Birch Lake, Ontario, resident served in England until he was transferred to the 58th Battalion in March 1918. He was wounded on September 29, 1918, and missed the remainder of the war. After the armistice, he eventually settled in Espanola, Ontario, where he raised his family of nine children and worked at the paper mill. Proctor served with the Veterans Guard during the Second World War. He died on December 16, 1973. (Submitted by Dale Proctor, William's grandson.)

1918

1919

August 8, 1918
The Allies launch the "Hundred Days Campaign," a major offensive against German forces. Earlier, in 1917, the Americans had entered the war, a key development that helped turn the tide of the conflict.

June 28, 1919
The Treaty of Versailles is signed, formally ending the war.

November 11, 1918
The armistice is declared, ending the war. Canada, with a population of only 8 million, suffered more than 60,000 deaths and another 172,000 casualties.

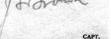

Form R. 231
780 10m 1 /219 D. 565

CIRCUMSTANCES OF DEATH OR MISSING REPORT

RGT. NO. 675904.   RANK Private.

AME POOLE. B.   UNIT 18th Cdn:Battn:

ASUALTY Killed in Action. 11.10.1918.

CIRCUMSTANCES

Private POOLE was instantly Killed by enemy shrapnel while taking part with his Battalion in Military Operations near IWUY North East of CAMBRAI on the 11th of October, 1918.

J L Brook

3/P.   CAPT.

Left: Families dreaded receiving news of the death of a loved one, but also often desired information on how the death occurred. Documents were kept recording the circumstances of soldiers' deaths. This report indicates that Private Bruce Poole of Norwich, Ontario, who enlisted in 1916, was killed instantly by shrapnel in October 1918—exactly one month before the armistice. (Submitted by Donald Poole. Bruce was Donald's cousin.)

Right: Canadian soldier Frederick Arthur Lee of the 3rd Canadian Engineers made this matchbox out of a German shell case while stationed near Lens, France. One side of the matchbox shows the Royal Flying Corps insignia, while the other depicts an engraving of a German soldier running.

210TH OVERSEAS BATTALION CAMP HUGHES AUG. 1916

Members of the 210th (Frontiersman) Battalion stand at attention at Camp Hughes, near Carberry, Manitoba. Raised in Moose Jaw, Saskatchewan, in early 1916, the Battalion was broken up upon arrival in England, with most of its members serving in either the 1st Canadian Mounted Rifles or the 46th Battalion. (Submitted by Clark Seaborn. His father, Walter, commanded the 210th Battalion.)

FOR MOST CANADIANS, THE
FIRST WORLD WAR CAME LIKE A LIGHTNING
BOLT OUT OF A CLEAR SUMMER SKY.

CHAPTER ONE

Before the Fall

CHRISTOPHER MOORE

Tuesday, August 4, 1914. The August long weekend—Canadians called it a bank holiday then—ended with the coming of war. "This war is the suicide of civilization," Prime Minister Robert Borden wrote privately, even as he prepared to lead Canadians into it. "It will be a terrible war," wrote Dr. John McCrae, a Boer War veteran. Here and there, other Canadians sensed the grim future. "The north wind blew wildly all night," the Ottawa socialite Ethel Chadwick told her diary on Sunday. "War was on it, blowing all over the world."

Until that weekend, very few Canadians had been thinking of war. Back in June, news of the assassination of an Austrian archduke was soon overtaken by events closer to home, such as the provincial election results in Ontario, where the Conservatives won a fourth term. For most in Canada, the war came out of what Stephen Leacock called "the clear sky of vacation time, the glory of Canadian midsummer . . . summer cottages and bush camps, and for the city population the soft evening sky, the canopy of stars over the merry-go-round resorts in the cool of the summer evening."

In 1914, Canada was a big country, and a small one, too. Not quite fifty years after Confederation, the nine provinces and two territories of Canada had barely more than 7 million people. Yet, except for Newfoundland and Labrador, Canada had today's immense geography, from Halifax, where thousands of immigrants landed every year, west to fast-growing Vancouver, and north to the Arctic Ocean, where that summer Newfoundland's Captain Robert Bartlett was mounting a desperate rescue of the ill-fated Canadian Arctic Expedition.

Canada was growing fast. In 1913, Canada received its largest number of immigrants ever, more than 400,000 people. Canada was still as much rural as urban, and the rural half was proud, prosperous, and growing. Saskatchewan's population was five times what it had been a decade earlier; the new province now boasted the third-largest population in the country. In rural Canada, that summer meant ripening orchards in the Okanagan and Annapolis valleys; pigs fattening for the big packing plants of "Hogtown" Toronto; and golden wheat fields across the prairies, where

Above: Two girls offer bouquets of flowers to the Duchess of Connaught and Princess Patricia at Indian Head, Saskatchewan, in 1912. At the time, the royals were touring Western Canada. Two years later, Princess Patricia lent her patronage to the raising of a new regiment, one that today is among Canada's most-storied fighting forces—Princess Patricia's Canadian Light Infantry. (Submitted by Ralph Lemon.)

Facing page: Nellie L. McClung, her son Mark and dog Philip in the front yard of her house in Edmonton, circa 1910.

Cities were thriving too. The manufacturers who had helped turn back free trade in 1911 boasted of new American branch plants providing employment and prosperity in their towns. Cities were bringing electric light to almost every home. In the summer of 1914, Toronto commuters were grousing about the newly electrified but overcrowded transit system. But automobiles were coming in fast. You could buy a Studebaker for $1,975 or a Ford runabout for $540, and that year saw Alberta's first oil strike at Turner Valley near Calgary.

Cameron Brant, twenty-seven, from the Six Nations Reserve in Ontario, was working in sheet metal in Hamilton, and was newly married. Rena McLean, "Bird" to her family in Souris, P.E.I., had gone to "the Boston states" to learn nursing and was head nurse in the operating room of a hospital in Massachusetts.

Above: John William Winchester, seated on the bench, fourth from right, in 1908 with fellow employees of Dalhousie Lumber Ltd. of Dalhousie, New Brunswick. Winchester enlisted in 1915, and served with the 26th Battalion (Victoria Rifles). Wounded in France in 1916, he returned to Canada and lived the rest of his life in Saint John, New Brunswick, where he and his wife, Marion, raised three children. (Submitted by Dawson Winchester, eldest son of Bill and Marion.)

the grain elevators could store 150 million bushels of grain for shipment. Harvesting was still mostly done by hand and by horse; "harvest excursions"—twelve dollars to Winnipeg on the Canadian Pacific—brought in temporary workers from Ontario and the Maritimes.

Englishman Gus Lambert, twenty, had come to Arelee, Saskatchewan, with his brother Tony in 1913, and they found work as farm labourers and drivers of ox teams. Ephrem Tremblay, thirty-two, was farming near his birthplace at St-Hubert, Quebec. Henry Norwest, thirty-four, a Cree saddler and cowpuncher, found work on a ranch near Wetaskiwin, Alberta.

As the holiday weekend approached, fortunate Canadians looked forward to special trains to the cottage or the shore. The Governor General—Prince Arthur, the Duke of Connaught—had been touring the lower St. Lawrence River by steamer. The finance minister was just back from enjoying the sea breezes of Dalhousie, New Brunswick. The prime minister had been golfing and boating in Ontario's Muskoka region, thinking that if there was an election in the fall the big issue might be Senate reform. At Niagara Falls, Ontario, they had marked the centennial of the Battle of Lundy's Lane, "when England and the United States were struggling for supremacy."

Above: Olympian Alexander Decoteau of the Red Pheasant Reserve in Saskatchewan runs in a road race in Calgary on Christmas Day, 1910.

Left: Harold Birkett and friends proudly display game shot during an afternoon of hunting in the Okanagan Valley of British Columbia in 1914. Birkett, sitting in the back seat smoking a pipe, enlisted in June 1915 at the age of thirty. The married Birkett was killed at the Battle of the Somme in September 1915. (Submitted by Daphne Randall. Birkett was Randall's mother's first husband.)

Above: Victoria Cross recipient Hugh Cairns.

For those stuck in the city, mass entertainment was all the rage. Earlier that year, Nellie McClung had presented *The Women's Parliament* in Winnipeg's Walker Theatre, part of the growing votes-for-women campaign. By August, the play *Sherlock Holmes* was touring, fresh from Broadway, and Arthur Conan Doyle himself was in Canada to help promote it. Vaudeville thrived, but movies were the coming thing. That summer, Marie Dressler of Cobourg, Ontario, moved from vaudeville to her first big movie feature, *Tillie's Punctured Romance*. Produced by fellow Canadian Mack Sennett, it helped launch the hot new comedian Charlie Chaplin.

Canadians followed American sports trends avidly—Babe Ruth, then still a pitcher, had just moved to the Boston Red Sox—but in every part of Canada, lively amateur leagues and small-town tournaments drew enthusiastic crowds all summer long. On the long weekend, St. Catharines, Ontario, hosted the Canadian Henley rowing regatta. There was particular joy for Toronto's sports fans that year. The Toronto Blueshirts had won the Stanley Cup back in March, and the Argonauts were on their way to the Grey Cup.

In Saskatchewan, Hugh Cairns, eighteen, was working as a plumber, but mostly he trained with his brother Albert for football season. In Woodstock, New Brunswick, Rankin Wheary, nineteen—a mixed-race kid with a black Loyalist father and a Scots mother—did some labouring jobs, but he was a star on the local baseball team and he travelled the province and into Maine for the summer tournaments. Alexander Decoteau, twenty-seven, of the Plains Cree was a sergeant in the Edmonton police in 1914. He had been an Olympian at Stockholm in 1912.

For one group of Canadians, summer always meant military drill. Canada's permanent force had barely 3,000 soldiers, but each year more than 70,000 Canadians took part in the precious ritual of summertime militia training. For leading citizens and young professionals, holding an officer's commission in one's local regiment was proof of being a gentleman, while workers and farmers learned skills, enjoyed camaraderie, and earned a little money. Few were thinking of war. In the summer of 1914, the social order was being sustained at parade grounds, rifle ranges, and cavalry stables across the nation.

Above: James Cleland Richardson was posthumously awarded the Victoria Cross on October 8, 1916.

Scots-born James Cleland Richardson, nineteen, did militia training with the pipe band of the Seaforth Highlanders in Vancouver. Albert Mountain Horse, twenty-one, born on the Blood Reserve in Alberta, was a cadet instructor in Calgary; his skill with horses and rifles had earned him rank as a militia lieutenant.

Canada was a North American nation in 1914. Though it looked to the United States for sporting heroes, movie stars, and much of its manufacturing trades, the vast majority of Canada's inhabitants were Canadian-born. Yet almost 60 percent of Canadians claimed British origins, and almost a million had been born in Britain. In trade and finance, in political culture, and in family ties, Canada remained a very British nation, too.

Above: A young recruit (middle, with haunches raised) is about to learn the hard way that there is a proper—and an improper—way to shoot his rifle. Behind him, raising a riding crop, ready to strike, is an increasingly frustrated drill instructor. In 1910, when this photo was taken, these green recruits of the 91st Regiment Canadian Highlanders could afford to treat the practice as a lark. But few were laughing five years later when Canada found itself mired in a trench war in Europe. (Submitted by Charles Pryke. His father, Boer War and Great War veteran George Pryke, took this photo at a firing range in West Hamilton, Ontario.)

Left: In the summer of 1914, this ice cream parlour in Alberton, Prince Edward Island, was a popular spot. Siblings Jennie (second from left) and Roy Campbell (second from right) ran the store. Also shown are sister Rita, centre, brother Kenneth, far right, and a family friend, Helen Agnew, left. Sadly, Roy died in 1918 after contracting the Spanish flu. (Submitted by Alan Leard, son of Jennie Leard, née Campbell.)

Britain was still the focus of many Canadians' loyalties. For British Canadians, the Crown, the Empire, and the British way of life were profoundly important. Canadians waved the Union Jack against free trade with the Americans and celebrated the knighthood Prime Minister Borden had accepted just that summer. They cherished "the rights of Englishmen" and the "mother country," even if their families had been Canadian for generations. They identified proudly as imperialists and wanted Canadians to share in running the world's greatest empire.

William Alexander, thirty-four, immigrated to Canada after serving in the British Army and found work with an automobile tire company in Winnipeg. In 1914, he opened the firm's Calgary branch. Scots-born Margaret Ann Low, *twenty-eight, a nurse who trained at Winnipeg Civic Hospital, was working in rural Binscarth, Manitoba.*

Some British Canadians saw their heritage and language threatened by non-British elements. Ontario, trying to build an English-speaking country, had recently put an end to French-language education in schools, to the fury of the three in ten Canadians who were francophone. Immigration from Eastern Europe provoked cries of "mongrelization," and harsh laws kept most Asians out altogether. Late in July, the Komagata Maru and its would-be immigrants from India had been driven out of Vancouver's harbour. But Americans, Ukrainians, Jews, South Asians, First Nations, the French, and others had already endowed Canada with a unique ethnic mix.

Above: Immigrants from India stand on the deck of the *Komagata Maru*, anchored in English Bay, Vancouver, circa July 1914.

Yoichi Kamakura, thirty-two, came to Canada from Hiroshima, Japan, with his family in 1908 and found work as an engine cleaner for the CPR in Vancouver. Wasyl Perchaluk, about twenty-three, had come from Ukraine a few years before and was doing agricultural labour near Lethbridge, Alberta.

For Canadians in the summer of 1914, did the sudden coming of global war simply mean following British command? Not quite. When King George V declared war on Germany, Canada was automatically at war, along with the rest of the British Empire. Yet had Canada decided to contribute only a corporal's guard to the war effort, such would have been Canada's choice. It was not England that sent Canada to war in 1914.

It was Britain that declared war, true; but the Canadian government, the Canadian Parliament, and the people of Canada determined Canada's role. "Canada is an autonomous nation within the British Empire, united to that Empire … by the free will of its people," Borden had declared.

Joining in the Great War was the overwhelming choice of Canadians. "If unhappily war should ensue," Borden said, "the Canadian people will be united in a common resolve to put forth every effort and to make every sacrifice."

The young men and women of Canada agreed. As the last weekend of peace ended, thousands volunteered. In three weeks, they filled the 45,000 places the Canadian forces had available. In barely a month, troop trains brought the new battalions to Valcartier near Quebec City. In another month, Canada's First Contingent was sailing to Europe, including one hundred nurses led by Major Margaret Macdonald of Bailey's Brook, Nova Scotia, who had been with the army's Nursing Service since Boer War days. By the end of 1915, roughly 200,000 Canadians had volunteered. Borden promised there would be half a million if they were needed. They would be.

Cameron Brant, the young sheet metal worker in Hamilton, enlisted three days after the declaration of war. He died at Ypres, Belgium, in April 1915. Lieutenant Albert Mountain Horse, the Siksika cadet instructor from Calgary, sailed with the First Contingent. Gassed at Ypres, he returned to Canada to die at Quebec City in November 1915. Ephrem Tremblay, the St. Hubert farmer, went to Montreal to enlist after the harvest was brought in and was killed in Belgium in October 1915.

Nurse Rena McLean went overseas with the First Contingent. She was tending wounded Canadians returning to Canada in June 1918 when their ship was torpedoed, and she and thirteen other nurses were among the lost. Bagpiper James Cleland Richardson went on active service in August 1914. At the Somme in October 1916, when his unit's morale flagged, he rose from the trench to pipe the men forward until he was killed.

At the outbreak of war, Wasyl Perchaluk, the farm labourer from Lethbridge, was interned as an enemy alien along with many other Ukrainian immigrants who had been citizens of the Austro-

Friends of Albert Mountain Horse attend his funeral in November 1915, held on the Blood reserve, Alberta.

Hungarian Empire. He enlisted upon his release in 1916, but someone thought he must be a spy and had him arrested again. Perchaluk hanged himself in his cell that December.

Saskatchewan farm labourer Gus Lambert found the ranks full when he tried to enlist in August 1914 and had to wait until December. He died at Vimy. Recruiters in Vancouver did not want Yoichi Kamakura when he tried to enlist in 1914, but the Calgary Mounted Rifles accepted him in 1916. He died at Hill 70 near Lens, France, in August 1917. Alex Decoteau, the Olympic distance runner, joined up in 1916

and died at Passchendaele in October 1917. William Alexander, the tire salesman and British Army veteran, joined up at once and served steadily in combat until September 1917. That month, when his unit was ordered to attack, his nerves failed him and he stayed back. He was court-martialed and shot by firing squad.

Manitoba nurse Margaret Ann Lowe joined the nursing corps in 1917 and was killed in an air raid at her nursing station at Étaples, France, in May 1918. Cowpuncher Henry Norwest, who enlisted at Wetaskiwin in June 1915, served as a sniper until he was killed near Amiens in August 1918.

Rankin Wheary, the mixed-race baseball star from New Brunswick, enlisted in 1916. He helped his team win the divisional baseball championship in the summer of 1918 and was killed at Cambrai in October.

Hugh Cairns and his brother Albert enlisted two days before the declaration of war. They served throughout the war until Albert was killed in September 1918. Hugh fought on without regard for his own life and was killed ten days before the armistice.

WISHING YOU ALL A MERRY CHRISTMAS AND A HAPPY NEW YEAR.

XMAS. 1906.

The Avery Smith Homestead N.E.¼ 28 of 40. 8. 3. Sask.

Above: Edward Vernon Callow of the 126th Overseas Battalion, far left, poses with fellow volunteers during training at Camp Borden, Ontario, circa fall 1915. Callow, a shoemaker from Brampton, Ontario, enlisted on November 24, 1915, at the age of nineteen. On May 25, 1918, he was struck by shrapnel while fighting near Arras, France. Hospitalized for months, he was declared medically unfit for service and discharged home. Following the war, he opened a shoe and leather shop in Alliston, Ontario. Callow died in 1960 at the age of sixty-four. (Submitted by Douglas Callow, Edward's son.)

Top: Jennie Avery Smith (right, holding baby Christine) stands on the porch of her home near Borden, Saskatchewan, circa 1906. With her are her sons, Eric and Stanley, with pitchfork and spade. Both boys later enlisted in the Great War. Eric, a fighter pilot, was shot down over France. Stanley survived the war and lived to the age of ninety-nine. Jennie's husband, Ted, not shown, died of Spanish flu near the end of the war. Jennie—an ardent feminist who had run for public office in Edmonton in 1916—returned to England and remarried. (Submitted by Avery Fleming, granddaughter of Ted and Jennie.)

Above left: This photo suggests times were good for William Penland in the years before the Great War. He was driving a Winton Six, which was an expensive automobile for the day, and he lived in a substantial home built in the popular Queen Anne revival style in the town of Medicine Hat, Alberta, where he owned a hotel (the first in town, it is said). In this 1912 photo, Penland is joined by his brother Charles, front seat, and Charles's wife Augusta, back. (Submitted by Lyle W. Fraser, Charles's son-in-law.)

Above right: Father Donald MacPherson of Port Hood, Nova Scotia, with his portable altar. He enlisted in 1915 and served on both the Eastern and Western Fronts. After the war, he served as the parish priest at Port Hood from 1919 to 1957. (Submitted by Joanna Watts.)

Colt Gun Section Canadian Scouts in action
South African War 1901.

BLAESER
Pretoria

Above: Walter Bapty (left, with bandolier) in South Africa in 1901 with fellow Canadian volunteers. Bapty grew up in London, Ontario, reading boys' adventure stories. Emulating the fictional heroes of the novels, he ran away from home in January 1900 to fight in the Boer War. He was fifteen. After the war, Bapty trained as a physician and later served in the Great War as medical officer. In the Second World War he commanded the 2nd Battalion, Canadian Scottish Regiment. (Submitted by Bruce Williams, Walter's grandson.)

Above: Canada tried many different tactics to encourage men to enlist in the Great War. Among them was the creation of units based on specific geographic or ethnic orientation. One such unit was the Winnipeg-based 223rd, or Viking Battalion. The majority of its members were of Icelandic origin. Few recruits realized that upon their arrival in England or France, such units were often broken up and the men reassigned to other battalions. In this photo, taken in late summer 1916 in Winnipeg, at least half of the men shown are from the same Icelandic Canadian settlement, Logberg, Saskatchewan. Sitting, front row, middle, is Lieutenant Jon Einarsson. Einarsson was killed at Passchendaele in October 1917. Second from right, back row, is Einarsson's younger brother, Villi. (Submitted by Joe Martin, nephew of Jon and Villi Einarsson.)

Above: A Japanese Canadian soldier, circa August 1917. When the Great War broke out, Japanese Canadians in British Columbia stepped forward to enlist—only to be turned away by recruiters due to the prevailing racist attitudes of the day. Undaunted, in 1916 more than two hundred Japanese Canadians travelled en masse to Alberta to try to enlist. They were accepted and sent to fight at the front. In total, 222 Japanese Canadians served in the war, many in combat roles. They were awarded eleven Military Medals for bravery, and fifty-four of the volunteers were killed.

Bottom left: William Martin, far left, standing with his parents and siblings, date unknown. William enlisted in March 1916 at the age of thirty-four. Just over a year later, his family received a telegram announcing his death. Mary Irwin—William's niece—was there when the telegram arrived, and in later years she described the scene to her son, Lane Gray, who remembers: "Mary—seven years old at the time—could not understand why the family was grieving, but she felt she too should cry. She went behind a door and cried." Martin was killed near Liévin, France. Gray still wonders what compelled his great-uncle to enlist. "Did he feel pressure from recruitment drives that were common during the war?" he asked. "Was farming not successful for him? Was he suffering from the loneliness of being a single man on a homestead? Did he feel patriotic and believe the war was a noble cause?" (Submitted by Lane Gray, great-nephew of William Martin.)

SOLDIER...
WHY DID YOU ENLIST?
HOW SOME CANADIANS ANSWERED.

"I had had no thought of being accepted for overseas after three failures for bad teeth, but when I heard old Dr. Baird was the recruiting medical officer for our town ... I headed for his office. In ten minutes I was in."

—WILL BIRD, AMHERST, NOVA SCOTIA

"I was getting restless, as about all the conversation these days was regarding enlisting and as I was eighteen now, I knew that I would be in the army before too long."

—JAMES JOHNSTON, MONCTON, NEW BRUNSWICK

"Out on the awful old trail again! And with very mixed feelings, but some determination. I am off for Valcartier tonight."

—DR. JOHN MCCRAE, GUELPH, ONTARIO

"It would have been rather peculiar not to have volunteered, for to be a soldier in peacetime and back out in war would be queer."

—FRANK CHADWICK, OTTAWA, ONTARIO

"One might reasonably hope to see a little service under such glorious conditions as the European war."

—AGAR ADAMSON, OTTAWA, ONTARIO

"It is because if the Christian religion is worth anything, it is the only thing I can do."

—HAROLD INNIS, OTTERVILLE, ONTARIO

Top left: Coverdale (Pat) Patterson attempted to enlist with his brother Goldwin (Goldie) but was refused by the recruiter. Goldie went on to serve overseas and was killed in France in 1917. Instead of going to war, Pat married Anna Johanssen and had four children, including Dona, seen here on a horse. (Submitted by Dona Norton, Pat's daughter.)

Top right: Herbert Harris, a member of the 31st Battalion, was killed in action in September 1916. Born in 1897, the native of Wiseton, Saskatchewan, was working as a farmer at the time of his enlistment. Harris was just shy of his twentieth birthday when he was killed. (Submitted by Karen Johnston, Herbert's great-niece.)

Above: Herbert Lyth from Knowlton, Quebec, enlisted in February 1916 and served as a lance corporal with the 24th Battalion (Victoria Rifles). He was wounded at Vimy Ridge. (Submitted by Juliette Brouillette, Herbert's daughter.)

Above: Francis Cuthbert Malcolm Cumming decided to enlist after his farm was destroyed. It happened during the summer of 1915 when a severe hailstorm hit his Saskatchewan farm and completely demolished the crop. With a wife and five kids to take care of and no crop to generate family income, Cumming enlisted. He served with the 46th Battalion and was killed in action on January 3, 1917. (Submitted by Rob Crang, Francis's grandson.)

MANUAL TRAINING CLASS
WHITBY 1918
INS. J. PHILIPS

Left: Like many young men at the time of the Great War, Vincent Aquilina was caught up in the passion of a great cause. He was born in 1900, which meant he was underage when he tried—and failed—to enlist in Toronto. Finally, in London, Ontario, someone turned a blind eye, and in January 1916 Vincent, known as "Joe," joined the cavalry. In France, he was wounded and had his leg amputated above the knee. He was not yet eighteen. Aquilina, pictured in the centre in white, is undergoing what we now call occupational therapy at a hospital in Whitby, Ontario. (Submitted by George Aquilina, the son of Vincent.)

Bottom left: Family lore suggests that Daniel Foley, centre, fled Scotland to enlist in Canada under the false name of Daniel Fowler because his mom disapproved of his joining the British Army; his brother Thomas had enlisted a year earlier. Foley served as a private in the 10th Battalion and was killed in April 1917 during the first offensive of the Battle of Vimy Ridge. (Submitted by Virginia Foley, Daniel's great-niece.)

Bottom right: Sisters Irene and Gertrude McGillicuddy of Skiff Lake, New Brunswick, both trained as nurses and then accepted nursing jobs in Massachusetts. When the United States entered the war in 1917, the sisters enlisted in the American military. However, although they were both eager to serve, the war ended with neither nurse ever receiving the call to head overseas. (Submitted by Anne Marie Beattie, the niece of Irene and Gertrude.)

A soldier tries on his small box respirator at Whitley Camp, Surrey, England, circa 1916.

ENTHUSIASTIC CANADIANS SIGNED UP BY THE THOUSANDS TO FIGHT. LITTLE DID THEY REALIZE THE HORROR THAT AWAITED THEM.

CHAPTER TWO

A Different Kind of War

TIM COOK

Most Europeans and Canadians expected the war to be over by Christmas. Most generals also predicted a rapid victory. While the leaders underestimated the slaughter that would unfold, they recognized the power of modern weapons: rapid-firing rifles, machine guns, and artillery. Since the generals came from a profession not given to despair, they convinced themselves that their armies would prevail if they were offensive-minded and willing to endure casualties in the pursuit of victory.

These armies, first made up of regular soldiers and then of great swaths of citizens who volunteered or were conscripted for duty, did not disappoint. Young men from across Europe, and then from around the world, embraced the offensive spirit. Even when that fighting spirit was overwhelmed by the big guns, the soldiers proved incredibly resilient as they endured ghastly living conditions and unrelenting brutality.

The new realities of warfare were fully revealed during the first months of the war on the Western Front. German and French armies consisting of hundreds of thousands of soldiers, with the smaller forces of Britain and Belgium, smashed into each other in the borderlands of multiple nations. While German Kaiser Wilhelm II's forces marched and fought through Belgium, the French armies to the south ran face-first into a German buzz saw and were cut down in sickening numbers. The Germans, too, in their sweep through Belgium and northern France came up short, eventually stopped by the massed guns and, less bloodily, by the logistical nightmare of ordering armies to march by foot for hundreds of kilometres.

The only way to escape the scythe of fire was to dig into the ground. Desperate scratches in the earth became ditches, and the ditches soon extended into long trenches. As the front congealed at the end of 1914, the trenches were soon enlarged into complex underground fortresses. It was there that the rebuilt armies, expanded by millions of civilians turned soldiers, would stay for the better part of the next four years.

Above: Tom Nowell enlisted in November 1915 at Montreal, and served as a private with the 87th Battalion (Canadian Grenadier Guards). At age forty, Nowell was considerably older than the typical recruit. He was killed in action in France on October 22, 1916, leaving behind a widow, Lucy Nowell. (Submitted by Elaine Fuller. Nowell was her grandmother's second husband.)

Canadian forces did not fight in the opening, crippling phase of the war. With almost no professional army, Canada was grossly unprepared for modern warfare; but that did not stop tens of thousands from enlisting. They were soon sent overseas with the First Contingent, 30,000 strong. After several months of training in England, the Canadian Division of 18,000 soldiers arrived at the Western Front trenches in February 1915. Another 420,000 Canadians would follow them over the next four years. In total, about 619,000 enlisted in Canada but not all were sent overseas.

These civilian-soldiers came from across the country, representing all regions and classes and almost all faiths, although in the first half of the war they were drawn predominantly from British-born Canadi-ans. Their average age was twenty-six, but many of the older men were kept from the Western Front. Officers were better educated than the enlisted men, but even then, more than half of the force had not passed out of middle school. This was a generation that had been raised to work long hours. Life in the army, while more regimented than that of civvy street, was not a difficult transition for many men. However, nothing prepared them for the trenches.

Running from Switzerland to the North Sea, the seven-hundred-kilometre-long trench system snaked through France and Belgium. The opening manoeuvres saw the Kaiser's armies occupying much of Belgium and the industry-rich northeast of France. They had dug their trenches to take advantage of the best terrain, with broad fields of fire and using the reverse slopes of hills and ridges to provide safety for reinforcements. A spider web of support trenches and communication lines moved back from primary trenches that faced off against each other across a dead zone known as no man's land. The two opposing sides were as close as fifty metres in some places, but usually the gap was wider at several hundred metres. Corrupted with the rotting bodies of the dead, strewn with garbage, and pitted with shell craters, no man's land was a terrifying space into which the sentries on both sides stared.

The trenches were not much better. This was as much a war of pick and shovel as it was of rifle and grenade. With the trenches dug down to two metres into the seeping earth, and then built up with sand-bags, a soldier spent much of his day staring into muddy walls. With the Germans also stuck in the ground, the battlefield was a strange, empty place. It was tempting to take a peek at the enemy, but merciless snipers lay in wait for any man foolish enough to put his head above the trench. Dozens of Canadians were killed with strikes through the head in the first months of the war.

Throughout the war, in fact, much of the time spent at the front was quite boring, as soldiers waited for something to happen. But officers did not allow their men to lounge around. There were constant digging parties to expand trenches or rebuild shattered ones. Latrines had to be constructed near the front, with new ones built when they overflowed. Dugouts, some ten metres deep, were excavated to provide protection from shellfire and mortars. In the first two years of the war, there were not enough dugouts to house the forward units, and so soldiers took to carving out holes in the trench walls. They burrowed into their "funk holes" to escape the rain and enemy fire, sometimes taking refuge with rotting corpses in the open graveyard the soldiers made their home.

Most of the labour happened at night to avoid the enemy's searching eyes. Work parties stealthily climbed over the forward trench to lay barbed wire that would slow enemy attacks and funnel the Germans into kill zones that were swept by machine-gun fire. Intelligence officers and a few men patrolled no man's land, testing the enemy defences. In late 1915, the Canadians began to organize trench raids. In these "butcher and bolt affairs," a few dozen men (and later hundreds) smashed the enemy lines in surprise

assaults. The Canadians soon acquired a reputation as elite raiders.

That same year, the Germans began to employ more trench mortars, which lobbed a high explosive bomb on an arc to land in Allied lines. Underneath the battlefield, sappers and miners pushed forward tunnels to lay explosives under the enemy garrison. Cave-ins were a constant threat, as was the enemy, who often broke into the tunnels from their own side; the result was vicious fighting with pistols, rifles, knives, and sharpened shovels; gasping, panting, oxygen-deprived men fought for their lives in the dark.

Above: A soldier wears a German sniper mask made of half-inch steel.

Above ground, chemical weapons added to the soldiers' horror. First, chlorine seared the lungs; later, there was phosgene, nearly invisible and eight times as lethal as chlorine. The front was fouled with chemical agents, delivered by gas clouds and then in artillery shells. In the summer of 1917, the Germans pushed the gas war to new horrible levels as they saturated the front with mustard gas, which burned the skin, caused temporary blindness, and created panic. The persistent

chemicals lay active in the mud and trenches for days and even weeks. Flimsy respirators offered some protection, but wearing them reduced oxygen intake to nearly suffocating levels.

Even without the never-ending casualties, the dirt and deprivation of the trench systems eroded the soldiers' morale. In the winter months, soldiers stamped their frozen feet and shivered against the blasts of cold. In the summer, the sweltering trenches were sticky and humid. Everyone felt like his brain was baking, but only a fool took off his steel helmet.

Body lice infected the soldiers all year round. These ugly bloodsucking insects lived in the folds of clothing and came out to feast at night. Men scratched themselves raw. When they could, the lice-infected men disrobed and used a candle to draw out the monsters before grinding them up satisfactorily between their fingers. This passed for fun.

Rats infested the front by the millions, thriving on refuse and the flesh of unburied corpses in no man's land. The squeaking beasts ran over the soldiers by day and bit them at night. Some were the size of cats. Vengeful soldiers took delight in hunting the rats. Only the massive chemical attacks wiped them out in sufficient numbers to lessen the hordes, although even then they repopulated with astonishing speed.

It is hard to imagine how the soldiers withstood it all. Rotation out of the front lines every four to six days offered a break, although rear areas could still be shelled, and always the next phase of the cycle—the return to the front—loomed large in the mind.

As soldiers on the front line watched their comrades being cut down, they could not help but do the math and realize that the odds of surviving were against them. And so each man found ways to cope. Some developed a fatalistic attitude, as summed up in

Far left: Private George Richard Cross of the 4th Canadian Mounted Rifles was gassed near Cambrai, France, in October 1918. The unit's war diary mentions that, during the battle, several units suffered heavy shelling, gas shell strafing, and the explosion of a cordite ammunition dump that left a crater "70 feet wide and 30 feet deep." Cross survived the war. (Submitted by Ron Cross, George's grandson.)

Left: Harry Norman Forbes of Hamilton was wounded in a mustard gas attack and sent to England for hospitalization; while there, he met a nurse, Charlotte Cackett, married her, and brought her to Canada after the war. (Submitted by Adrene Schmidt, Harry's granddaughter.)

Below: Canadian soldiers line up for a hot lunch, circa 1914. This photo is part of a collection of images owned by Michael Snell, who retired as a colonel after thirty-nine years in the Canadian military. (Submitted by Michael Snell.)

Above: A Canadian soldier examines "dummy" heads used in the trenches to fool snipers, circa July 1918.

the popular soldiers' quip of the day: "You'll get it when your number's up."

Despite the nightmarish conditions, the soldiers remained resilient. The small pleasures in life kept many men from cracking. Almost all soldiers smoked, non-stop. It calmed the nerves and masked the stench of unwashed bodies, burnt earth, and rotting corpses. While the food was monotonous and heavy, no one starved. When soldiers grew tired of canned bully beef, they pooled their food into large stews augmented with eggs, poultry, and other fresh food obtained from local farmers behind the lines. Packages from home provided chocolate and other sweets. Equally important was the daily ration of rum. Served at the discretion of the officers, the two-ounce shot of over-proof rum burned all the way down, but it provided much fortitude. The rum was so important that it was used to reinforce discipline: It was denied to men who were in the

bad books and offered liberally to those who volunteered for dangerous tasks.

Army discipline provided control and comfort in times of high stress and battle. But those who did not follow orders suffered the full wrath of the system, with brutal punishments that included death by firing squad. Twenty-five Canadians were executed by their comrades during the course of the war, most of them for deserting from their units.

Survivors inevitably wore down. Any service at the front beyond a year began to break most soldiers. Good officers watched for the signs—nervous tensions, facial tics, and nightmares—and tried to relieve tottering men by giving them safer jobs to the rear. But few could be spared from the firing lines. It was usually a single traumatic event that caused a man to snap—a near-death experience or seeing a mate killed. The breakdown was categorized as shell shock, and it included both physical trauma and mental strain. More than 9,000 Canadians were diagnosed with shell shock during the course of the war.

Considering the terror and turmoil of the trenches, one might have expected more shell shock or mutiny. In fact, the numbers were quite small in relation to the total number of soldiers who fought. Most men at the front learned to endure the terrible strain. The Canadian soldier was young, tough, determined, and proud. In the end, it was the Canadian soldier, with his Allied comrades-in-arms, who delivered victory.

Below: George Leslie Scherer, front row, second from right, poses with members of his Lewis gun brigade. He enlisted in January 1916 with the 48th Highlanders of Toronto. He received the Military Medal for refusing to leave an ongoing battle for treatment despite being wounded in France at Hill 70. He added a bar to the medal for leading his Lewis gun section across open ground under heavy machine gun fire at the Battle of Amiens in August 1918. (Submitted by Norman MacInnes, George's grandson.)

THE SHRINE OF HONOUR.

"WHO GOES THERE?"
"I HAVE NO NAME. I DIED FOR MY COUNTRY."
"PASS, UNKNOWN WARRIOR."

Top: Charles Switzer, left, with friends the day after the end of the Third Battle of Ypres, June 15, 1917. Switzer enlisted in December 1914 and served with the 8th Canadian Mounted Rifles. He was awarded the Military Medal in 1917 and later added a bar to the medal. (Submitted by Fay Tidd, née Switzer, Charles's daughter.)

Above: Thomas Judge, first on the right, enlisted in the 83rd Battalion and served as a driver in the 4th Division Motor Train. (Submitted by Brian Hutchinson, Thomas's great-nephew.)

Left: This illustration is part of a collection of papers and documents belonging to the family of Harry Murney of Toronto. Murney enlisted in August 1914 and was killed by shrapnel during a June 1916 attack on a German position. Murney was twenty-three at the time of his death, and had been serving in the 13th Battalion. (Submitted by Mrs. A. Alder.)

Clockwise from top left: Wilbert Robinson Ferguson, middle, front row, and his fellow teaching students at normal school in Ontario, circa 1915. The Stayner, Ontario, native enlisted in the 14th Battalion. An expert shot, he was made a shooting instructor at Shorncliffe Army Camp in England and quickly rose to the rank of sergeant. He was killed in action on June 3, 1916, in the Ypres Salient in Belgium. (Submitted by John Borthwick and Ruth Borthwick, née Mitchell. Wilbert was John's great-uncle.)

Daniel Edmond Booth enlisted in the 52nd Battalion on April 29, 1915, and served in England and France. Booth was raised in North Sydney, Nova Scotia. He survived the war but was killed in an industrial accident in New York City in 1949. (Submitted by George Ingham, Daniel's great-nephew.)

Harold Eston Fowler, Sr., of the 1st Canadian Motor Machine Gun Brigade, second from right, stands in front of an armoured car as part of an armed escort for General Arthur Currie in Bonn, Germany, January 1919. (Submitted by Les Fowler, Harold's grandson.)

Thomas Lowry enlisted in Calgary on February 12, 1916, joining the 137th Battalion. His brother Timothy also served in the Great War. Tom survived the war. He was a lifelong bachelor and died at the age of seventy. (Submitted by Maureen Lowry, Tom's great-niece.)

Sarcee Camp in Alberta, where Kenneth Thomas Ferguson—shown in the final photo—enlisted in Edmonton in 1916. He survived the war and in later years told the *Vegreville Review* about a close call he had during the conflict. It happened while he was building a rail line near the front in France. Finishing for the day, he and his crew left. Returning the next morning, they found a massive shell crater at the exact spot where they were to resume working. "The Germans had dropped a shell right in the middle of it," Ferguson recalled in the article. "We were lucky we weren't there when it hit!" (Submitted by Joyce Fingland, Kenneth's granddaughter.)

Clockwise from top left: Edward Shirtraw, right, and a friend shortly after enlisting in September 1915. The Brockville, Ontario, native joined up at age thirty-eight and survived the war. (Submitted by Wendy Rudd, Edward's great-granddaughter.)

When William Tilley was ten, he was rounded up, put on a boat, and shipped to a farm in Northern Ontario, far from his home in England. It was 1899, and Tilley was one of a host of "home children" fetched from Britain's slums to be put to work as labourers in Canada, Australia, and New Zealand. "My grandfather . . . was a cockney lad who had likely never seen a farm," said grandson Kenneth Tilley. "He was sometimes beaten by his employer and, at some point, ran away and made his way in the world on his own." Despite this traumatic upbringing, Tilley enlisted in 1916 to fight for "King and country." In France, Tilley was shot, seriously gassed, and eventually discharged in February 1919 for medical reasons. (Submitted by Kenneth Tilley, William's grandson.)

Charlie MacDonald of Souris, Prince Edward Island, second from right, in France in 1917. He enlisted in 1914 at the age of eighteen. Following the war, he returned to P.E.I. to farm. (Submitted by Bernie MacDonald, Charlie's son.)

Arnold Moses, front right, gathers behind the lines with friends from the 107th Battalion for a souvenir photo. A Delaware from the Six Nations of the Grand River, Moses survived the war and served as band council chief of the Six Nations for a term in the 1940s. (Submitted by John Moses, Arnold's great-nephew.)

William James Proctor, Sr., enlisted in December 1915 at Massey, Ontario. He was wounded on September 29, 1918, seven weeks before the armistice. During the Second World War, Bill served with the Veterans Guard. (Submitted by Dale Proctor, William's grandson.)

BEHIND BARBED WIRE

FOR SOME, BEING A POW DURING THE GREAT WAR WAS NOT MUCH BETTER THAN BEING IN THE TRENCHES.

NATHAN M. GREENFIELD

"Für Sie ist der Krieg zu Ende." (For you, the war is over.)

These were the words that Canadian soldiers like Captain Thomas Scudamore never wanted to hear; indeed, the disgrace attached to surrender was so great that Scudamore's father assumed that his son, captured in April 1915, had fallen into German hands unconscious.

Though the POWs may not have faced death or dismemberment on a daily basis, being a prisoner of war in Germany during the First World War was a trial. German soldiers beat Scudamore and the men who surrendered with him with their rifle butts and threatened them with their bayonets. Nor were they alone in receiving ill treatment. One Canadian—a Private O'Brien—reported being kicked and spat on by the Germans after being captured at the Battle of Mount Sorrel in 1916. O'Brien later recalled seeing

German guards shoot a Toronto-born soldier in cold blood.

Despite the German reputation for maintaining order, the handling of prisoners of war and the operation of the POW camps were conducted in a haphazard manner bordering on neglect. Some POWs were transported in manure-covered cattle cars. Many grew sick during their time in capture.

Incidents such as these took place despite Kaiser Wilhelm's signature on the Hague Convention of 1899, which defined the humane treatment of prisoners of war. Under the convention, POWs were entitled to the same quality and quantity of food served to their captors. In reality, the rations they received were vile—often only weak soup that left stomachs achingly empty and sapped strength, thus lessening the chances of escape attempts. Lieutenant J. C. Thorn, a Canadian captured at the Second Battle

of Ypres in 1915, lamented the general lack of fats and protein in his diet. At times, the stew given to the POWs at Holzminden, Germany, was made from a cow's head and once from "half a horse's head, complete with the eye."

The Hague Convention allowed the Germans to require what the military calls "ordinary ranks" to work. But it didn't allow labour to be extorted by beatings and the withholding of vital rations and food parcels from home. Nor did the convention allow the running of a gauntlet if you didn't meet your mining quota or, as happened to one Canadian at Osnabrück, Germany, being "lashed to a furnace for two hours" for refusing to manufacture munitions.

Of the 3,800 Canadians captured during the Great War, 300 died. Another 175 escaped, although the Canadian government suppressed knowledge of this. In one case, Major

Above: Robert Howard, second from right, at German prisoner of war camp Celle Lager IV, near Hanover, Germany, in 1916. His family recalls Howard as a very determined and even arrogant man, who may have tried to escape this camp. (Submitted by Robert Wilkes, Robert's great-nephew.)

Left: In 1916, William John (Jack) Gray traded life in the trenches for a commission in the Royal Flying Corps, only to be shot down and captured by German forces. While a POW, Gray was made to sign the following pledge: "I will not escape nor attempt to make an escape, nor will I make any preparation to do so, nor will I attempt to commit any action during this time to the prejudice of the German Empire." The Weyburn, Saskatchewan, man enlisted on August 6, 1914, just two days after the war was declared. In 1916, he joined the Royal Flying Corps as an aerial observer. Shot down near Péronne, France, he was held in five different German prison camps before finally being released on December 8, 1918. (Submitted by William [Bill] Gray, Jack's son.)

Peter Anderson of the Canadian army managed to escape to England, arriving there in October 1915, only to find himself accused of being a German agent.

Some POWs went to great lengths to escape. In his memoir, *Three Years a Prisoner of War in Germany*, Thorn recounted how, during one escape attempt, he hid in the bottom of a wheelbarrow filled with manure, and, during another attempt, he hid at the bottom of a laundry basket.

After several failed escape attempts, Thorn was sent to Holzminden, a camp for inveterate escapers. Holzminden's most brazen escape occurred on July 23, 1918, when twenty-nine men fled through a tunnel designed by a Canadian POW. Thorn was not part of that group. However, he did later manage to escape with a fellow prisoner, a Brit; the pair, dressed in fake German uniforms, simply walked out Holzminden's main gate.

According to Thorn, his comrades in camp bought him time by covering for him during inspection. One POW, Lieutenant J. G. Colquhoun of the Princess Patricia's Canadian Light Infantry, even poured cayenne pepper in Thorn's old shoes to throw off the Germans' bloodhounds. Unfortunately, Thorn's flight to freedom ended after only nine days, when he and his partner were recaptured.

Returned to Holzminden, Thorn was sentenced to a month of solitary confinement, which exceeded the period allowed under the Hague Convention. Thorn was ultimately released as part of a prisoner exchange.

Above: Heber Rogers of Peterborough, Ontario, was reported killed in action in April 1915 near Langemark, Belgium, during the Second Battle of Ypres. So, imagine his mother's surprise at receiving a letter from him dated May 5, 1915. Hit in the face by shrapnel, he had been captured by the Germans and placed in a POW camp. In the letter, he reassured his mother that he was okay. "My right eye has got a band and I cannot see out of it yet. Beyond that, I am feeling fine." He also urged his mom to send him a care package of sweets: "some cake, chocolates, candy, biscuits, jam, potted meats, etc." Despite two escape attempts, Rogers remained a POW for the remainder of the war. (Submitted by Robert Rogers, Heber's cousin.)

Above: Joseph Francis (Frank) MacDougall served as a guard at the Spirit Lake internment camp in northern Quebec. A private in a composite regiment, MacDougall made it as far as England before he was sent back to Canada because of an injury he suffered while working on a farm before elisting on August 17, 1917. (Submitted by Patricia Meko, Joseph's granddaughter.)

Above: Worlend Errol Nicholson, foreground, right, stands before a group of German POWs, somewhere in Europe. He served in the camp for a time during the First World War. He was honourably discharged in 1919 and returned to Alberta. (Submitted by Laurel Fitzsimonds, Worlend's great-niece.)

Left: Great War veteran Fred Armstrong served in the Veterans Guard of Canada during the Second World War. He worked as a guard at several POW camps, including this one, Camp 20, on Lake Muskoka, at Gravenhurst, Ontario. The camp, mostly used to house captured officers, operated from 1940 to 1946. (Submitted by John L. Armstrong, Fred's son.)

Right: Lieutenant Colonel Hugh Dale-Harris enlisted in September 1916 at the age of twenty. The Germans captured Hugh in March 1918 and he remained a POW until the end of the war. (Submitted by W. Hugh Dale-Harris, Hugh's son.)

ENEMY ALIENS

CANADA WAS QUICK TO INTERN THOUSANDS OF RECENT IMMIGRANTS DEEMED TO BE THREATS TO NATIONAL SECURITY.

NATHAN M. GREENFIELD

Within days of the First World War being declared, eighty-four German merchant mariners were seized from a ship docked in Montreal and classified as prisoners of war. By the end of August 1914, the sailors were transferred to Fort Henry in Kingston, Ontario, which had been hurriedly pressed into service as a prisoner of war camp. Soon, more than 3,000 German and Austrian reservists or civilians, who were deemed by the Dominion government to be enemy agents, were also imprisoned.

Some, however, managed to slip through the porous Canadian dragnet. Joachim von Ribbentrop, thirty-one, was among those who made their way to the neutral United States. He later became Hitler's foreign minister.

On September 2, 1914, Robert Borden's Conservative government promised that immigrants from Germany and Austria-Hungary would "not be arrested, detained or interfered with, unless there is reasonable ground to believe they are engaged" in hostile actions. Yet, within weeks, a system was in place to register some 80,000 immigrants from Central and Eastern Europe as "enemy aliens." Of them, a total of 5,204 men, 81 women, and 156 children were placed in internment camps. The vast majority of these enemy aliens were Ukrainian immigrants,

Ice Palace at Banff, Alberta: built by interned aliens. 1916 - 17.

camps, men who refused to work were not fed, which violated the Hague Convention, as did the corporal punishment some guards routinely used to enforce discipline. Not surprisingly, given the harsh conditions in which they lived, many men tried to escape. In his final report, Major General Sir William D. Otter, who ran the internment camps, told the minister of justice that six would-be escapers had been killed and four were wounded by gunshots. Otter gave special praise to Captain T. W. Kirkconnel for leading a detail of three men up the Kapuskasing River, across twelve portages over a distance of almost 130 kilometres, to capture two "delinquents."

It took almost a century for the Canadian government to recognize the injustice done to many innocent internees. In 2001, Parliament passed Bill C-331, which recognized the wrongs done to the Ukrainians and other Eastern Europeans during the First World War and provided $10 million to fund educational and other projects.

the very "Ruthenians" considered hostile to Austria-Hungary and thus friendly to the British Empire.

The internees formed a pool of cheap and easily controlled labour, which became more important as hundreds of thousands of men joined the Canadian army. Paid a quarter a day (and thus, much less than a labourer) the internees felled trees, removed rocks, and built roads in national parks in Western Canada. In northern Ontario and Quebec, they cleared land for experimental farms. The *Vernon News* of British Columbia estimated the internees' labour as being worth $1.5 million a year or more than $30 million in today's dollars.

Food was so scarce in Banff, Alberta, that the censor allowed one internee—Nick Olynik—to write, "We are not getting enough to eat—we are hungry as dogs." In some

A VIRULENT AND POISONOUS AFFAIR

THE SECOND BATTLE OF YPRES

JOEL RALPH

By the time the Canadians arrived in the Ypres salient in the spring of 1915, the devastation caused by the war was on full display. The ancient city of Ypres, Belgium, had been flattened by German shellfire the previous October, the crumbling shells of former structures serving as a daily reminder of the destruction that had passed through and that would surely return.

In the late afternoon of April 22, 1915, the German army took advantage of a favourable wind to release a cloud of chlorine gas. A yellow-green fog crept over the ground, descending into the trenches occupied by Algerian and Moroccan troops. Chaos ensued as panicked soldiers inhaled the lethal chemical; gasping and choking, the men felt their insides burn as the chlorine made contact with fluid in their throats and lungs.

Lacking gas masks, the colonial soldiers retreated from their chemical-filled trenches, leaving a six-kilometre-long hole in the Entente front line. The Canadians rushed to halt the Germans, who now easily advanced through the vacated lines, and the two opposing sides clashed throughout the night.

On the morning of April 24, nearly thirty-six hours after the initial attack, the Germans released a second wave of gas, this time directly against the Canadian lines. The Canadians improvised, finding limited protection against the gas by breathing through urine-soaked cloth.

The Canadians struggled to hold their position as fighting continued throughout the day. They were eventually forced back, with British forces sent to relieve them. In only a few days, the Canadians had suffered more than 6,000 casualties.

It was a horrible introduction to war on the front made even more hellish by the first large-scale use of poison gas. But in the face of the Germans' blindsiding attack, the Canadians proved that they could hold their own amid utter chaos.

An airplane flies over the ruins of Cloth Hall, Ypres, Belgium.

Left: Percy Bradshaw, a private in the 4th Battalion, was shot during the Second Battle of Ypres and lost mobility in his hand. Even so, he played baseball into his sixties and kept the bullet as a memento. (Submitted by Roger Bradshaw, Percy's son.)

Facing page: A pair of Canadian soldiers wear heavy bandages covering blister burns caused by exposure to mustard gas.

NOTHING LIFTED THE MORALE OF SOLDIERS MORE THAN THEIR CORRESPONDENCE WITH LOVED ONES BACK HOME.

A Canadian writes home from somewhere at the front, circa May 1917.

CHAPTER THREE

Letters from the Front

CHARLOTTE GRAY

Letters sent from the First World War battlefields take us deep into the experience of that shocking bloodbath. Whether writing in untidy scrawls or in carefully formed script, battle-worn soldiers wrote to distant loved ones about their daily routines, their homesickness, and their moments of terror.

For generations, families hung on to bundles of such dog-eared letters, tied up with hair ribbon, binder twine, or pink tape. Some letters lay forgotten because the writer had returned home and life had moved on. More often, the letters remained as painful reminders of the grinning young men who had marched away full of life and ended up dead and buried in a foreign field. Only when the carnage of the trenches had passed from living memory were many of these letters reread, transcribed, or donated to archives.

Now, at websites built by Canada's History Society, the Canadian Letters and Images Project, the Canadian War Museum, and others, those who lost their lives as well as those who made it back to Canada can speak to us across the years.

Soldiers craved letters. "How we all eagerly wait for mail when the rations arrive every night," John Sudbury, twenty-two, wrote from France to his family in Montreal in June 1916. "It's the first thing thought of and asked for and you should see the faces when there's nothing for this one or that one and away they turn, mostly to think of home . . . But how the same faces brighten when from the dugout he who sorts the mail shouts their names! The contrast is wonderful to behold."

Letters helped revive spirits when a recruit found himself in disorienting, terrifying circumstances. Five months after Frank Cousins, a twenty-four-year-old Saskatchewan student, arrived at the front, he feared that his family had forgotten him. "I get so mad when mail comes in and there is none for me," he wrote his sister Nellie in April 1918. "Since coming from Canada I have had but three letters from Mother . . . You cannot imagine how, over in this land, a letter from home cheers and encourages. Without it one feels lost and, as it were, stranded in a sea of desolation."

I WONDER IF YOU MISS ME SOMETIMES (1).
I stand on a lonely seashore,
    And gaze o'er the waters blue;
I picture a land of sunshine,
    And dream all the time of you.
The waves of the ocean divide us,
    But still in my heart you reign;
I'd give all I have in the world, love,
    To see your dear face once again.

Above: In this Great War–era postcard, a soldier looks out to sea as he thinks about the love he has left behind.

Above: Norman Ewart of the 47th Battalion, second from right, and friends hang out a train window as they depart for the war in 1915. Ewart, from Toronto, enlisted in September 1915. He served in France and survived the war. Throughout, he maintained a correspondence with Kit Faris, whom he described in his letters as his "little pal." She's shown above right, on the right, standing with a friend. In one letter, dated October 13, 1916, he raves about the treats he's received. "I am fine & everything is jake. I want to thank you very much for the swell parcel of candy . . . believe me Darling Kit it sure came at the right time."

Right: Alexander Parnell of Montreal carried this 1914 photo with him throughout the war. It shows, from left, his children Jean, two, John, eight; wife, Harriet (née Creswick); and infant daughter, Annie. (Submitted by Sandra Adams, Alexander's granddaughter.)

Far right: John Pritchard Sudbury of Montreal enlisted in July 1915. He served at the front and was wounded at Passchendaele in October of 1917.

However banal the news from home, a handwritten letter was a tangible connection with another life. "How is the weather over there now?" George Tripp, a nineteen-year-old from Huttonville, Ontario, wrote to his childhood friend Lola Passmore in 1916. "I guess it will be skating time again soon."

"Do you remember . . . ?" is a constant refrain. Soldiers yearned for family, friends, and familiar sights, but in the middle of the unprecedented, dehumanizing conditions of trench warfare, they also clung to memories of their civilian identities. They thought wistfully of the days when they were individuals, making their own way in the world, rather than numbered cogs in a giant killing machine. Dreams of walks through local woods, fantasies of waking up in bed at home, visions of family celebrations—all provided an escape from the relentless thud of mortars and whine of sharpshooter bullets. A husband lapped up details of his son's first haircut; a single man asked about his sister's job in a munitions factory and about the neighbour's tea party. Soldiers pined for reminders of the timeless routines of the family farms, small towns, or city streets where they had grown up.

First Nations soldiers often felt particularly alone. About 4,000 status Indians served at the front, in units where all the other civilian soldiers came from British backgrounds. A young Saskatchewan soldier, Mountain Horse, sadly wrote home: "I have not talked Blackfoot for over six months." Another, Abel Watech, told the local Indian agent, "I am quite interested in the news of our reserve. Many is the time I wish I was back in my native country."

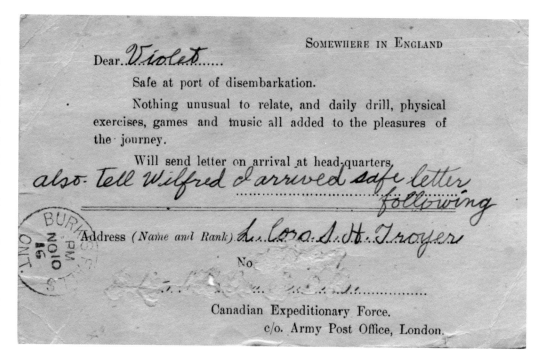

Parcels from home were welcomed, since they contained precious luxuries for men living in filthy dugouts. Will Mayse, a Baptist clergyman from Emerson, Manitoba, listed with glee the contents of one package he received in February 1917: "1 towel, 1 pair socks, 1 box cream crackers, 1 tin of pork & beans, 1 small glass of honey, 1 package of seedless raisins, 1 cake of real bar soap, Wrigley's Spearmint, 1 packet of tobacco, + 2 small candles—pretty good!" Oxo cubes were particularly popular because they dissolved quickly in water heated by a candle stuck in a discarded tin.

When John Sudbury received a parcel from home, he wrote, "My dearest Mother . . . Oh! That little bread pudding took my fancy so much so that I kissed it before I ate it because I thought of the hands that made it. The pastry and cake were also lovely." Some recipients complained of receiving too many pairs of hand-knitted socks and mitts; and some were very specific about what

Above: To save time, many soldiers chose to fill out form letters to send to their loved ones back home. Here, Sutherland Henderson Troyer of Hensall, Ontario, has written a short note to his sweetheart—and future wife—Violet MacMillan, circa November 1916. (Submitted by Judy Modray, Sutherland's granddaughter.)

they wanted: "Please send me a pound of Hudson's Bay tobacco, two pipes, some cigarettes and some Canadian matches," wrote Ed MacNachtan, a young sergeant from Cobourg, Ontario. "It is impossible to buy anything smokeable here."

Boxes of apples or tins of fruitcake were often shared with brothers-in-arms, even if the food was stale or mouldy after the long trip across the Atlantic. Jars of peanut butter and homemade jam cemented new friendships within the alien landscape of ruined villages and blasted trees. George Scherer, a young Ontario recruit, wrote with exhilarating gratitude to his sweetheart, Catherine, about the fudge she sent: "Believe me, it was swell and the rest of the boys said the same thing."

The military mail service established in 1911 by the Militia Department in Ottawa kept the boys in touch with home. Canadian mail was sent to London, where it was sorted into bags for units in the field, then delivered on the ration train. Mail in the other direction took longer to leave Europe, because officers had to censor their subordinates' mail—a task most officers hated as much as the men resented. Soldiers were not supposed to discuss troop movements, armaments, or morale, or to criticize operations or superiors—though some of the letters are surprisingly graphic about horrific injuries and day-to-day squalor.

They were not permitted to send pieces of shrapnel home, although some couldn't resist doing so in response to requests from their children. Those caught breaking the rules were punished, with repeat offenders risking court martial. Many—especially those who didn't have much education—used the standard Field Service Postcard, with its multiple choice approach to communication: "I am quite well / I have been admitted into hospital / sick / wounded / and am going on well / and hope to be discharged soon . . . Letter follows at first opportunity . . . " A weary soldier simply crossed out the inapplicable lines and added his signature.

A tone of stubborn bravado permeates many of the letters mailed from the trenches. Reverend William Beattie, a forty-three-year-old Presbyterian minister who spent three and a half years with Canadian troops in France, marvelled at his fellow countrymen's bravery: "They are a wonderful bunch of fellows so cheerful & take danger so splendidly," he wrote to his mother in 1915. "My

Above: Gordon McMahon did his best to write to his sister during the war. Sometimes it was a longer letter, and at other times, simply a standard soldier's form letter, in which you indicated your general health and status through a series of standardized answers such as "I am quite well" or "I have been admitted to hospital." Sadly, McMahon was killed in action in France in 1917. (Submitted by Edith Bannerman, Gordon's niece.)

old Colonel was telling me that on Sunday the Germans dropped nine shells right into our trenches. The first hit the parades at the back of the trench. Several boys . . . spilled their tea & they got up laughing & blaming the mean Germans for spilling their tea. When each shell fell & hurt no one they yelled across at the German trenches, 'Have to do a little better than that Fritz.'"

John Sudbury would fight within the Ypres Salient and on the Somme in 1916, and at Vimy Ridge and Passchendaele in 1917. Sudbury's letters tell of someone who kept his head when there was danger and raised morale around him. "What else can I spout about?" reads a letter dated October 8, 1916, one of dozens of letters he sent back to his family in Montreal during the war. "Oh! I'll give you the latest parody on 'Keep the Home Fires Burning': Keep the Huns retiring / Keep the guns afiring / Keep the rifles cracking till the Huns are done / Keep the bayonets flashing while the boys are dashing / Turn the Germans inside out / And we'll all go home."

But even Sudbury's optimism sometimes deserted him. Two months later, he was in the trenches with a bad cough and could only stutter out a few lines: "I haven't anything more to write for I feel absolutely void of inspiration." Later wounded at Passchendaele, Sudbury lost his leg to gangrene.

Perhaps the bravado sometimes reflected what the lower ranks felt the censors expected. On other occasions, it seems prompted by naive optimism. In April 1917, Earl Johns, twenty-four, wrote to his mother in Elimville, Ontario: "Fritz throws a few shells near us at a little village once in a while. But that is nothing to what he gets in return. It must be awful over in his lines. One cannot help but pity the poor beggars that have to stay in them." Five months later, Johns was dead.

It was hard to sustain bravado and esprit de corps when conditions were disgusting and fear pervasive. As I read the accounts of life in the trenches, I realize that few twenty-first-century Canadians could cope. A century ago, most Canadians consumed far

Above: Thomas Rayner enlisted on November 15, 1915, in Winnipeg at the age of twenty-three. In a letter to his sister Ada, he jokes about the beating the Germans will receive once he makes it to the front: "Wait til the little black devils get loose we'll make Fritz run round a bit . . . " In September 1916, he was killed in action during the Battle of the Somme. (Submitted by Sherill Zellis, Thomas's great-niece.)

Left: Matthew Archer of Bradford, Ontario, sent this embroidered postcard (above) to his family in 1916. In an October 1916 letter to his mother, Jessie, he wrote, "Dear Mother, in one of your letters you showed a little anxiety that I should be a good boy. I am well aware of the dangers to be faced in England in the way of temptations and drink and women but when I am faced with those temptations the memories of my mother and my Evelyn will keep me pure." He ended by promising to look for the "silver lining" in the war, but added a postscript: "Seeing as I can't see a silver lining, I will try to polish up the dark side, mother." Archer received the Military Medal for bravery at Vimy Ridge in April 1917. He was killed a few months later near Lens, France. (Submitted by Anne-Mae Archer, Matthew's niece.)

fewer calories and performed more physical labour than we do today. They bathed only once or twice a week and lived in unheated houses. But nothing had prepared the troops for the mud, the rats, the lice, the day-to-day horror of being at the front, or the boredom and menial routines of periods spent behind the lines. The citizen-soldiers struggled to convey to folks back home that this was no Boy's Own adventure story.

Howard Curtis, who would lose his life in the closing stages of the 1916 Battle of the Somme, confessed to his mother in Peterborough, Ontario, a year earlier: "We see terrible sights out here that I can't describe to you." Curtis had just spent ten days under brutal shellfire, day and night. "Our casualties were heavy, mostly wounded. It is nerve shattering to be under shellfire. No matter how strong a man's nerves are, they are affected. I have seen many a poor fellow break under the strain."

On June 21, 1916, young George Tripp wrote to his friend Lola Passmore: "We [are] living underground part of the time. I had seen some awful sights before but the last few days I have seen things I'll never be able to forget. I'm only just beginning to find out what war really is." In October 1916, nineteen-year-old Jay Moyer wrote to his sweetheart, Violet, in Toronto: "Modern warfare is not hell, it's worse." Both Tripp

and Moyer would be killed at Vimy Ridge the following April, before reaching their twenty-first birthdays.

Alongside deadening fear and horror was disgust with the living conditions. Chief amongst them was the glutinous mud, which clung to clothes, blocked gun barrels, and left boots soaking and smelly. Private Harry Jennings of Princess Patricia's Canadian Light Infantry received a bullet wound in his skull within weeks of arriving in France from Ontario. Hospitalized in England, he told his mother in a letter dated February 22, 1915, that the war was "absolutely worse than the people ever imagine. The weather is not as cold as Canada of course but it rains or sleet[s] every day nearly." Before he

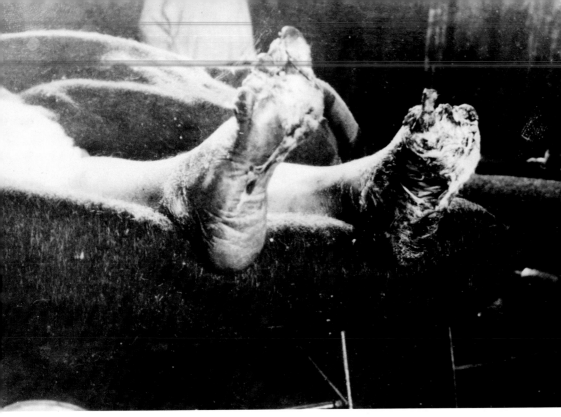

Above: This unidentified soldier is suffering from a case of trench feet, circa 1918.

Right: Earl Johns of the 58th Battalion is holding his infant niece prior to being sent overseas. He enlisted in April 1916. On September 12, 1917, his mother in Elimville, Ontario, received a letter from G. E. Kellett: "I do not wish to write this but knowing you would like to hear from one who was near to Earl at the time of his death and I being a chum of his ever since our coming to France and I assure you it meant a blow to me and also to all the other boys. He died a hero." Johns had died instantly after being hit by an enemy shell.

Pte. Earl Johns with niece Margaret Coultis, c. 1916 Usborne Tp., Huron, ON

was wounded, he had stood for forty-eight hours in knee-deep water, "raw and miserable . . . [and] kept my back humped up and my head down below the trenches all the time." When he was finally rescued, semi-conscious, from no man's land, medical orderlies had to cut off his boots because his feet were so swollen.

Had Jennings stayed at the front, he risked contracting the dreaded trench foot, a crippling condition in pre-antibiotic days. Henry Crozier Smith, a British Columbia rancher, suffered terribly when his artillery unit was sent forward in October 1916. "I had a bad foot and it was all I could do to get to the front. Miles and miles of muddy trenches with mud so sticky that one had to be pulled out at times." As he told his wife, "The journey out [three weeks later] was even worse than in, my foot was very bad and I could hardly make the trip at all." A month later, his wife received the dreaded telegram: "We regret to inform you. . . ."

Many correspondents dealt with the endless discomfort with grim humour. John Sudbury wrote to his mother on May 17, 1916: "We got yesterday what we had eagerly awaited, dreamt of by the hour, thought of, talked of, and smacked our lips over for 16 days previously and the realization was even more enjoyable than the anticipation. We had a bath!" Ron McKinnon from Toronto told his father on February 25, 1917: "We get a clean change at the bath house: socks, towel, two shirts, and drawers. But they are generally lousy but we get used to that; in fact, we are lonesome without a louse or two and new underwear would get lousy as soon as it landed in France. It is always amusing to a tenderfoot to see the old timers lousing a shirt, that is, pulling your shirt off and making a night attack on the lice!" McKinnon was killed in action at Vimy Ridge six weeks later.

David McLean, a Scotsman who had emigrated to Toronto, tried to make a joke of the hardships when he wrote to his young son, George, on November 5, 1916: "You can tell mother she would like it here. We've got such nice company lots of nice big rats so we have lots of fun killing them and tell mother if ever she sends anything be sure and put in some insect powder." He was more candid in a letter to his wife, Lettie, a month later: "I tell you a man hasn't got a fighting chance for his life out here for the shell fire is terrible and I have had some pretty narrow escapes." Little George would grow up fatherless; McLean lost his life in April 1917.

Religious convictions helped some soldiers cling to their sanity. On March 17, 1917, his twentieth birthday, Harold Simpson, who worked in wireless signals, wrote to his mother in Prince Edward Island: "We are not fighting for our king and country merely, we are fighting for humanity and

On Active Service

WITH THE BRITISH EXPEDITIONARY FORCE

you asked me if I ever see any vine yards, no, I see plenty of hop, wheat, oat & rye fields though and the crops are fine about 7 or 8 miles behind the firing line, oh we see life although we don't get much now. I am in the machine gun section now as I could not shoot fast enough with a rifle to suit me so my adress will be M.G. Sec. instead of C. Coy.

I never cared much for Athens and its

Above: Ida Collier stands beside an unidentified friend who is about to head off to the front. Collier, from Portage la Prairie, Manitoba, was a prolific letter writer and corresponded with many friends fighting in the Great War. (Submitted by Julie Duncan, Ida's niece.)

God, and death should hold no terror for the man who does his duty faithfully and well." Perhaps Simpson relied on the terminology of religious crusades to explain the slaughter around him; more likely, his simple Christian faith was his only resort at a time of desperate confusion.

News from Canada about falling recruitment and the 1917 conscription crisis left front-line soldiers feeling betrayed and abandoned. Harry Morris, a Montrealer who had been wounded early in 1917, was furious. "Why don't the boys enlist?" he asked his wife, Lillian. "We need men. What is death on the battlefield compared with what the poor French and . . . Belgians . . . had to put up with? Do the slackers on St. Catherine Street realize that their mothers, wives, sweethearts, and sisters would be in danger if it were not for these English-women who say to their husbands, sons and

brothers, 'Enlist to save the laws of humanity and right'?"

First Nations soldiers at the front also expressed political frustrations. They were being killed and wounded in defence of a country that did not recognize them as citizens—and, at war's end, would not give them the benefits to which non-Native veterans were entitled. Private M. E. Steinhauer, of Saddle Lake, Alberta, a Cree, sent a letter about this from the front to Duncan Campbell Scott, who headed the Department of Indian Affairs in Ottawa: "I have been wondering since I joined the army whether . . . [there is] a possible chance of us getting our franchise . . . after the war is over? I do not think it would be fair not to get anything out of a country that we are fighting for." The plea would go unheard by Scott.

Canadian nurses were an important element in the front-line war effort. Most were part of the Canadian Army Nursing Service, which by 1918 had a total enrolment of 3,141 personnel; 2,504 of them served in Europe—most in Canadian military hospitals in England. But large numbers also staffed casualty-clearing stations close to battle, where the wounded were assessed, treated, or evacuated.

May Grenville was a nurse who served with the American Expeditionary Force and often found herself attending to wounded men while "Fritz . . . bombed all around us and over us." She was never allowed "off the post without gas masks and helmets." On November 23, 1918, she wrote to her mother in Thorold, Ontario: "'Finio La Guerri'— Hurrah! . . . I am very glad it is over. There will be no more poor broken bodies brought

Above: Margaret Munro, shown here in 1915, was engaged to marry Wellington Dennis Murray when the Weyburn, Saskatchewan, man enlisted in April 1916. Murray was killed in action on August 9, 1918. On August 28, Munro received a blunt telegraph from Murray's mother, which read: "Our Murray fell in action. August ninth. Be Brave. Mother."

to us. We had a trainload of patients yesterday who had all been prisoners, and oh, my, how they must hate the Germans!"

But most of the participants of the grim "war to end all wars" limped away from the battlefields with heavy hearts. Harry Morris, John Sudbury, and Harold Simpson were among those lucky enough to make it home. As Simpson set sail from Liverpool in the spring of 1919, he wrote, "There are not a great many of the two hundred and eighty who left Charlottetown on that November morning going back with us." Some of his best pals, he reflected, "will never go back."

MINISTER'S OFFICE

OTTAWA August 11th, 1916.

Personal.

Dear Mr. Lennie,-

Will you kindly accept my sincere
sympathy and condolence in the decease of that worthy
citizen and heroic soldier, your son, Private Lewis
Frederick Lennie.

While one cannot too deeply mourn
the loss of such a brave comrade, there is a consolation in knowing that he did his duty fearlessly and
well, and gave his life for the cause of Liberty and
the upbuilding of the Empire.

Again extending to you my heartfelt
sympathy.

Faithfully,

Sam Hughes.

Major General,
Minister of Militia and Defence,
for Canada.

Charles Edward Lennie, Esq.,
Lindsay,
Ont.

Left: Families dreaded receiving official letters or telegrams from the front, as they often brought news of the injuries or deaths of loved ones. After the July 14, 1916, death of Lewis Frederick Lennie of Lindsay, Ontario, his family received a letter of condolence from Minister of Militia and Defence Sam Hughes. (Submitted by Al Lennie, Lewis's nephew.)

Below: Soldiers often injected humour into their letters to ease the fears of loved ones back home. Here, Bjorn Christianson of Langruth, Manitoba, has written a self-deprecating note on the back of a picture postcard: "It is rather hard luck that cameras should always tell the truth." His photo is on the reverse. (Submitted by Hope Caroll, Stephanie Christianson, and Shirley Christianson, Bjorn's daughter, granddaughter, and daughter-in-law, respectively.)

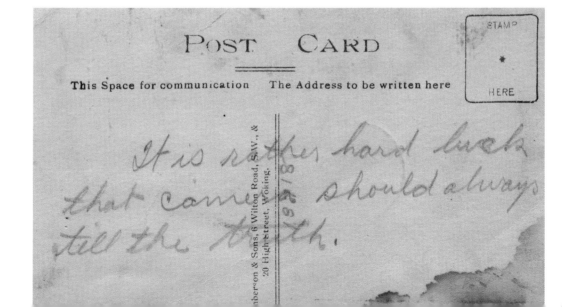

TIES THAT BIND

WHEN THE WAR ERUPTED, ENTIRE FAMILIES ANSWERED THE CALL.

During the Great War, it was not uncommon to see several siblings or close relatives enlist from the same family. For many men, the notion of seeing a brother or cousin march off to war without being by his side was unthinkable. Sadly, with casualty rates so high, blood ties often ended in tragedy for family members back home when not just one but several relatives were injured or killed at the front.

Above: From left, brothers Norman, Jack, and Gordon Mitchell, circa 1917–1918. Norman, a medical doctor, served in the navy, while Jack and Gordon were in the army. All three brothers survived the war. (Submitted by Ruth Borthwick, Jack's daughter.)

Left: When Robert Elderkin's son was born, it was no struggle to find the right name: William. That's because the infant was named after Robert's oldest brother, who went off to war and never returned. Bill Elderkin, left, was one of two Elderkin brothers to serve in the war; Robert was too young to sign up, but middle brother Angus, far left, also served. Bill was killed in action in June 1916. (Submitted by William Elderkin, Robert's son.)

Top: From left to right, friends Gilbert Edward Dryburgh, Karl Mizener, Jerry Pettes (killed in action), and James Harold Maynard Dryburgh from Knowlton, Quebec, in 1918. Brothers Harold and Gilbert were privates in the medical corps. (Submitted by Bev and Gary Crandall; Bev is James's daughter and Gilbert's niece.)

Henry and Isabella Deacon of Monitor, Alberta, saw three of their six sons sign up to fight. Frank, not shown, enlisted in August 1915. In France, he served with the 1st Battalion, Canadian Mounted Rifles, and was shot in the leg at the Somme. He spent more than two years in hospital in England before being sent home to Canada in May 1919.

Fred, middle left, enlisted in October 1915. In November 1916, he was wounded by shrapnel at the Somme and eventually sent home in August 1917.

The youngest brother, Albert, middle right, enlisted in March 1916, at age twenty-one. On September 27, 1918, he was killed in action at the Canal du Nord. (Submitted by Shirley Waldon. The Deacon brothers were her great-uncles.)

Bottom left: Brothers Ervin, left, and Angus McDonald, circa January 1918. The men were living on their family cattle ranch in remote Lac des Roches, British Columbia, when the war broke out in 1914. They, along with younger brother Dan, tried to enlist but were twice rejected on the basis that their farm—and the cattle it produced—was essential for the war effort. In 1917, a letter arrived informing them that two of the three brothers would be permitted to enlist, but the third must stay home. Their father tossed a coin, and Dan lost. Angus enlisted on November 27, 1917, and Ervin followed on December 12.

Bottom right: Dan, shown with his wife, Maude, circa 1919, stayed home and worked the ranch throughout the war. (Submitted by Ervin McDonald's daughter, Ruth McDonald Roberts.)

Top: When brothers Robert and John Gillespie of Winnipeg enlisted, Robert's wife, Annie, had a dark premonition that one of the brothers would not return. Sadly, her vision proved prescient—John, a lieutenant with the 16th Battalion (Canadian Scottish), died of wounds suffered at the Battle of Passchendaele in 1917. Robert, a lieutenant colonel, raised the 226th Battalion and brought it to England, only to see it broken up and its members sent to reinforce other, under-strength battalions. After the war, Robert returned to Manitoba and had a brief stint in politics, helping to found the "Reconstruction Party." Annie later said that, due to the stress and hardships of the war, her husband returned to Canada "a changed man." (Submitted by James Gillespie. Robert was his great-grandfather.)

Page Twenty
Lieutenant J. W. Gillespie
Commanding No. 11 Platoon

Page Ten
Lieutenant-Colonel R. A. Gillespie
Officer Commanding

Bottom left: You can say this about Roy Macfie: he had a great sense of humour. Macfie, shown seated in this 1916 photo postcard, wrote a quick note to his brother: "Dear Bro: Here's a picture I've carried around a long time. I was afraid to send it to anybody. But we weren't nearly so drunk as we look. We only had a beer or two at the time. We look about starved to death too. Be careful who you show it to." Roy was the first of three Macfie brothers to fight in the Great War. Roy and his brother Arthur survived the war, but their brother John was killed during the Battle of Fresnoy in May 1917. (Submitted by John Macfie, Roy's son.)

Bottom right: Brothers Griffin, left, and Charles Mulligan, likely in Medicine Hat, Alberta, in early June 1916. Both men were members of the 27th Battalion, and both survived the war. (Submitted by Mike McMullen. Griffin and Charles were Mike's great-uncles.)

Above: The pain of losing two of her three sons to war was so unbearable that Jean Murray, far left, died of a broken heart at age fifty-five in 1918. "The death of her sons hit her very, very, very hard. Her health just kind of went down-hill," said her great-grandson, John Calvert. "It was all too much for her to take." John Murray, middle, and Alexander Murray, right, were killed just a few weeks apart in 1915. (Submitted by John Calvert. Alexander was his great-uncle.)

Above: Leslie Hale, a sniper with the 46th Battalion, was killed in November 1917 in Belgium. Leslie's brother Victor enlisted in 1916 and was gassed during the war. A third brother, Gerald, survived the war. A fourth brother, Frank, intended to enlist, but before he could, he was injured by a threshing machine during harvest. His arm was amputated to save his life. (Submitted by Grant Hale, great-nephew of Leslie, Gerald, Victor, and Frank Hale.)

Above: Enlisting was a family affair for these Leslie, Saskatchewan, men. On the right is forty-four-year-old Moses Green, a married father of six. He stands next to his son, Arthur, nineteen. Next is Harold Farrer, Moses's cousin, and finally, his son-in-law Percy Edwin Biggs. The men enlisted together in the spring of 1916. Sadly, Arthur was killed a little over a year later during the Battle of Hill 70 in France. (Submitted by Brian Green, Moses's grandson.)

Above: In this 1905 photo, the Smales and Dale families are meeting for a picnic in the Qu'Appelle Valley, with Allister Smales and George M. Smales sitting on their horses. Both would serve overseas during the First World War (Submitted by H.G. Bartlett. Bartlett's mother was Dolly Smales.)

DISORDER AND LOSS

THE BATTLE OF FESTUBERT

JOEL RALPH

Despite standing their ground at St. Julien near Ypres in April 1915, the Canadians and the rest of the Entente forces still had a great deal to learn about attacking an enemy trench. This lack of experience revealed itself at Festubert, France, during a battle that has all but disappeared from the annals of the Great War.

As part of a larger British offensive, the Canadians were hurried into exactly the kind of attack that today summons up all the worst images of trench warfare. Not only were there few clear objectives, but the maps provided also identified them incorrectly.

Artillery barrages, which at the time were considered to be quite large, proved ineffective at best.

And despite repeated requests for more time to prepare, the confused Canadians crossed no man's land in a futile attempt to push the enemy back. Free from harassing artillery fire, the Germans fired at will at the Canadians as they emerged from their protective trenches.

Rushed into a war for which they were not yet prepared, Canadians suffered more than 2,500 casualties in the debacle.

Early defeats in the war, such as the one at Festubert, highlight the transformation of the Canadian Corps over the two years that followed. Within this short time they would learn and develop new tactics of war that would help them capture Vimy Ridge and pave the path to victory over the last one hundred days of the war.

HEROES OF St. JULIEN AND FESTUBERT

Here's to the Soldier who bled
To the Sailor that bravely did fa'.
Their fame is alive, though their spirits have fled
On the wings of the Year that's awa'.

SHALL WE FOLLOW THEIR EXAMPLE?
APPLY AT RECRUITING STATION

The landscape at Festubert remained a wasteland four years after the battle when this photograph was taken in April 1919.

FOR THE PIONEERS OF FLIGHT, AERIAL COMBAT WAS GLAMOROUS YET EVERY BIT AS DANGEROUS AS FIGHTING IT OUT IN THE TRENCHES.

A Royal Flying Corps cadet in Ontario practices with a mounted "camera gun."

CHAPTER 4

The Cavalry of the Clouds

WAYNE RALPH

I met him on Easter Monday, April 1, 1991, in Toronto. He was ninety-five and dying of cancer. He dressed for my visit in a dark blue blazer with a Royal Flying Corps (RFC) gold badge, a tie, and grey trousers. As I came into the room, he was standing with his back to me at the dining table. The falling snow outside the picture window beyond the table was so thick that the other high-rise apartments could be seen only as pale shadows. Introduced by his daughter Virginia, Gerry Birks shook my hand and invited me to sit down.

I knew nothing of him beyond a brief entry in a history book. I didn't know it then, but I was meeting the last living Canadian-born RFC fighter ace of the Great War. To be an ace, you had to have shot down, or forced down, at least five enemy aircraft or balloons.

His daughter had warned me that he was deaf and an interview might be difficult. I didn't know that Sopwith Camel pilots who were lucky enough to get old went deaf due to the damage caused by the noise of the engine and machine guns. I wrote my questions on notepaper, and he read them, answering me in a loud, quavering voice.

"Did you shoot anybody down in the war?" He looked at the paper, looked up at me, and said, "Twelve. Six in flames." He was still proud of that record and the evidence of his accurate gunnery. Relentlessly, he had searched for and found the body of his fifth victim to confirm his status as an ace. One of his proudest moments happened high above the Italian Alps on a spring day in 1918, when he fought against one of the highest-scoring Austro-Hungarian aces, József Kiss, sending him to his death.

At 4:00 p.m., he asked if I wanted a drink. "He'd really like to have a drink with you," said Virginia. He went to a polished cabinet, mixed us gin tonics, and toasted the day and my visit. Later, wearing a wool overcoat and a fedora, he got into a cab to attend a family dinner; the snow had melted on the streets and the sun was shining. I never saw him again, as he died the following month. He had, in the expression of his fellow flyers of that long-ago war, "flown west."

Above: Pilot Gerald Birks in a studio shot taken in July 1918 in London, England. (Submitted by Virginia Alexander, Gerald's daughter.) Inset: Gerald Birks in Toronto, circa 1991. (Courtesy of Wayne Ralph.)

Above: Herbert Gardiner, middle, and fellow Royal Flying Corps members pose in front of the wreckage of a plane. Gardiner has written "not mine!" across the photo. Gardiner was attending the University of Toronto at the time of his enlistment. He survived the war, only to die from complications related to injuries he sustained during the conflict. (Submitted by Jane Dimock-Mahoney, Herbert's great-niece.)

Right: Royal Flying Corps cadets at Camp Borden, Ontario, are taught the proper technique to swing an airplane propeller, circa 1917.

Gerry Birks was one of the grandsons of Henry Birks, the silver and jewellery merchant from Montreal. It was the custom for affluent middle-class families to offer their sons up to the war effort, and many of Henry Birks's descendants volunteered. Gerry enlisted with Montreal's 73rd Battalion, the Black Watch (Royal Highland Regiment) of Canada, on August 31, 1915. He was wounded at the Somme in 1916. After recovering in Montreal, Birks volunteered for pilot training for RFC Canada, established in 1917 as a training organization of the British RFC.

Birks might have signed up as an airman earlier, but like those of many Canadian young men who wished to serve as pilots, his opportunities to do so were limited. The Canadian government in 1914, faced with the enormous cost of raising the Canadian Expeditionary Force (CEF), did not want to fund a Canadian Flying Corps. Thus, at the outbreak of the war, the only way for a young man in Canada to become a military flyer (only men were considered candidates) was to apply with a British air service—the RFC or the Royal Naval Air Service (RNAS). To qualify, he first needed to obtain a civil pilot's certificate. The few schools in existence, founded by the pioneers of powered flight, Orville Wright or Glenn Curtiss, were overburdened by the demand, and the cost was enormous—one dollar a minute, with about four hundred minutes in the air to qualify. Few sons of farmers or of working-class families applied.

Above: In 1917, Lieutenant Ralph Sausmarez Carey had his portrait taken. "I didn't expect then that I would ever get back alive to my family so I wanted them to have a picture to remember me by," the Royal Flying Corps officer from Winnipeg later wrote. He honed his dogfighting skills by practising with a "camera gun" mounted to his plane; the goal was to line "enemy" pilots in the sights and snap them with the camera. (Submitted by Christine Willis, Ralph's granddaughter.)

With an acceptable flying certificate, a Canadian could receive a probationary or temporary officer's commission, a paid ship passage to England, and further training. Some affluent young men paid their own way across the Atlantic to volunteer directly with the British air services.

Among the first Canadians to fly were a couple of graduates from the Royal Military College of Canada (RMC) who were already with the RFC, having been commissioned before the war in the imperial forces of Britain. Others gained officers' commissions in the first months of the war in British regiments and then transferred quickly from their regiments to flying schools. Though not in Canadian uniforms, these adventurers were among the first Canadians to be wounded or killed in action. Theirs was an individual glory that did not adhere to the Dominion of Canada.

In the first two years, flyers were the eyes of the army, the so-called "cavalry of the clouds." Aerial photography; artillery fire coordination (corps co-operation); and ground attack (contact patrol), bombing, and air superiority all evolved from visual observation. One hundred years later, however, it is only the aerial fighting between pilots that we remember; the legendary figures are all fighter pilots. By war's end, ten out of the twenty-seven highest-scoring British Empire fighter aces were Canadians. The most familiar names in 1918 were Billy Bishop, Raymond Collishaw, Donald MacLaren, and William Barker.

Students of aerial warfare recognize by name the first flyers of Canada: from Montreal was Frederick Wanklyn (RMC, class of 1909); from Winnipeg was Redford Mulock (McGill University, Engineering, class of 1909); from Vancouver, William Gladstone Murray (Rhodes Scholar at New College, Oxford, 1913); and, from Toronto, Arthur Knight (born in Bedford, England, but educated in Canada and a student at the University of Toronto). The wealthy Bell-Irving family from Vancouver contributed two

Above: An unidentified Canadian airman grins as he sits in a biplane bearing a special message for Germany's leader: "To Hell with the Kaiser." (Submitted by Jo Ann Alexander and Heather Rider.)

Left: Zeppelins were used throughout the war for observation and for bombing, but quickly grew obsolete due to improvements in airplane technology. This photo is part of a collection owned by Arthur Russell Attridge, who served with the Royal Flying Corps. (Submitted by Ross Attridge, Arthur's great-nephew.)

Hangars at Amric.

daughters and five sons to the war, two of whom, Malcolm and Duncan, became decorated flyers by 1916. "Red" Mulock, Duncan Bell-Irving, and Arthur Knight shared honours as the first three Canadian flyers to achieve the status of ace.

Mulock had a versatile war career, participating in bombing raids and an unsuccessful night attack against a Zeppelin airship. Born in 1886, he had maturity and leadership that resulted in his promotion to colonel, the highest rank held by a Canadian flyer in combat.

Arthur Knight had fought aerial battles against some of the great flyers of the German air force and, in October 1916, was in the air on the morning that the legendary Oswald Boelcke died. The German tactical genius, while attempting to shoot down Knight, died when his Albatros fighter and that of his wingman collided. But Boelcke's protegé Manfred Freiherr von Richthofen (soon to be more famous as "the Red Baron") shot down and killed Knight two months later. Knight was von Richthofen's thirteenth victory in a score that rose to eighty.

The Red Baron was the highest-scoring ace of any nation in the war. He fought frequently with Canadians, shooting down, among others, Geoffrey Brichta of Battleford, Saskatchewan; Duncan McRae of Alexandria, Ontario; Albert Cuzner of Ottawa; and Allan Switzer Todd of Georgetown, Ontario.

On the morning of April 21, 1918, the Red Baron was chasing Canadian flyer Wilfrid "Wop" May of Edmonton at a very low altitude. Arthur Roy Brown of Carleton Place, Ontario, seeing his inexperienced friend in

Above: Roy Everton Goodfellow served as a pilot for the Royal Flying Corps, later the Royal Air Force, until 1919. (Submitted by Audrey McDowall, Roy's daughter.)

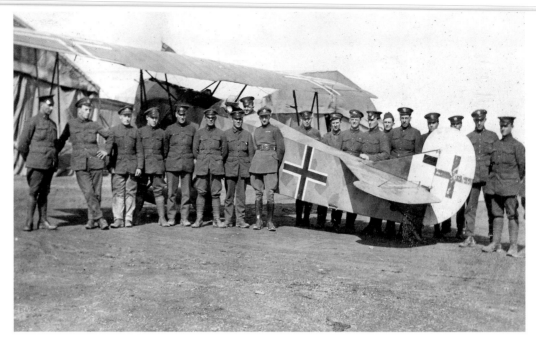

Above: Norman Fitzsimonds, fifth from right, and a group of Canadian servicemen pose with a plane that was surrendered by the Germans following the armistice, circa late fall of 1918. Fitzsimonds, from Huntingdon, Quebec, enlisted in the army on October 1917 but was loaned to the Royal Air Force to work as an airplane mechanic. (Submitted by Laurel Fitzsimonds, Norman's granddaughter.)

trouble, dived at high speed at von Richthofen's Fokker triplane.

With tracer bullets coming at him from an invisible enemy concealed by the sun, von Richthofen turned sharply right toward higher ground. But his escape path over a ridge to home exposed him to ground fire from Australian army machine gunners and riflemen. One of their bullets mortally wounded him. He died in his cockpit shortly after crash-landing. Within hours, all knew the dramatic news that Germany's deadliest air fighter was dead. Politically, it was important to know who was responsible. Brown's own combat report was noncommittal about the encounter: " . . . dived on pure red triplane which was firing on Lieut. May. I got a long burst into him and he went down vertical . . . "

But his squadron commander insisted that Brown's actions were decisive, and two other pilots testified that they saw the Fokker triplane crash after Brown's pass. Higher-ranking commanders of the newly formed RAF accepted the combat report, and Brown became, and still is, officially the flyer who finished off a legend.

But Brown took no pleasure or pride in it. Already an experienced and decorated fighter ace, he knew how the military hierarchy worked. The next morning, Brown viewed von Richthofen's corpse propped upright on a plywood board. He wrote his family to say how heartsick he was to see the dead body of the fine-looking young man: "It is a terrible thing when you think of it that they should examine a body to see who should have the credit of killing him."

By 1918, the training system of the RFC in Canada and, in the winter of 1917 to 1918, in Texas, was graduating over one hundred pilots and observers every month. More than 30 percent of the RAF flying personnel in Italy in 1918 were Canadians. Canadians were flying in all types of operations and in every far-flung theatre of war, from East Africa to the Middle East.

We do not know how many Canadians served in or flew with the imperial forces of

Great Britain. The most common figure is about 22,000, but this includes thousands of Americans who learned to fly in Canada in 1917 to 1918 before joining U.S. Air Service squadrons, as well as many others who happened to live in Canada but were not born here. The total number of ground crew and aircrew together likely exceeded 15,000 in the last months of the conflict. But no comprehensive records were kept to say where aviation recruits were born, so there is no definitive number.

About fourteen hundred Canadian flyers were killed in action or died in service, a tiny fraction of the more than 60,000 of the CEF, but thousands more were wounded or taken prisoner. The survival rate in aerial combat was not much better than in infantry operations. An inexperienced flyer in April 1917 or September 1918, two particularly high-loss months of the Great War, might last only a few days, perhaps a couple of weeks, before being injured or wounded, taken prisoner, or killed.

Gerry Birks's friend William Hilborn of Cariboo District, British Columbia, is buried at Montecchio Precalcino, Italy. He died about a month after his twentieth birthday

Above: Pilot William Hilborn of Caribou District, British Columbia, recorded seven kills before dying in August 1918 of injuries sustained in a crash. (Submitted by Margaret Sawyer, William's niece.)

in August 1918 from crash-related injuries. At the time of his death, he was already a captain, a seven-victory ace, and a recipient of the Distinguished Flying Cross. But, as he wrote not long before his death, "Decorations are very nice, but I don't believe in taking foolish chances to get them. I have just gone along, and done my work, and with a little luck have done pretty well."

Birks survived and was awarded the Military Cross and bar. But after the war, he never flew again. He went to work at Henry Birks & Sons following his return to Canada and later founded his own investment firm.

The flight commander of Birks and Hilborn, William Barker of Dauphin, Manitoba, came home from the war as Canada's most decorated war hero. He was awarded the Empire's highest medal, the Victoria Cross (VC), and established the first scheduled air transport service with fellow VC recipient Billy Bishop. In 1924, Barker became the acting director of the newly created Royal Canadian Air Force (RCAF). He died in a plane crash six years later. It's clear, though, from a letter he wrote to his family during the war, that his wartime experiences had weighed heavily on him. "I always seem to get the . . . sad job of writing to relatives of men killed here, and I am going to stop. A person doesn't know what it is like until they have tried it several times."

Many of Canada's First World War pilots went on to lead celebrated postwar lives. Wop May became a famous bush pilot. Conn Smythe founded the Toronto Maple Leafs hockey team. William Gladstone Murray became the first general manager of the Canadian Broadcasting Corporation radio network in 1936.

Some returned to serve in the Second World War, with their faces displayed on RCAF recruiting posters to entice a new generation. Billy Bishop became the director of recruiting for the RCAF. Raymond Collishaw of Nanaimo, British Columbia—who finished the Great War as the RAF's second-highest-scoring ace—commanded all RAF forces against the Axis in the Western Desert in 1940 to 1941.

The birth of aerial warfare produced outstanding leaders who, if they survived, contributed immeasurably to the growth and evolution of Canadian society. They were the founding generation of air transportation, which opened the North and shrank a huge country. Aviation makes Canada work in a way that no other technological invention does. Our Great War flyers, courageous and resourceful in all of life's challenges, made it possible.

Right: This July 1916 photo is unique for what is written in the margins—the men's ethnicities: "Irish . . . English . . . Delaware . . . Mohawk . . . Irish . . . Scotch." These officers are members of the 107th "Timber Wolf" Battalion. Raised in November 1915, it was the only fully integrated First World War battalion featuring First Nations soldiers. More than half of its nine hundred members were Aboriginal, with many of those volunteers hailing from Ontario and Manitoba. Among them was Lieutenant James David Moses, back row, far right. Moses was a Delaware from the Six Nations of the Grand River Reserve near Brantford, Ontario. At the time of his enlistment in February 1916, he was also active in his local militia unit, the 114th Battalion, which was comprised entirely of First Nations volunteers. In 1917, Moses was seconded to the 57th Squadron of the Royal Flying Corps as an aerial observer and gunner. On April 1, 1918, he and his pilot disappeared during a bombing mission against the Germans. The man in the front row, far left, Lieutenant Oliver Milton Martin, a Mohawk also from the Grand River Reserve, survived the war and went on to serve in the Second World War as a brigadier, the highest rank ever attained by an Aboriginal Canadian. In total, more than 4,000 First Nations Canadians served in the Great War. (Submitted by John Moses, great-nephew of James.)

Above: Harold Austin Boettger, second from left, and his fellow Royal Flying Corps cadets pose for a photo at the RFC training base in Toronto, circa 1917–1918. (Submitted by Jo Ann Alexander, Harold's daughter, and Heather Rider, his granddaughter.)

Top right: Royal Air Force pilot John William Grant sits in the cockpit of an R.E. 8 biplane near Archangel, Russia, sometime between 1919 and 1920 as part of Britain's support of anti-Bolshevik forces during the Russian Civil War. During this period, Grant flew over enemy lines with an observer (seated behind him in the picture) who photographed landscapes and facilities for intelligence purposes. (Submitted by Charles Grant, John's son.)

Bottom right: Harold "Gus" Edwards, a flight sub lieutenant in the Royal Naval Air Service, in England in June 1916. Edwards was shot down and captured by German troops on April 14, 1917. He later wrote to a friend, "I am a prisoner at Karlsruhe. I was shot down after lengthy engagement with several enemy machines. My observer . . . was wounded in about fifteen places and died a few minutes after we came down. Luckily we struck the ground in such a way that I was unhurt. Since then I have sombered away with a gnawing in my stomach like many others who have shared this fate." After several failed attempts, he and two others managed to escape, but were recaptured after ten days on the run. He spent the remainder of the war in various prison camps. After the armistice, he served in the Canadian Air Force, retiring with the rank of air marshal. (Submitted by Suzanne K. Edwards, Harold's daughter.)

WITH JUST TWO AGING WARSHIPS AND ONLY A THIRD OF THE CREW NEEDED TO MAN THEM, CANADA WAS FORCED TO QUICKLY BRING ITS NAVY UP TO PAR.

CHAPTER 5

Seaworthy

ROGER SARTY

On June 27, 1918, a German submarine launched a brazen attack that would fuel the fury of Canadian troops in a later battle. The *U-86* torpedoed the hospital ship *Llandovery Castle* in the Atlantic, about 224 kilometres off the coast of southern Ireland. The British vessel was under charter to Canada to transport injured and sick troops home from the Western Front. The ship was returning from Halifax, and had no casualties aboard, but only 24 members of the 258 crew and Canadian army medical personnel on board survived.

Among those lost were all fourteen nursing sisters, whose lifeboat failed to get clear of the suction produced by the hull's rapid descent below the surface. Sergeant Arthur Knight, who was in the boat and lived, reported that the nightmare unfolded over a period of eight minutes:

"In that whole time I did not hear a complaint or a murmur from one of the sisters . . . There was not a cry for help or any outward evidence of fear. In the entire time I overheard only one remark, when the matron, Nursing Sister M. M. Fraser, turned to me as we drifted helplessly towards the stern of the ship and asked—'Sergeant, do you think there is any hope for us?'—I replied 'No,' seeing myself our helplessness without oars and the sinking condition of the stern of the ship. A few seconds later we were drawn into the whirlpool of the submerged afterdeck and the last I saw of the nursing sisters was as they were thrown over the side of the boat."

Knight, who sank and surfaced three times, eventually clung to a piece of wreckage and was rescued. Several boats with many more people got clear of the wreck, but the submarine surfaced and opened fire, evidently

Facing page: As the saying goes, any port in a storm. Robert Percival Webber of Paris, Ontario, finds a comfy perch aboard a troopship while en route to Canada, circa 1919. After the war, Webber worked at *The Toronto Telegram* as its financial editor and as a columnist. His column was titled "How Thomas Richard Henry Sees It." He would say the column was about every man—any Tom, Dick, and Harry. (Submitted by Frances McColl, Robert's daughter.)

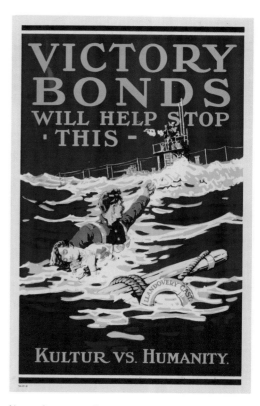

Above: A propaganda poster promotes the sale of Victory Bonds by denouncing the German submarine attack on the Canadian hospital ship *Llandovery Castle*.

Above: Sailors of the Royal Naval Canadian Volunteer Reserve, circa 1917–1918.

Above: Members of the Royal Naval Canadian Volunteer Reserve march in a Victory Bond parade at Sydney, Nova Scotia, circa 1918.

in an effort to erase evidence of an attack on a clearly marked hospital ship. When the Canadian Corps on the Western Front next attacked, at Amiens on August 8, 1918, the battle cry was, "Remember the *Llandovery Castle*."

When the war broke out in August 1914, the Borden government was convinced that Canada could not and should not involve itself in operations at sea. That was why the country focused its effort on raising land forces. Those land forces—the Canadian Corps that fought on the Western Front—were always the first priority. But Canada also became deeply committed to the war on the oceans.

There was no choice. Britain's most important source of vital imports of food, raw materials, and industrial goods came in merchant ships that either sailed from Canadian ports or followed routes from U.S. ports that passed close by the Maritime

provinces and Newfoundland. Demands for North American supplies multiplied as the war continued, straining even Britain's vast merchant marine. Defence of the vulnerable merchant vessels against determined enemy attack stretched Britain's Royal Navy to the limit.

In 1914, Canada had a navy, but just barely. Founded in 1910, the Royal Canadian Navy had nearly been throttled at birth by political controversy that was still unresolved at the beginning of the war. The service possessed only two warships—out-of-date British cruisers taken over in 1910 for training duties—and about 350 personnel, only a third of the number needed to crew the two vessels. Newfoundland, then a dominion of the British Empire and separate from Canada, had established a division of the Royal Naval Reserve at St. John's,

where, in the off-season, fishermen received naval training from British instructors.

British cruisers soon arrived at Halifax and at Victoria-Esquimalt, British Columbia, to protect shipping in Canadian and Newfoundland waters. Fast German cruisers were known to be at large in the eastern Pacific and western Atlantic. German merchant ships, moreover, were taking refuge in U.S. ports under the protection of American neutrality. These vessels were well-positioned to rush to sea to support the fast cruisers with fuel and supplies or to take on armaments and attack British Empire shipping in Canadian and U.S. waters.

As luck would have it, the single Canadian warship on the West Coast, HMCS *Rainbow*, was ready for sea. Local volunteers—the first units of what was known as the Royal Naval Canadian Volunteer

Top: The sailor's life was not for everyone. Such was the case for John "Jack" Harding, shown here aboard HMS *Suffolk*, circa 1915, centre, holding a cat. Harding joined the British navy in 1914 as a sixteen-year-old. In 1916, while serving aboard HMS *Cumberland*, the sailor jumped ship while the vessel was undergoing repairs in Nova Scotia. Hiding his naval uniform under a rock, he enlisted with the Canadian army, using the alias John Jones (his mother's maiden name), and went on to fight at Vimy Ridge. After the war, the British Admiralty— citing his service in the trenches—pardoned Harding for going AWOL. Harding settled in Toronto. (Submitted by Mitch Bubulj, Jack's grandson.)

Bottom: Canadian naval cadets aboard HMS *Berwick* at Portsmouth, England, in April 1914. These men were among the first class of officer cadets who in 1911 sailed with a British cruiser for sea training because of the poor state of the Canadian Navy.

Reserve—had prepared the ship for a fisheries patrol. Since there was no major Royal Navy warship in the eastern Pacific, the British Admiralty urged that she put to sea on August 3, the day before the outbreak of war, and head south to San Francisco to protect British shipping against a German cruiser heading north from Mexican waters. *Rainbow* carried out her mission and returned to Esquimalt on August 13, 1914—much to the relief of the navy and the local population. The out-of-date ship with mostly only partially trained reservists in her crew wouldn't have stood a chance against the more modern and fully efficient German vessel.

British warships were able to reach the East Coast more quickly. Rear Admiral Christopher Cradock's small squadron at Bermuda was reinforced by additional ships that came to Halifax from the United Kingdom. On August 17, at sea south of Halifax, Cradock shifted from the cruiser *Suffolk* to the larger, newly arrived cruiser HMS *Good Hope* and headed for South America with three other warships. This was in response to moves by the German navy's China squadron, under the command of Vice Admiral Maximilian Graf von Spee, which was heading across the Pacific, evidently to break into the south Atlantic.

On *Suffolk* were seven young Canadian midshipmen—officers under training from the first class of officer cadets that had entered the Royal Canadian Navy at the beginning of 1911. Because of the parlous state of the Canadian service, the young men were assigned to British ships for sea training. *Good Hope* was short of midshipmen, and thus four of the Canadians transferred with Cradock. Ten weeks later,

they were lost, the first Canadians killed by enemy action in the war.

The action took place on the evening of November 1, 1914, when Cradock engaged von Spee's superior force off Coronel, Chile. After forty-five minutes of combat, *Good Hope* was a flaming wreck. An officer on the fast British cruiser *Glasgow*, which escaped, described what happened: "At 1950 [hours] there was a terrible explosion onboard between her mainmast and her after funnel; the gust of flames, each a height of over 200 feet, lighting up a cloud of debris that was flying still higher in the air. She lay . . . a low black hull lighted only by a dull glow [of internal fires]."

Good Hope went down with all nine hundred of her people, including midshipmen Malcolm Cann of Yarmouth, Nova Scotia; John Victor Hatheway of Fredericton, New Brunswick; and William Palmer and Arthur Silver, both of Halifax.

Canada's only warship on the Atlantic coast was HMCS *Niobe*, a cruiser less out of date and much larger than *Rainbow*. In 1914 to 1915, *Niobe* and its crew worked as part of a British squadron based in Halifax, patrolling off New York and intercepting German ships heading into or out of harbour.

To help bolster strength on the seas, the Royal Navy sent recruiters to Canada. In the spring of 1916, the recruiters' campaign persuaded Arthur Lower, a twenty-five-year-old teacher at the University of Toronto Schools, to join the British service. Within a few months, Lower (later to become one of Canada's foremost historians) was a junior officer in a seventy-five-foot-long wooden "motor launch." Motor launches were driven by

powerful gasoline engines and carried a few light guns and depth charges. The British had ordered 550 of the vessels from the United States, but, in view of American neutrality, the parts were shipped to Canada and assembled at Montreal and Quebec City. Lower's boat operated in the English Channel, which the Royal Navy tried to block to prevent German vessels from reaching the open sea.

He described his first winter in service, in 1916 to 1917, as featuring mainly "boredom," punctuated by occasional flashes of sheer terror. As he wrote in his memoirs:

"There took place one of those hit-and-run destroyer raids that the Germans organized from their bases on the Belgian coast. German destroyers . . . would dash through the straits, firing on everything in sight. Sinking ships was secondary, the primary objective being to run submarines through, for these had to go through on the surface, the British minefields preventing their submerging. The raid . . . cost us a fairly heavy price . . . and I don't know why the little M.L. on which I was did not meet its fate, too, for we were subjected to the concentrated fire of several German destroyers at short range and in the full glare of their searchlights."

The submarines that ran clear of the British defences had become the main German offensive weapon. The Germans had lost von Spee's south Atlantic squadron to a powerful British force near the Falkland

Above: Arthur Lower, a Toronto teacher who joined Britain's Royal Naval Volunteer Reserve, on his anti-submarine motor launch at Dover, England, 1916.

Islands on December 8, 1914. Meanwhile, the main German battle fleet was bottled up in the North Sea by the superior British battle force. By contrast, the submarines, once out on the high seas, were able to avoid the Royal Navy and to strike with devastating effect against unprotected merchant ships.

The answer to the submarine menace was finally implemented in 1917; merchant ships started sailing in groups—convoys—under the protection of warships equipped with depth charges. Frank Houghton, who entered the Royal Canadian Navy as an officer cadet in 1913 and, like his colleagues, was sent to the Royal Navy for training and experience, was assigned in early 1918 to a small anti-submarine warship that escorted convoys in British waters. He described the challenge of the relentless duty at sea in a letter home:

"I am on watch on the bridge twelve hours out of twenty-four on one day; ten hours the next; and six the next. Then round again. I don't seem to have had more than five hours of sleep at a time for years . . . The ship falls over herself at the slightest provocation; for the first three days I was deathly seasick and ate nothing at all. Had to keep my watch on the bridge just the same—perhaps the best cure . . . This job is just an existence—nothing more. One eats, works and sleeps, round and round in a never-ending circle. There is neither the time nor the inclination to think; the instinctive part of the brain only is in use."

The Royal Canadian Navy, in addition to helping Britain raise anti-submarine forces, urgently built up a force of small patrol vessels to protect shipping in Canadian waters, where the overextended Royal Navy could give very little help. The new Canadian flotilla ran convoys that kept shipping clear of the submarines, but there were attacks on vessels that sailed independently.

On the morning of August 5, 1918, the tanker *Luz Blanca*, under charter to Imperial Oil of Canada, sailed from Halifax. She was armed with a single small twelve-pounder gun for self-defence and crewed by two members of the Royal Naval Reserve. The ship was attacked at 11:40 a.m., when it was about fifty-five kilometres southwest of the Halifax headlands. "The shock of a terrific explosion was felt . . . A German torpedo had found its mark in Tank Number Eight. The concussion was so great as to shift the compass from its tripod on the bridge," the ship's captain, John Thomas, said in a later interview.

Thomas ordered his crew to man the gun and then head full steam toward Halifax. For the next two hours, the German

Above: The tanker *Luz Blanca*, circa 1918.

Above: Frank L. Houghton, seated, right, and his fellow officer cadets, Royal Naval College of Canada, Halifax, circa 1913.

submarine harried the ship, firing forty-five-kilogram projectiles with its fifteen-centimetre deck guns. "High explosive shells struck the water in all directions . . . each one sending a geyser spouting seventy or eighty feet into the air," Thomas said. The *Luz Blanca*'s gun crew was handicapped because a torpedo had damaged their gun mounting, and they had to swivel it by hand. This meant the Germans

Above: Lieutenant Colonel Walter Ernest Seaborn, second from right, of the 210th Battalion, joins the RMS *Carpathia* gun crew during firing drills using the ship's six-inch deck gun in April 1917. The Moose Jaw, Saskatchewan, lawyer raised his own battalion, which made the passage to England aboard the *Carpathia*, famous for its role in rescuing survivors of the *Titanic* disaster of 1912. The *Carpathia* was later sunk by a German submarine in 1918. (Submitted by Clark Seaborn, Walter's grandson.)

could fire several shots for every one returned by the *Luz Blanca*.

The submarine strafed the *Luz Blanca* with gunfire, forcing the crew to abandon ship. Luckily, a U.S. Navy anti-submarine vessel, on loan to the Canadian navy, appeared over the horizon, "and the U-boat disappeared."

This was *U-156*, which had already created havoc off New York and Cape Cod, before heading to Nova Scotia. Her orders, transmitted in coded radio messages that

British intelligence had decrypted and passed to the Canadian navy, were in fact to operate in U.S. waters, which was why *Luz Blanca* had been allowed to sail without escort. With the obvious German interest in Halifax, the British and Canadian authorities quickly shifted the most valuable shipping into convoys that assembled at Quebec City to sail out of the Gulf of St. Lawrence, either through the southern entrance by Cape Breton or north of Newfoundland, through the Strait of Belle Isle. The small Canadian escort ships, based at Sydney, Cape Breton, in hastily improvised facilities on that city's ill-equipped waterfront, struggled in the late summer and fall storms to shepherd these convoys through the long St. Lawrence passage.

Unable to find any other large ships, *U-156* ran amok among the scattered fishing fleet—mostly sailing schooners that sat immobile while the dories connected to them

were out tending fishing lines. On August 20, 1918, off Cape Breton, the sub captured the Canadian steam trawler *Triumph*. The Germans ran the *Triumph* as a sea raider for a few days, sinking six schooners: "I thought the captain was joking with us," was the reaction of one schooner man when the familiar trawler that had been hijacked by the Germans approached and ordered him to stop. The trawler's coal ran out within a couple of days, and the Germans sank her. In total, during her cruise in Canadian waters, *U-156* destroyed twenty-one fishing vessels (including those sunk by *Triumph*) together with a small Newfoundland steamer and *Luz Blanca*.

By the war's end, the Canadian navy had recruited nearly 10,000 personnel, who served in both the Canadian and British navies, while many other Canadians, like Arthur Lower, entered the Royal Navy directly. More than nineteen hundred Newfoundlanders served in the Canadian and British navies, and their superb seamanship won plaudits from both services. Thousands of Canadian and Newfoundland merchant seamen faced the perils of enemy attack while carrying supplies essential to the Allied war effort or fishing to provide vital high-protein food for the armed forces and populations of the Allied countries. Some 900 Canadian and Newfoundland naval and merchant seamen lost their lives during the course of the war; 578 of them were merchant mariners.

Despite the government's early reluctance to commit to a naval force, the Royal Canadian Navy's contribution to the war effort proved significant in the end.

Above: John Newton, second from right, and his mates enjoy a lighter moment aboard the RMS *Grampian*, circa October 1916. Newton, a football star, helped the University of Toronto Varsity Blues win the first Grey Cup championship in 1909.

Right: John Henry McVittie, circa 1920. He joined the Royal Naval Canadian Volunteer Reserve on November 2, 1917, and served on HMCS *Margaret*, a patrol ship that sailed out of Halifax. On December 6, 1917, while the *Margaret* was in port, the ships *Mont-Blanc* and *Imo* collided in Halifax Harbour, resulting in the devastating Halifax explosion. Moored about two kilometres away, the *Margaret* was only lightly damaged.
(Submitted by Brian Latham, John's nephew.)

WHEN THEY WEREN'T DODGING DEATH, SOLDIERS OF THE GREAT WAR FOUND WAYS TO KEEP THEIR SPIRITS HIGH.

Bottoms up! Here, Arthur Elsegood of the 15th Battalion, left, and his new pal—identified only as a "Norwich man"—share a bottle of wine in this 1917 photo postcard sent to Elsegood's brother Sidney.
(Submitted by Janette Kasperski, Arthur's granddaughter.)

CHAPTER SIX

Hope amid the Madness

TIM COOK

The shell-shattered Western Front, with its hundreds of kilometres of trenches, barbed wire, and unburied corpses, is the most powerful motif of the Great War. A hundred years later, we shudder at the thought of soldiers crouched beneath the earth, cowering under the fall of shells or the raking fire of bullets, trapped in a struggle of suffering, deprivation, and despair.

Yet there was more to the soldiers' experience in the trenches. They banded together, drew strength from one another, wrote letters home to loved ones, and were cycled to the rear for a rest every four to six days. They also found ways to cope by developing and sustaining a rich and closed culture.

Historians have studied the culture of the Great War, but usually through the eyes of the elite poets, novelists, or painters. While this small group has left a powerful legacy of cultural artifacts, most of the Canadians who enlisted averaged a grade-six education; they would never paint in the official war art program or write poignant prose or poetry like the university-educated officers who have

Above: New recruits horse around at Camp Hughes circa 1916. Did all these smiling men survive the war?

become the memory guides for generations.

Yet rank-and-file soldiers also had a culture that emerged in the trenches. This was a lowbrow, popular culture, and it can be partially reconstructed through the rumours and songs that were wildly popular on the front lines. There were also soldier-published newspapers that captured their thoughts, poetry, and cartoons in print. Often steeped in humour, this culture normalized the abnormal, helped make sense of the war, and even offered hope during the long nightmare of trench warfare.

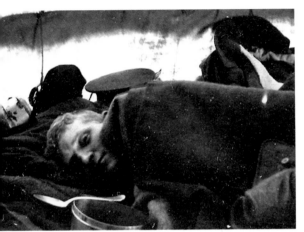

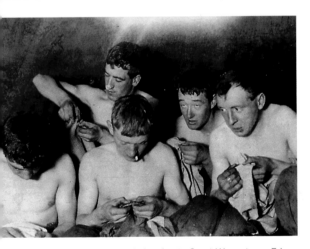

A series of photos belonging to Great War veteran Eric Hearle of Hamilton offers a candid glimpse of life during training in England. Here, Hearle and other members of the 4th Battalion are seen playing cards, smoking, relaxing, and even picking their clothes free of lice while at the training camp at Salisbury Plain, England, circa 1914. Hearle died in 1934 at age forty-one.

RUMOURS

"The closer we got to the war the less we knew of it," wrote Lieutenant James Pedley of the 4th Battalion. Although the soldiers were at the coal face of battle, information was fragmented and filtered through censorship. Newspapers that were a day or two old could be bought behind the lines, usually from Belgian or French boys who braved the shellfire and poison gas, but the papers were heavily censored and laced with patriotism that skewed the truth of what was happening. On the questionable content of newspapers, Percy Willmot of the 25th Battalion wrote in early 1917 to his sister, "As a rule . . . to find the soul of truth in a tissue of falsehoods: Read the story, divide it by two, add 0000, subtract 100% and take the remainder with a pinch of salt."

Stories bred rapidly in the trenches. While standing sentry, searching for lice in their clothes, or visiting the latrine, trench soldiers shared and passed on what they had heard. There were constant dark rumours about how the home front had abandoned them to rot in the trenches. Resentment against senior officers was common. There was always some snide insinuation circulating about a special food delivery or a rich meal to be prepared behind the lines for the officers, at the expense of the rank and file. Every few months, a wishful yarn circulated about the death of Germany's Kaiser, and therefore the end of the war. In winter, there were hopeful tales of the Canadians being sent to Egypt or some other warm theatre of battle. In summer, they were to be cycled to cooler northern climes.

There was wild speculation about German atrocities. For instance, the story of a Canadian crucified during the April 1915 Second Battle of Ypres was widely believed, despite the lack of credible witnesses. Captain W. W. Murray recounted that before a battle the "rumour-factory worked overtime" and the "Battalion just revelled in these mysteries." Rumours, gossip, and wild stories effectively bound the soldiers together, helping them to make sense of the war, pass the time, cling to hope, and get motivated for battle.

SONGS

Amid the crash of deadly explosives, the soldiers sang. At night, as men sat in holes carved out of the trench walls, or in their dark dugouts in the ground, they often joined together in song. Soloists and groups, perhaps accompanied by a mouth organ, fiddle, or violin, ran through their favourites. The pre-war hit "It's a Long Way to Tipperary" was popular throughout the English-speaking armies. "Everyone is singing it; without doubt it is the song of the war," wrote Private Louis Keene.

The men drew on a wide variety of songs. Church hymns were easily incorporated into the new soldiers' society, as were folk songs. Comrades on leave in Britain brought back sheet music containing popular music hall ditties. Sometimes records were played on battered gramophones that were fiercely protected by their owners.

Popular songs were taken and remade with new lyrics that better fit the harsh reality of the trenches. Infused with soldiers' slang—such as "Jack Johnsons" (the name of a popular boxer) for the impact of heavy shells, and "Alleyman" for the Germans—the songs were difficult for outsiders to understand. "I Don't Want to Die" was based on "I Want to Go Home":

I want to go home, I want to go home.
I don't want to go in the trenches no more,
Where whiz-bangs and shrapnel they whistle
*   and roar.*
Take me over the sea, where the Alleyman can't
*   get at me.*
Oh my, I don't want to die, I want to go home.

Other songs trivialized mud, lice, and sudden death and reminded soldiers that they had to find ways to endure the discomfort and distress. "Never Mind" offers insight into the bravado—perhaps forced—of those in the trenches:

When old Jerry shells your trench, never mind.
And your face may lose its smile, never mind.
Though the sandbags bust and fly you have only
*   once to die.*
If old Jerry shells the trench, never mind.

There were countless songs devoted to pursuing women and sex, with the most popular being the ever-changing "Mademoiselle from Armentières." In their singalongs, soldiers added filthy verses on the fly, and most of them related to sexual relations with the lady from Armentières, or her daughter and neighbours, in all manner of shocking situations. While soldiers might sing out these smutty songs one minute, they could easily turn to sentimental and sappy ballads like

Top: Edward Brogden, middle row, sixth from left, poses with his military bandmates—and friends—circa 1916. Brogden enlisted in Toronto with the 126th Battalion on February 14, 1916. He was thirty-two, married to Nelly Scully, and working as a conductor at the time. (Submitted by C. Betty Greenwood. Edward was her great-uncle.)

Above: For many soldiers, a trip behind the lines for leave, or perhaps minor medical care, was a welcome relief—especially if it meant meeting members of the opposite sex. Here, Ralph Clark, left, and a friend pose in Belgium with two unidentified Belgian sisters, circa 1916–1918. For Clark, the Great War was no adventure. In later years, when prodded by his youngest son, Peter, Clark would only utter, "It was terrible—so many of my friends were killed." (Submitted by Peter Clark, Ralph's son.)

66th BATTERY

The best artillery Battery,
That came to France this year,
Was the Sixth-Sixth — from Montreal,
With fourteen kegs of beer.
They marched right up to Windsor Station,
And got aboard the train,
They said good-bye — with tears in their eyes
And kissed ten thousand Janes.
When the train pulled out,
They were heard to shout,
Hurrah, hurrah, hurrah.
And when they reached Smith's Falls that night,
The boys were heard to say —

Chorus:

Won't you come to camp with us,
And be a soldier — a soldier,
If you can't sit on a horse,
Why then we'll hold you — we'll hold you,
It is the greatest life in the world — that's true.
You get baked beans and Irish stew
And your meals grow colder — and colder
And when you wash your dishes
               in the water — dirty water.
You hear the trumpets shouting out with glee
You run like Hell and curse like sin
And the God Damned Sergeant shouts "fall in"!
Oh — it's the soldier's life for me.

IN 'WAWA

In 'wawa — Petawawa
There's sand and tents and horses
'n we never get a minute
Hard work was never in it
Sand for breakfast, sand for dinner,
Sand for supper-time
All this God damn drilling
For a dollar and a dime
In 'wawa — Petawawa.
There's bombadiers and corporals
'n the bull they shoot
Would make you want to scoot
From Petawawa to Montreal.

ROAD TO PETAWAWA

Said a certain Sergeant
Now listen to me,
I've heard you fellows brag
About your drill in Montreal, were talking pretty tall
Next week I'll see
How smart you can be.
For when you go away
I'll drill you till I think you've earned
Your dollar ten a day.
Oh battery! Oh battery!
Wait till you get there.

Chorus:

On the road to Petawawa.
We were swinging along, singing a song,
No drink to quench your thirst boys,
Like you had in Montreal,
And when you've marched,
Till your throat was parched,
'n your feeling, sore and blue,
You say tonight, "no late leave for me,
It's bed for you and me"
And your thoughts of dear old barracks
Seem to carry you back
To that rickety shack
How you long to be there once again,
You write your wife and say to her,
Dear, this is the life,
Along the road to Petawawa.

Key hole in the door —

Strolling down the sea-shore —

Petawawa —

We haven't seen the Kaiser for a hell-avah while.

Above: Many regiments created lighthearted spoofs of popular songs, such as these ditties composed by members of the 66th Field Battery, Canadian Field Artillery. The songs built camaraderie and helped alleviate the stress of battle.

"Roses of Picardy" and "Keep the Home Fires Burning," which brought a lump to the throat as men dreamed of one day returning home to loved ones.

"A common song (even now and then a dirty song)," wrote Lieutenant Henry Simpson, "can make one glad and sad beyond words."

NEWSPAPERS

The army of citizen soldiers had editors, journalists, and cartoonists in its ranks. As a result, throughout the summer of 1915, soldiers founded a number of trench newspapers for their comrades-in-arms. Some lasted only a few issues, sometimes stopped cold when the editorial team was killed or wounded, while others, like *The Listening Post*, grew to a circulation of 20,000 and survived into the postwar years.

Infantry, artillery, engineering, and medical units published dozens of newspapers during the war, with titles like *The Dead Horse Corner Gazette*, *The Brazier*, *Tank Tattler*, *The Iodine Chronicle*, and *R.M.R. Growler*. Published every couple of weeks, they varied in length from four pages to dozens.

The editor of *The Forty-Niner*, in seeking copy for the fifth edition of the newspaper in early 1916, nearly begged his comrades for stories, jokes, and poems, reminding the recalcitrant that "this was a medium where he [the soldier] can make himself heard." With everyone under tremendous strain and fatigue, it was never easy to get material from

soldiers. Yet the papers limped on, published behind the lines using French or Belgian printing presses and with paper that was borrowed or stolen.

Independent of the high command, most of the papers avoided sounding like propaganda rags. In fact, the content could be quite biting, with casualties bemoaned and officers lampooned. In a grousing column in *The Listening Post*, one writer demanded, "Who is the officer who remarked to the sergeant when he went for the rum ration in the morning, 'The supply is very low, I guess I will have mine now.'"

The newspapers also published soldiers' poetry. At the time, poetry was a widespread and popular means of communicating one's emotions and of capturing one's experiences. Much of the soldiers' poetry was downright awful, but it reflected their closed society and unique environment. There were odes to cigarettes and rum, attacks on shirkers at home who refused to enlist or do their duty, laments to honour fallen comrades, and hyper-patriotic cheers to the Empire. Most of the poems were humorous, such as this ditty:

Oh where do we go from here, boys?
Where do we go from here?
We've been from Ypres to the Somme
And haven't found good beer.
We're sick as hell of shot and shell
And generals at the rear—
We've got no rum and we're feeling bum,
Where do we go from here?

And then there were simple but powerful poems, like this one from *The Brazier*:

*There were nine of us camped at West Down
   South,
And nine of us crossed to France,
And we grew to savvy each other's gaits,
When all of a sudden we fouled the fates,
And the only one left of all my mates
Is me, by the grace of Chance.*

The trench newspapers poked fun at subjects that were a constant source of complaint, such as food and work fatigue, or taboo subjects, such as uncaring officers and shell shock. The content was not meant for those outside of the soldiers' culture. The *R.M.R. Growler* apologized half-heartedly in its first issue: "Should any layman be unfortunate enough to secure a copy, we can only sympathize with him and apologise, as it was not intended that the 'Growler' should wander from the family circle."

The soldiers' closed culture of rumours, songs, and poetry functioned as a powerful means of escape. It brightened the soldiers' lives, allowing them to cope, endure, and make sense of their cruel environment.

Top left: A group of soldiers read the *Canadian Daily Record* in trenches near Lens, France, circa February 1918.

Above: A page from *The Listening Post*, a trench newspaper.

OFFICER (to applicant for transfer to M.T.): "What do you know about motors?"
PRIVATE: "Only that they don't go into the trenches, sir."

Left: A cartoon typical of those found in trench newspapers during the First World War.

Bottom left: A Canadian soldier enjoys a quick swim in a shell hole.

Bottom centre: Many soldiers stiffened their resolve prior to an attack with a generous dollop of rum. In Samuel Watson's case, his rum ration may have saved his life. According to family lore, Watson, shown here in France in 1918, was given a stiff drink of rum on the eve of a bayonet charge. It clearly went straight to his head, because, as Watson's nephew, Mick Watson, related, "Uncle passed out, since it was the first shot of rum he ever had." The Pincher Creek, Alberta, man was carried out of the trench on a stretcher, thus avoiding the bayonet attack. (Submitted by Mick Watson, Sam's nephew.)

Bottom right: Organized sporting events helped keep soldiers' minds off the war. Here, soldiers test their skills in the pole pillow fighting competition at the Canadian Championship Athletic Meet in France, 1917.

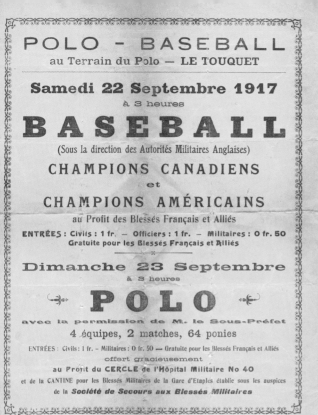

POLO - BASEBALL
au Terrain du Polo — LE TOUQUET

Samedi 22 Septembre 1917
à 3 heures

BASEBALL
(Sous la direction des Autorités Militaires Anglaises)

CHAMPIONS CANADIENS
et
CHAMPIONS AMÉRICAINS
au Profit des Blessés Français et Alliés

ENTRÉES : Civils : 1 fr. — Officiers : 1 fr. — Militaires : 0 fr. 50
Gratuite pour les Blessés Français et Alliés

Dimanche 23 Septembre
à 3 heures

POLO
avec la permission de M. le Sous-Préfet

4 équipes, 2 matches, 64 ponies

ENTRÉES : Civils : 1 fr. — Militaires : 0 fr. 50 — Gratuite pour les Blessés Français et Alliés
offert gracieusement
au Profit du CERCLE de l'Hôpital Militaire No 40
et de la CANTINE pour les Blessés Militaires de la Gare d'Étaples établie sous les auspices
de la Société de Secours aux Blessés Militaires

Above: Sports provided a welcome distraction from the war and were also a way to build camaraderie among the troops. Here, a poster advertises an exhibition baseball match between the Canadian and American "champions." The game was played in September 1917 behind the lines in France. Officers paid a franc to attend, while enlisted men got in for half that price. (Submitted by Jane Dimock-Mahoney, who had several relatives who served in the war.)

Top: Men from the 72nd Batallion take part in the Tug of War finals in September 1917.

Above: Guy Dunmall, seated second from the left (holding fan), in drag, and friends pose for a photo in spring 1919 at a masquerade party held to celebrate his promotion to sergeant. Dunmall emigrated to Canada prior to the war and enlisted in September 1915. The Toronto resident served with the 11th Battalion of the Canadian Expeditionary Force and was gassed in September 1917. In 1918, he transferred to the 75th Battalion. He returned to Canada in May 1919. (Submitted by Kevin Grobsky and Lynne Grobsky; Lynne is Guy's granddaughter.)

A GLIMMER OF HOPE

THE BATTLE OF MOUNT SORREL

JOEL RALPH

By early 1916, the Canadian Corps was starting to take shape. The 2nd Canadian Division had arrived at the front in September of the previous year, and the 3rd Canadian Division had arrived and taken a position in the Ypres Salient in Belgium.

Furthermore, the Canadians had received a new British commanding officer—a cavalry officer by training, and Canada's future Governor General, Julian Byng. General Byng proved to be the perfect match for the young Canadian Corps when only a few short days into his command of the Canadians, he was thrust into an emergency situation.

On June 2, 1916, the Germans launched a massive artillery barrage that pounded the newly arrived 3rd Division's position for several hours. In the attack that followed the artillery barrage, the Germans seized nearly the entire Canadian position, capturing vital high ground in a move that threatened to collapse the Ypres Salient.

The Germans were determined to hold the area, and the Canadians had been thoroughly overpowered— but Byng was determined to retake the lost ground. He moved the 1st Canadian Division forward and provided them with additional artillery support. Aerial photographs gave gunners a clear list of potential targets, and for more than five days, Canadians pummelled exposed German positions.

Finally, during the morning of June 13, the 1st Canadian Division launched a daring attack under the cover of darkness. Desperate hand-to-hand fighting took place throughout the night. Despite heavy casualties, the Canadians were able to recapture all of the lost territory and push the Germans back to their original lines from two weeks before.

The bloody fighting around Mount Sorrell cost the Canadians more than 8,700 dead and wounded. The 3rd Canadian Division was particularly hard hit, losing its commanding officer and thousands of men who had only just arrived on the Western Front. But out of the battle came a glimmer of the exceptional fighting unit the Canadians were to become. There were still lessons to be learned, but it was clear that proper planning and overwhelming artillery fire could create the conditions for a successful attack.

Post-battle image of the June 1916 Mount Sorrel battlefield. The debris is all that remains of a dugout and shelter destroyed by artillery fire. Prior to the war, most of the terrain there was heavily wooded.

O.4569

Mary Winter holds a bouquet of wildflowers as she walks along a grassy pathway behind the Beaumont Hamel war memorial in France in 1938. Accompanying her is a man believed to be the memorial's park caretaker, William Brown, and a Newfoundland dog. Winter and her husband, James Winter, Newfoundland's Commissioner of Home Affairs, were taking part in an official tour of Newfoundland's war memorials in France and Belgium.

NEWFOUNDLANDERS HAVE THEIR OWN UNIQUE WAY OF REMEMBERING THE GREAT WAR.

CHAPTER SEVEN

The July Drive

DEAN F. OLIVER

I knew the war for the longest time as the "Ju-ly Drive." I don't remember it ever being obvious to me what this phrase actually meant, save that it was serious in a way that most subjects for young Newfoundland lads never seemed to be. It juxtaposes in memory with "Sun-dee drive," a welcome family ritual usually ending in ice cream at Portugal Cove, overlooking the Bell Island Ferry, or Holyrood, where fish and chips were sometimes involved. The phraseology and emphasis were similar—"Ju-ly" and "Sun-dee"—but never the context. Grandparents and parents used it often enough to make it resonate, however hushed.

The July Drive never seemed immediately relevant to us as kids, anyway, save in its implied gravitas—much as "dead," or "sex," or "murder" might have, as words alone, if overheard dimly by any child on the margins of adult conversation. Ears might tweak, questions might be asked, or not, but, either way, impressionable minds would be awash in images and imaginings, squishing inferences this way and that alongside the known or the merely suspected.

We "make meaning" in this way, I think—to borrow from the idiom of museum professionals—long before we know what anything could possibly mean in the first place, intuitively crafting myths from half-understood soundings of reality. My mother, who is nearly ninety, uses the phrase with precisely the same tone that I recall from my youth, and still perhaps without full knowledge of the real war, or its impact, or the grand, incessant debates it occasioned. Does it matter that myth trumps history most of the time? I have long since known the historical reference in substantial detail, but I still stumble on its meaning. And, at times, I would just as soon know less but believe more.

"Drive" or "push" was the language of wartime optimism, as though mere effort, mental as much as physical, stood between one's own sodden trenches and the victory just behind the enemy's lines. The war in 1914 would be over by Christmas, for Newfoundland's would-be generals, as for France's or for Britain's. The other side reflected

Above: The striking caribou memorial at Beaumont Hamel, France, is one of five along the Western Front. The woodland caribou was, and remains, the emblem of the Newfoundland (from September 1917, Royal Newfoundland) Regiment.

Top left: The first commissioned officers of the Newfoundland Regiment, circa September 1914, at the Pleasantville Training Grounds, St. John's.

Above: Transport officer Stanley Goodyear, one of the strongest men in the regiment, hoists a horse in this undated photo. He was killed in action in October 1917 at the Battle of Poelcapelle.

Top right: Roy Spencer, shown here circa 1914–1915, was shot in the arm during the doomed July 1, 1916, attack that nearly wiped out the Royal Newfoundland Regiment. A native of Fortune, Newfoundland, Spencer enlisted in December 1914 at the age of seventeen. A year after Beaumont Hamel, Spencer was wounded again—and nearly died—at the Battle of Arras. (Submitted by John King, Roy's grandson.)

Bottom right: This still from footage shot on the morning of July 1, 1916, shows the massive explosion of a British mine, dug secretly beneath German defences along Hawthorne Ridge. The explosion marked the beginning of the costly Somme offensive.

unalloyed evil, while one's own chaps died in a worthy cause. We would beat them quickly and teach them something ("spanking" was a common metaphor, along with "thrust," "slice," and "punish"). Just one more heave might do it or another, or another after that.

War news came slowly, and deliberately askew, from the slaughter abroad. Propaganda was imperfect but tried earnestly to improve: only the grim casualty lists suggested that pyrrhic victories and stymied offensives concealed rather more than the heroic cant of official cyphers.

The language of wartime optimism also mirrored the sheer ignorance of the era. Donkeys did not lead all armies, as postwar pundits would slanderously charge, but far too many did graze up and down the front, defeated—or dazed—by combinations of science, topography, technology, and tactics that mutated and defied mere human courage. Learning came slowly, and not quite in time for the Somme, which opened on July 1, 1916 (the "Ju-ly Drive"), two years into the struggle.

That first day of battle would be the British Empire's bloodiest in history, with more than 60,000 casualties. Confidence ebbed. Recruitment fell. Propaganda struggled. "Pushing" was not so easily believed in. Victories would be measured by inches and yards, not miles and countries. Faith in the big breakthrough never entirely died—

certainly not for Britain's most senior generals—but hope alone no longer sufficed. Economies struggled, dissent gained voice, determination shuddered. Dedication to the cause was now, more than ever, important, or so the patriotic gore intoned.

Above: Members of the "First 500" aboard the SS *Florizel* at Devonport (Plymouth), England, on October 15, 1914. Back row: R. W. Bartlett, H. C. Herder, J. M. Irvine, S. Janes. Middle row: S. Green, A. Penny, E. Churchill, J. Williams. Front: R. J. Stick.

The Somme made it harder to be glib, but glibness limped on. The outlines are familiar: a vast push, a botched attack, horrendous British (and German) losses, a massacre that epitomized anew the war's near-daily massacres. The war can be missed entirely when seen in aggregate, like a flaccid narrative without protagonists. The Newfoundland Regiment, a single unit among hundreds and hardly new to fighting (it had been in the Dardanelles Campaign

against Turkey), was, on July 1, 1916, annihilated in mere minutes.

The names and families and religions of the dead are known and have been plotted for decades now by genealogists, historians, and demographers. When I viewed the current monument at Beaumont Hamel, France, for the first time in the 1990s, the surnames could have been the roll call of my high school graduating class. It was too much for grieving families, for editorialists, for pastors, and for politicians. In Newfoundland, as elsewhere, the war overwhelmed.

As historian Robert J. Harding has argued, paeans to heroic sacrifice soon transformed the tragedy into a rallying cry; the dead became "Christian knights engaged in a modern crusade." Corps commander Major General Sir Henry de Beauvoir de Lisle's thrilling epitaph—"It was a magnificent display of trained and disciplined valour and its assault only failed of success because dead men can advance no further"—still forms the essential descriptor in Remembrance Day speeches, regimental gatherings, and proud reflections. Beaumont Hamel was to Newfoundland what Gallipoli was to Australia and New Zealand, and it remains a site of secular pilgrimage for Newfoundlanders abroad.

Newfoundland's war was distinctly local, as most wars are, and thoroughly imperial. Connections of heart and kin to

the Empire were broad and deep, if criss-crossed by complex skeins of religion and class, politics and economic interest. Commemoration tends to forget the latter—the divisions occasioned by war—or it ascribes to them crude categories of pro and anti, loyalist or some equally conjured opposite. The lived war was subtler. In Newfoundland, as in Canada, calls for non-partisanship in the face of crisis were both ubiquitous and passionate, and predictably impermanent. A "National Government," struggling with wartime loss and home front challenge, later enacted conscription (compulsory service), as unions and others complained loudly about inefficiency and war profiteering.

Postwar scholarship waxed poetic as monuments rose from Grand Falls, Newfoundland, to Gueudecourt, France—consecrating ground, lecturing the living. The braying stag caribou, the regimental emblem, was iconic, atop rocky mounds

of transplanted shrubbery and sombre plaques. In St. John's, British sculptor Captain Basil Gotto's twin pieces, *The Caribou* and *The Fighting Newfoundlander*, continue to define the city's sprawling Bowring Park, itself opened—ironically enough—in July 1914, amidst the Balkan crisis that would lead the world to war.

The conflict imprinted deeply on the Dominion at large, aided by patriots and energetic veterans, and by the same commingling of grief and gratitude that marked other national efforts. It wasn't just the men who'd left from home, but the ways in which their services were marked. Plum Street in St. John's became Aldershot Street in 1922, for example, while Spruce became Cairo. Hamel (after Beaumont Hamel) replaced Oak; Beech became Monchy (after Monchy-le-Preux). Rabbittown, the area of St. John's in which I lived, is thoroughly martial in this respect: Malta Street and Liverpool Avenue, Suez and Suvla Streets, Edinburgh (we pro-

nounce it "Edin-burrow," of course) and Salisbury, edged what was, in the 1920s, the very outskirts of urbanity: the east-west-running Empire Avenue.

Monuments appeared in communities across the island, many purchased and installed by local patriotic associations and often bearing—as at Musgrave Harbour—an image of the fighting caribou. A memorial park took shape at Beaumont Hamel itself, encompassing the tiny battlefield with its jagged craters and slowly eroding trench lines. Memorial University College opened in 1925 as a "living memorial" to those Newfoundlanders who had died in active service during the war (it is now the

Above: A ceremonial remembrance parade marches along Water Street to the National War Memorial in St. John's on July 1, 1924.

Above: Members of the Royal Newfoundland Regiment wolf down rations near Berneville, France, May 1917.

Above: Members of the Newfoundland Royal Naval Reserve in St. John's Harbour during the First World War.

Memorial University of Newfoundland and retains proudly this "living" function). One of its first students, Thomas Ricketts, was the British Army's youngest Victoria Cross recipient during the war. A postwar druggist, his pharmacy in west-end St. John's was among the struggle's quietest and most dignified memories—an old soldier's home and business, the warrior aging gracefully, far from the limelight of feckless politics or boisterous veterans' advocacy.

The Grand Falls memorial, erected in the 1920s and modelled after the London Cenotaph, speaks to the wages of sacrifice paid by the island's still sparsely populated interior: fifty-five names of Great War dead and, added later, thirty-one from the Second World War and one from Korea. Of the First World War fallen, three are Goodyears, including one, O. R. (for Oswald Raymond), who later formed the centrepiece of author David Macfarlane's brilliant bestselling family memoir (and subsequent National

Film Board production), *The Danger Tree*.

The numbers here track something else as well: Newfoundland, like Canada, suffered less in the Second World War than in the First. The later war was bigger, grander, more reassuring in the madness of its fascist, maniacal enemies; the earlier war was more brutal, more tragic, and more difficult to explain or justify. Newfoundlanders fought in many battles in the Second World War, but there was nothing for them in that war to compare to Beaumont Hamel, or to the Dardanelles, where the Newfoundland Regiment received its initial, but milder, baptism by fire in 1915. Myth loves tragedy, and tragedy therefore endures.

In Newfoundland, Canada Day was never about red-and-white face painting, Pearson's flag, or bone-rattling rock concerts. It was Memorial Day, focused on mourning (and mourning) ceremonies around war memorials with flags at half-staff, bowed heads, and ranks of Legion blazers. Come-

dian Rick Mercer has expressed it better: "In one of those great Newfoundland in Confederation ironies, Canada Day is actually an official day of mourning in Newfoundland." We dressed up for the morning, or had a service at school, at 11:00 a.m., and watched the more Canadian fireworks at night. We knew little about historiography or the bitter legacies July 1 embodied: the war as Newfoundland's proudest, if costliest, moment, and the war as the precursor to national penury, humiliation, and, by 1949, consensual obliteration.

As my parents' generation celebrated one myth and recalled with sadness those whom it had claimed, another—the lack of political or economic options—subsumed them.

Newfoundlanders entered Canada in 1949 as torchbearers, reminding errant youth of a Memorial Day untainted by the bitter pill (for anti-Confederates, but not just for anti-Confederates alone) of Confederation,

of—somehow—the old Newfoundland, the old country. I think there was the scent of this in *Secret Nation*, the brilliant 1992 film that has a Newfoundland-born graduate student (played by Cathy Jones) on the verge of discovering the "conspiracy" by which Britain sold off Newfoundland to Canada. They all died in vain along the Somme, a reasonable interpretation might run, for an empire that soon would cast them out.

As Raymond Blake, a history professor at the University of Regina, has argued in his 1994 book, *Canadians at Last: Canada Integrates Newfoundland as a Province*, the transition to Canada in 1949 was anticlimactic: well planned, well funded, and well executed. It was the same for veterans and for remembrance. Canada's benefits regime was at least as good as Newfoundland's and, in many areas, a great deal better. Overseas sites were maintained, pensions paid, and programs run.

But military history suffered in the decades that followed Newfoundland's joining Confederation. The Royal Newfoundland Regiment, always the centrepiece of Newfoundland's collective memory of the war, ebbed from public view. A small regimental museum in St. John's, seldom visited and virtually unknown, housed a handful of treasures and fading documents. There was little curriculum, post-secondary study, or public history devoted to the cause of remembering—and understanding—Newfoundland's war history.

As emotionally committed as Newfoundland remained to its myths of heroic sacrifice and selfless service, understanding eroded as surely as the trench walls of Beaumont Hamel. We studied ancient Greece and Rome in grade school, a smattering of First Peoples, great events, and civics, but little of either war. Year after year, we graduated historically illiterate, "lest we forget" as much mockery and meaning.

Since the mid-1990s, there has been a shift in the opposite direction, so much so that critics have bemoaned the threatened militarization of the national past. Less noted have been the more grassroots efforts of schools, communities, service groups, and individuals who have worked to rescue the military past from obscurity and refashion a pantheon of heroes—we should use the word shamelessly—from the forgetfulness that has at times appeared endemic to the national memory.

The Rooms, Newfoundland's provincial museum, archives, and art gallery, launched a major online project on the First World War, while a small group of Ottawa-based, Newfoundland-born citizens orchestrate, each July 1, a Memorial Day morning service at the National War Memorial. A retired Newfoundland police officer, Gary Browne, reintroduced compatriots to Padre Thomas Nangle, the regiment's beloved wartime chaplain, whose work was instrumental in building home-front and overseas memorials that now, one hundred years later, form the war's most powerful points of reflection for Newfoundlanders. Memorial University has embarked on a major commemorative effort. Bay Roberts has a street named for the Newfoundland Regiment's first wartime enlistee, Leonard Stick. It is easier to be curious and harder to be dim.

Literature and art, music and film have made "the Danger Tree," "the Blue Puttees," "the First Five Hundred," and other wartime references as commonplace now as perhaps at any other time since the 1930s. There is a permanent exhibit on the Newfoundlanders at the Canadian War Museum. Where once we argued stupidly, as children do, over whose grandparents had served in the Newfoundland Regiment (ignorance being no check on passion), the variety of tools now available to verify such conceits would have seemed fantastical to us, and perhaps unwelcome. As long as all granddads had fought at Beaumont Hamel—its numerical impossibility notwithstanding—honour was served!

If such knowledge, or its availability, is the fruit of "militarized discourse," an oft-heard charge in light of recent or upcoming commemorations of military anniversaries, it is, as my maternal grandfather might have said, "no burden to carry around." I cite him here in some considerable shame, having once falsely enlisted him as a Blue Puttee when other mates, in schoolyard spats, were trumpeting their own lineage to the regiment. In truth, Fred Mills had been a merchant sailor, torpedoed by the Germans for his troubles. He was in no need of childish assertions of his wartime courage, the latter having been demonstrated well enough in a rowboat in the mid-Atlantic. He flew the Union Jack from a rough-hewn spruce pole in his front yard in Dildo, Trinity Bay, to his last day. It was, he'd say, good enough to serve under.

There is another reminder here, just below the surface: such loyalty was real and freely given, near limitless in its depth. It is the answer, for me, to the one great question: the war went on because we believed it should, because we believed that we were right.

Scholarship still wrestles with the First World War. The debates are sometimes caricatures but are no less fascinating for this: The Germans started it all. The Yanks won it. The Brits were idiots, and the French cowards.

The Canadians and Australians were twelve feet tall and indestructible. The Italians were weak and turned coat halfway through. The Austrians were incapable, the Russians weak, and the Turks inscrutable. Submarines were the key, and maybe airplanes, or was it tanks? Horses were useless. Generals were useless. Generals with horses were the most useless of all. Militaries learned a lot, but slowly, or a little and not fast enough. We were the good guys, meaning the other guys were just as certainly bad. It ended in armistice, or was it a sellout? The armistice stopped one war but started another. Or was that another convenient half-truth? Opacity encrusts obscurity. The presses roll on; the conferences continue, as well they should.

The one hundredth anniversary of the First World War will revitalize hoary myths, refight old battles, chew through reputations, and ask, occasionally, an intriguing new question. Works of scholarly creation or artistic beauty will jostle with vapid polemics and slimly sourced nonsense. They will all carry the banners of education, remembrance, and civic responsibility. Some will be worth such monikers. Most will be forgettable and, sadly, non-refundable.

And in one small corner of the old Empire, the dreadful war will remain, for another generation or so, the "Ju-ly Drive."

Top: Members of the Women's Patriotic Association of Newfoundland gather for either a sock-knitting drive or a wound-dressing packing bee, at Government House, St. John's, circa 1915–1918.

Above: Invalided soldiers, along with members of the Newfoundland Royal Naval Reserve, hold a recruitment drive at Harbour Grace, Newfoundland, in 1917.

A BITTERSWEET VICTORY

THE BATTLE OF THE SOMME

JOEL RALPH

The Canadians had been lucky to avoid the bloodbath at the Somme that started on July 1, 1916. The first day of the campaign, the single worst in the history of the British Army, saw more than 60,000 British and Allied casualties.

But by September, even the Canadians were called in for a series of new attacks. On September 15, the 2nd Canadian Infantry Division launched successful attacks towards the small French hamlet of Courcelette. The French-Canadian 22nd "Van Doos" Battalion and the 25th Battalion (Nova Scotia Rifles) captured the objective and then held off seventeen German counterattacks through four days of extreme and bloody close-quarters fighting.

The fighting that continued throughout September and October, however, left the first three Canadian divisions exhausted. They were withdrawn, and British troops, along with the newly recruited 4th Canadian Division, arrived to renew the attack.

It was blistering artillery barrages that eventually pounded the German position into a smudge on the landscape and enabled Canadian and British soldiers to declare victory. With both sides shattered and winter setting in, the Battle of the Somme came to an end.

However, these months of fighting only shifted the front lines by eight kilometres, and at a horrendous cost of more than 1 million casualties, with 24,000 dead and wounded Canadians. Consequently, the human toll of the battle remains as controversial today as it was at the time.

Facing page, top: Poison gas drifts over the battlefield during the Battle of the Somme circa 1916.

Facing page, bottom left: William Downes is seated in a postcard photo taken during the Somme offensive in 1916. Downes, a bombardier, sent the postcard to his parents back in Canada. (Submitted by Bruce Gillespie, William's nephew.)

Facing page, bottom right: Lorne Lamont Saunders sits in the cockpit of his Sopwith Camel in this undated photo. Saunders was an officer in the Royal Air Force. He died on October 4, 1918, during the Second Battle of the Somme. He was nineteen. (Submitted by Donna Davies. Lorne was the uncle of her husband, Charles Davies.)

503 - Attaque aux gaz - Somme -

SOMME
WAR

THE GREAT WAR REVOLUTIONIZED MEDICINE, AS DOCTORS, NURSES, AND PHYSIOTHERAPISTS STRUGGLED TO SAVE LIVES AND MAKE SHATTERED MEN WHOLE.

CHAPTER EIGHT

Bacilli and Bullets

SUZANNE EVANS

At the beginning of the war, volunteers standing in line at local enlistment offices across the country were likely not thinking about the shots that might save them. However, the Royal Canadian Army Medical Corps was paying attention to the need to vaccinate soldiers going overseas. Sir William Osler, the Ontario-born doctor considered to be one of the fathers of modern medicine because of his work in medical education, was adamant about the need for compulsory vaccinations for the military. His lecture "Bacilli and Bullets," given to officers and men at Churn, England, was distributed throughout the Empire in pamphlet form. He was clear about the lessons learned from the Boer War (1899–1902): "Of the 22,000 lives lost in that war—can

you believe it?—the bullets only accounted for 8,000, the bacilli for 14,000!"

Initially, typhoid inoculation was not compulsory for Canadian troops, but most accepted it, along with the smallpox vaccine, in spite of public debate about the safety of the procedure. Captain Percy George Bell, a thirty-year-old doctor from Winnipeg, was well aware of the heated arguments going on at the time. Less than two months into the war, he noted in his private war diary the ready acceptance of inoculation he found among the men aboard the *Tunisian* heading to Plymouth: "30 September 1914: Vaccination still in progress—did ninety-eight today myself. There are no 'conscientious objectors.'" He then dryly observed, "The insertion of some five hundred million little corpses into their bodies apparently not worrying them very much."

Typhoid wasn't the only preventative shot to come into use on a massive scale for the military during the war. In the early months, nurses and doctors all over the Western Front watched in horror as thousands of

injured soldiers under their care developed severe muscle stiffness that started with the jaw and took over the entire body. The bacteria *Clostridium tetani*, thriving in the manure-fertilized fighting fields of France and Belgium, had infected their wounds. Many died of tetanus poisoning even before succumbing to their injuries.

Medical authorities reacted quickly, mandating that all wounded men receive a tetanus shot. Within a few months of this decision, there was a worldwide shortage of the serum. The Canadian Red Cross was called upon to find 10,000 doses of the antitoxin for the Canadian Expeditionary Force. It ended up being purchased at great cost from an American supplier. After this experience, a small antitoxin laboratory at an old farm nineteen kilometres outside of Toronto took on the immense task of producing all the tetanus antitoxin the Department of Militia and Defence required at close to cost price. By March 1917, the lab, which became known as Connaught Laboratories of the University of Toronto, had produced over 75,000 packages of the antitoxin. Building on its strengths after the war, Connaught became the world's first large-scale producer of insulin. It was produced under the direction of war veteran Charles Best, who, along with decorated veteran Frederick Banting, had discovered the drug.

Although vaccines required expert planning and organization to produce and distribute, they were by far the easiest treatments to deal with for both men and medical staff. The effects of the Great War on body and mind were new, appalling, and hideous to treat. To help cope with the carnage, 2,504 Canadian military nursing sisters served overseas, a vast increase from the twelve who served in the Boer War. Nursing sister Lieutenant Clare Gass enlisted in 1915 and kept a diary of her experiences. She mentioned but

a few of the horrors she witnessed while she was at No. 3 Canadian General Hospital near the coastal town of Étaples, France.

On June 7, 1915, Gass wrote, "Some of these new patients have dreadful dreadful wounds. One young boy with part of his face shot away both arms gone & great wounds in both legs. Surely Death were more merciful." By the time this Nova Scotia woman had been transferred to No. 2 Casualty Clearing Station (CCS) near Poperinghe, Belgium, her diary no longer mentioned the sight of "heads shattered to pieces or limbs hanging by a thread of tendons." Like so many involved in the Great War, she buried the horrors inside herself and never wrote of them again.

Her time at No. 2 CCS overlapped with that of Major Lawrence Bruce Robertson,

MD, of Toronto. The workload was exhausting. On August 16 and 17, 1917, alone, No. 2 CCS admitted 1,202 casualties and Robertson performed 162 operations. He patched men back together, amputating when necessary, only to have some go into shock from blood loss.

With so many desperate cases, Robertson decided to experiment with blood transfusion techniques he had studied before the war and had used to save infants at Toronto's Hospital for Sick Children. To keep track of the continued well-being of the men who survived his blood transfusions—and most did—he gave them self-addressed envelopes so they could write to him. Captain A. C. Gayler's letter of August 14, 1917, sent from the Royal Free Hospital in London, was full of thanks as well as medical information. Knowing how busy

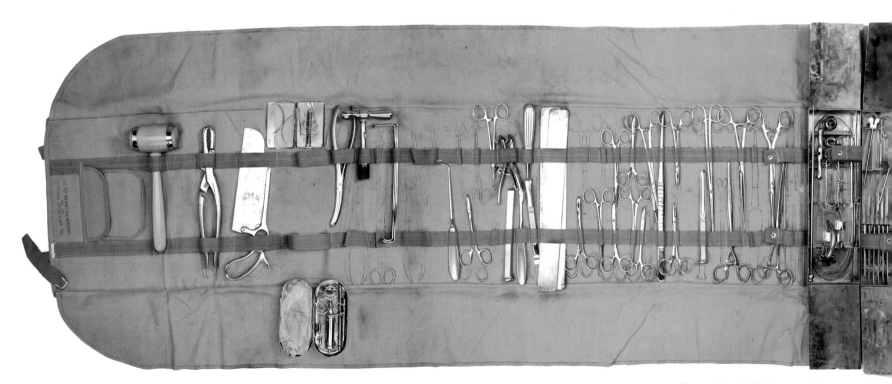

Above: A typical field surgery kit.

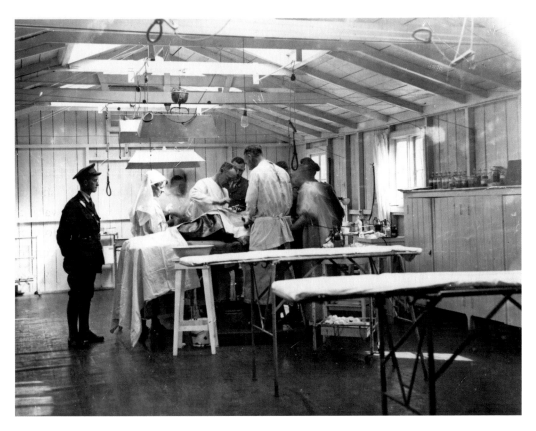

Above: A soldier waits patiently while a new hand is designed for him.

Left: Lawrence Bruce Robertson, the tall man seen from behind, operates on a patient at No. 2 Canadian Casualty Clearing Station in Poperinghe, Belgium, October 1917. Robertson pioneered work with blood transfusions during the war.

Robertson was at that time, Gayler thought to remind him of some of the finer details of his own case. "On 13th June you took my leg off above the knee, and until I received blood from someone else you countered the betting about 3 to 1 on my pegging out." In the same wry tone, he stated that "from a medical point of view my stump is now a thing of beauty and many compliments have been paid to the surgeon who did the operation." He thanked Robertson for adding years to his life and extended his gratitude further to another partner in the healing process. "Can you find time to let me know the name and address of the man who gave me blood? I should much like to write to him."

Men like Gayler faced months, if not years, of recovery, but many had the luck to encounter the help of a medical service just coming into its own at the time: physiotherapy. The wounded who were invalided back to Canada were sent to military hospitals across the country, as close to their home as possible. Toward the end of the war, they began encountering young women dressed in uniforms who looked much like nursing sisters but whose expertise was in therapeutic massage and medical gymnastics. Many had trained at the Military School of Orthopaedic Surgery and Physiotherapy at Hart House, University of Toronto, which had just opened in early 1918. They studied under the watchful eye of twenty-four-year-old supervising masseuse Enid Finley, originally from Montreal.

One of the men invalided home who would in time need physiotherapy treatment was Dr. Lawrence Bruce Robertson. Fate took him to the Dominion Orthopaedic Hospital for veterans on Toronto's Christie Street, where Finley was working after the war. Not long after meeting, the two were married, but the union ended in tragedy when Robertson died of pneumonia in 1923. Finley would, however, go on to be an organizing force, helping to ensure that physiotherapists—who suffered from the Victorian-era stigma that linked massage to prostitution—would, in the next war, attain the status that nurses had achieved in the First World War.

Physiotherapists' services were also needed to aid those suffering from what the Australian-born Sir Grafton Elliot Smith referred to as the "hydra-headed monster"— shell shock. As the dean of the faculty of

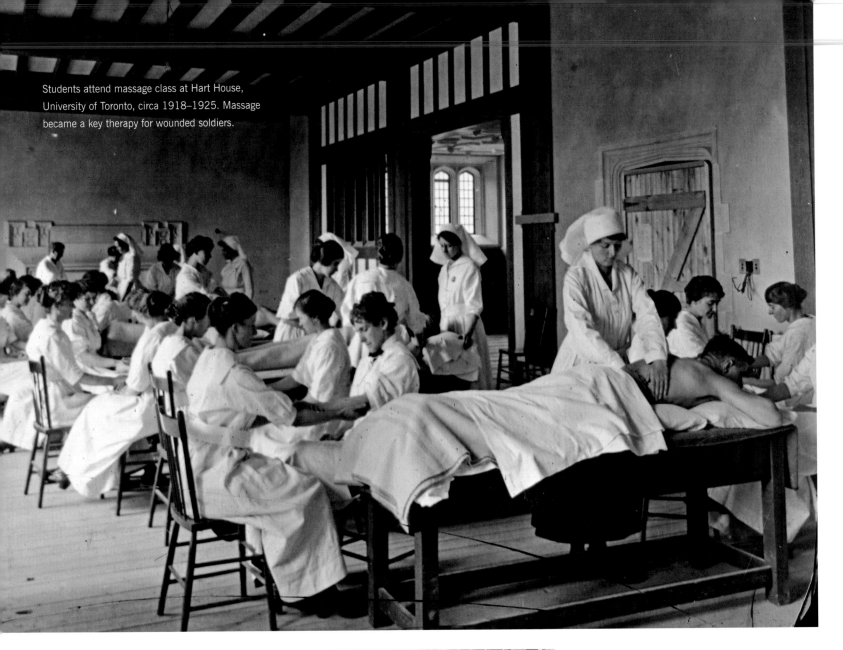

Students attend massage class at Hart House, University of Toronto, circa 1918–1925. Massage became a key therapy for wounded soldiers.

Far left: General Arthur Currie visits injured soldiers at Christie Street Hospital, Toronto, circa 1916.

Left: Machinist Frank W. Ellis, far right, poses with artificial limbs he helped make for veterans who suffered amputations during the Great War. Ellis enlisted in November 1914 and served in Belgium with the 18th Battalion. Discharged from the military on compassionate grounds in 1916, he eventually moved to Vancouver, where this prosthetics factory operated. (Submitted by Marion Coulter-Mackie, Frank's granddaughter.)

medicine at Manchester University Medical School during the war, Smith took particular interest in this puzzling "chemical compound of diseases." Without so much as a scratch on the skin, shell shock could produce symptoms ranging from blindness, mutism, paralysis, or uncontrollable tremors. Smith realized that a shell-shocked soldier does not usually "lose his senses." Rather, such soldiers function with "painful efficiency." He urged doctors to approach the stricken soldier without prejudice: "The doctor who wishes to be of real help to him must make up his mind to examine and ponder over the sufferer's mental wounds with as much, nay, even more, care and expenditure of time than would be given to physical injuries."

Many doctors were not so understanding. Almost 10,000 Canadians were diagnosed with shell shock and many more suffered in secret from a condition that became stigmatized as cowardice. In his *Official History of the Canadian Forces in the Great War 1914–1919: The Medical Services*, Sir Andrew Macphail claimed: "Shell shock is a manifestation of childishness and femininity. Against such there is no remedy." Smith, on the other hand, thought "war-strain" came about because "never in the history of mankind have the stresses and strains laid upon body and mind been so great or so numerous as in the present war." It took another world war before general attitudes toward shell shock began their glacially slow shift. A diagnosis of "lack of moral fibre" (LMF), used early on in the Second World War, was, by the end, replaced with the less demeaning phrase "battle fatigue."

Despite the efforts of those in the medical corps, over 60,000 Canadians died in the First World War. At home, an estimated 50,000 people would die from the influenza epidemic in 1918 and 1919, which was in part spread by returning soldiers. By 1920, 60,203 former soldiers qualified for pensions—often inadequate—because of disabling wounds. Fifteen years later, the number of pensioned veterans had risen to 77,855, in large part due to the poverty of the Great Depression and the after-effects of a war experience that had aged them unnaturally.

There will always be an unequal balance of power between the instruments of destruction and the tools of medicine. However, many in the Great War steadily fought back every inch of the way with needles, scalpels, bandages, and caring.

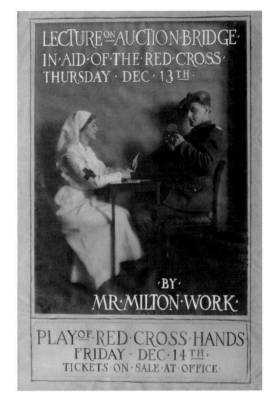

Top right: Physiotherapist Enid Gordon Finley and an unidentified soldier play a mock game of bridge in this wartime Red Cross fundraising poster. (Courtesy of the Enid Graham family.)

Bottom right: A nurse with veterans who suffered amputations in the Great War. This photo is from the collection of Sarah Livingstone, not shown, who served overseas as a nursing sister during the war. (Submitted by Dawn Livingstone. Sarah was the great-aunt of Dawn's husband, Jack Livingstone.)

Above: Angus Sutherland came home traumatized from his time in the trenches. The Presbyterian minister suffered from shell shock and was later diagnosed with Parkinson's disease. By his mid-thirties, he was barely able to speak. In applying for an invalid pension, Sutherland wrote that it was "true I was never in hospital for shell shock but that fact did not prevent my having it in a very pronounced [way] . . . In the presence of shellfire I could make no progress, but would fall to the ground screaming like a baby, and start shaking like a leaf." (Submitted by Robert Sutherland, Angus's son.)

Above: Clarence Edgar Kenney of Saint John, New Brunswick, rarely spoke of his Great War experience. What little he did tell grandson David Kenney was chilling: "I still recall him telling me that he witnessed the execution of deserters." Clarence enlisted in September 1914. In November 1916, he was hospitalized with "melancholia and neurasthenia" related to his chronic fatigue. In January 1917, Clarence was sent to Hastings, England, where he served out the remainder of the war, working in military hospitals. (Submitted by David Kenney, Clarence's grandson.)

Above: For Abenezer "Abie" Evans of Stratford, Ontario, the First World War didn't end with the armistice. He brought it home with him, replaying it in his mind over and over again. "My mother said that right after they married . . . he would hide under the bed nearly every time he heard a noise. He would think he was back on the battlefield. This persisted for quite some time," said James Evans, Abie's son. Evans enlisted with the 56th Regiment in 1915. The military provided Evans with a small medical pension for his injuries due to trench foot, but his shell shock was largely dismissed as trivial. (Submitted by James Evans, Abie's son.)

Left: A veteran, his left leg amputated, sits in a wheelchair at "Wizz-Bang Corner" on Davisville Avenue in Toronto. The term "whiz-bang" was soldier slang for an artillery shell. (Submitted by Eric Hearle.)

Top left: A group of women in Edmonton wear masks to protect against Spanish flu, which hit the city in 1919. The women were co-workers of Mabel Harper at Edmonton City Dairy. Mabel's husband, Lester Harper, enlisted in January 1916. He was reunited with his wife and young child after the war. (Submitted by Barbara Dalby, daughter of Lester and Mabel Harper.)

Top right: Arthur Robinson, a married thirty-one-year-old, enlisted with the 13th Battalion. He contracted influenza and pneumonia and died on December 18, 1918, in France. (Submitted by Donna Cochrane, Arthur's great-great-niece.)

Left: The death certificate of Albert Giles indicates that he succumbed to influenza and pneumonia.

Left: These medals belonged to a Canadian nursing sister.

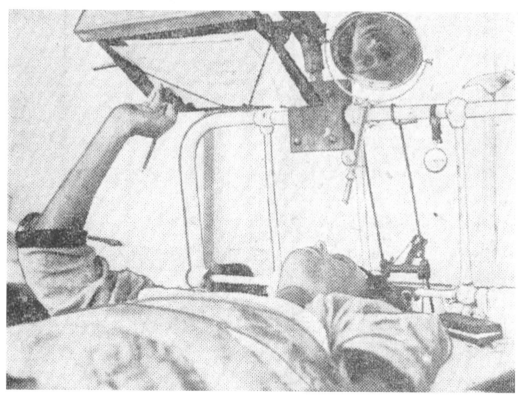

Above: It's likely there were times when Robert Mills thought his treatment was worse than the disease. The veteran of Vimy Ridge spent almost five years, between 1918 and 1923, receiving an experimental therapy to treat the spinal tuberculosis he contracted while serving overseas with the 48th Highlanders. This was before antibiotics, and doctors at Toronto's Dominion Orthopaedic Hospital (DOH) hoped to cure Mills by immobilizing him for hours at a time and placing him in the hot sun. The treatment was known as heliotherapy, and Mills, along with others suffering from the same disease, came to be known as "the rooftop gang" during their time at the DOH. Each day, they would be strapped to their hospital beds, arms and necks locked in place, and relocated to the hospital's roof for heavy doses of sunshine. During the therapy, Mills had to view the world through a mirror fastened above his bed. While in hospital, he met the love of his life—the hospital's head masseuse, Kathleen Jones. "Fifty years later, Mills loved to tell his seven grandchildren that he met their grandmother in a body rub parlour," granddaughter Patricia Staunton said with a laugh. (Submitted by Patricia Staunton. Robert and Kathleen were her grandparents.)

Above: Dr. Herbert Rogers was rejected as too old when he tried to enlist in 1914. The forty-eight-year-old travelled to England to petition to join the fight, and was finally accepted in September 1915. He served in the Royal Canadian Army Medical Corps. (Submitted by LT(N) Robert J. Rogers, UE, RCN [retired]. Herbert was Robert's cousin.)

Clockwise from top left:

Nurse Christina Mary Watling of Chatham, New Brunswick, enlisted in the Royal Canadian Army Medical Corps in Montreal on April 22, 1915. She served in France, England, and Canada, and was awarded the Royal Red Cross—a military decoration for "exceptional services in military nursing"—by King George V. (Submitted by Judy Watling, Christina's great-niece.)

Nursing Sister Mary Helen "Molly" Donerty served overseas during the war as a member of the Royal Canadian Army Medical Corps. Born in 1892 in Campbellton, New Brunswick, she enlisted in July 1916 in Montreal. (Submitted by Ian Bartlet, Molly's grandson.)

Dr. Victor McWilliams enlisted in 1915 and was stationed at Surrey, England, where he instructed members of the Royal Army Medical Corps. McWilliams later served in Egypt and France with the 16th Field Ambulance. He returned to Toronto in May 1919 and resumed his medical practice. (Submitted by Robert McWilliams, Victor's great-nephew.)

John Oliver, shown here, was a stretcher-bearer in the Great War, and later served as a chaplain during the Second World War. He died in 1979. His son, Lloyd, wrote this biography in his father's honour. (Submitted by Doug Oliver, John's grandson.)

Racism forced Charlotte Edith Anderson Monture, a member of the Six Nations of the Grand River Reserve near Brantford, Ontario, to travel to the United States in 1914 for training as a nurse; she couldn't find a Canadian nursing school that would accept her. In 1917, when the United States entered the Great War, Monture volunteered with the U.S. Medical Corps and served in a hospital in France. Following the war, she returned to the Six Nations reserve, where she worked as a nurse until 1955. (Submitted by John Moses, Charlotte's grandson.)

Pharmacist John Woolverton, far right, and his fellow Canadian Army Medical Corps medics on leave in Troisdorf, Germany, in January 1919. (Submitted by Ralph Woolverton, John's son.)

Top: Gerald Herbert Ryan, left, training in Petawawa, Ontario, in 1918. He was an ambulance driver in the 75th Depot Battery and a proud Irishman—he signed his attestation papers "Gearld," the Irish pronunciation of his name. His family said he was an emotional casualty of war and his life was never the same after. (Submitted by Kevin Gerald Ryan, Gerald's great-nephew.)

Above: Roberta MacAdams used this photo in the 1917 election campaign that made her a member of the Alberta government. Of the 25,601 ballots cast for twenty-one candidates, MacAdams received 4,023 votes, making her the second woman elected to a legislature in the British Empire. She was the first woman to introduce a bill—the "Act to Incorporate the Great War Next-of-Kin Association"—in any legislature in the British Empire.

German prisoners of war are made to carry wounded Canadians from the trenches, circa 1915–1918.

Above: While physical treatment was crucial for wounded soldiers, equally important was the spiritual solace provided by members of the chaplaincy. In this photo—which made the front page of newspapers around the world—the first man to enlist in Canada is offered a drink and some words of encouragement after being wounded during the Battle of Hill 70 on August 15, 1917. The wounded man is Alexander Reginald Bawden, who held regimental number 1. With him is Captain James W. Whillans, chaplain of the 8th Canadian Battalion, Winnipeg Rifles. Shortly after this photo was taken, Bawden died on the stretcher. Realizing Bawden's significance, the photographer rushed the photo into print, first in a Paris newspaper, and then later in Montreal, London, and Melbourne. As for Whillans, he served at the front for twenty-two straight months with no relief. After the armistice, the Presbyterian minister returned to Canada and held pastorates across the prairies. In Regina, he made history as the first clergyman in the British Empire to broadcast a sermon over the radio. He died in June 1954 at the age of seventy-four. (Submitted by Lee-Anne Penny, James's great-granddaughter.)

The Sailorettes drill team performs during a Victory Loan Parade in Toronto, circa November 1918.

WITH THEIR MEN FIGHTING IN EUROPE, CANADIAN WOMEN STEPPED FORWARD TO HELP THEIR COUNTRY. THAT THEY DID SO BEHIND A UNITED FRONT REMAINS A PERSISTENT MYTH.

CHAPTER NINE

Divided on the Home Front

JOAN SANGSTER

In 1918, *Women's Century*, a magazine dedicated to reform and women's suffrage, declared that the war was creating a "new sisterhood of women" cemented by the ideal of sacrifice and the just crusade against Germany. Unfortunately, that was wishful thinking.

Existing divisions of class, language, ethnicity, and political ideology intensified considerably during the war, although women's experiences were crosscut by multiple, competing identities. For instance, among the working class, British-born women with male relatives fighting overseas might support the war, while Ukrainian women—designated "enemy aliens," their husbands possibly interned—did not share their enthusiasm.

Why, then, was the war idealized at the time as a moment of sisterhood, and remembered later as a turning point for Canadian women? The idea that the war brought new respect for women workers, or was a wake-up call for politicians—who rewarded loyal and capable women with the vote—has been largely shattered by histori-

cal research. Women experienced marginal but not major alterations in gender ideology, work roles, and political citizenship. If the war became etched in historical memory as a watershed for women, this was partly the result of hopeful thinking by articulate and privileged women who anticipated that their contributions to the war would alter prevailing views of female inferiority and bring social progress.

Middle-class, professional, and politically astute women used their roles as volunteers, fundraisers, recruiters, and allies of the federal government to stake out a claim for enhanced respect. At the Women's War Conference, called in 1918 by the Union government to shore up support for the war effort, it was declared that British and Canadian women were creating a new soul of the nation through their dedicated volunteerism.

Suffragist Nellie McClung believed that women suffered the most painful loss of war, sacrificing their sons to the military, but she took comfort from the idea that her enlisted son was fighting for a just cause. "When I

Above: Two women wear soldier uniforms, circa 1916, in this photo belonging to Great War veteran George Dorman. Written in the corner is the following: "Have courage everyone, fear not. There's not a thing can harm ye. No foe can enter this burg now for we have joined the army!"

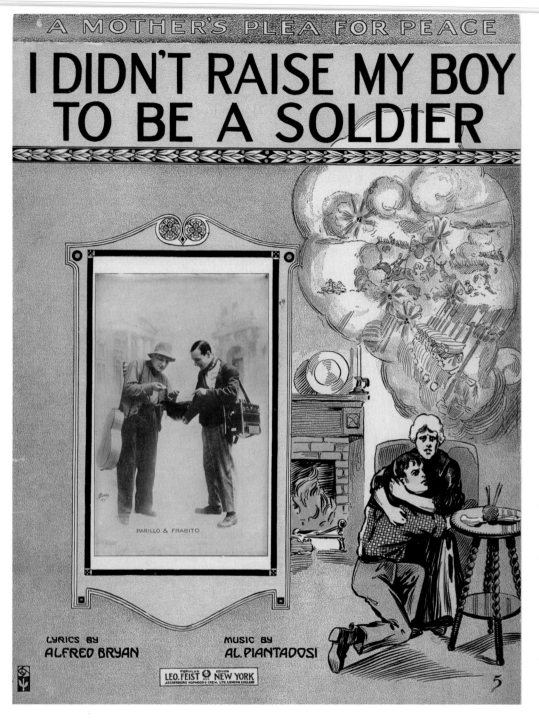

A MOTHER'S PLEA FOR PEACE

I DIDN'T RAISE MY BOY TO BE A SOLDIER

PARILLO & FRABITO

LYRICS BY
ALFRED BRYAN

MUSIC BY
AL. PIANTADOSI

POPULAR EDITION
LEO. FEIST NEW YORK
ASCHERBERG HOPWOOD & CREW. LTD. LONDON ENGLAND

5

Above: "I Didn't Raise My Boy to Be a Soldier" was one of the more popular pacifist songs to come out of the Great War.

on the very Prince of Darkness. I knew that it would be better—a thousand times better—to be dead than to live under the rule of people whose hearts are so utterly black."

Adopting the moniker "the Mothers of Consolidation," the women at the war conference believed they were taking up the nation-building work of the Fathers of Confederation. While they hoped that women would assume more public leadership in postwar Canada, they also believed in preserving their most important social roles as mothers and protectors of the family.

Women were not wrong in calculating the importance of their volunteer work. By 1918, it was estimated that women's organizations had contributed $90 million to the war effort, on top of tonnes of clothing and medical supplies. In 1914 alone, the Imperial Order of the Daughters of the Empire helped fund a naval ship, a hospital wing, and many ambulances. Women of all backgrounds rolled endless bandages and knitted countless socks for soldiers in the trenches.

Women also aided enlistment. They welcomed army recruiters to speak to their organizations and graced the platforms of recruiting leagues; a few also engaged in "white feather" campaigns, shaming men who would not sign up. Only selfish women would "hold back their husbands, fathers, and brothers," recruiters told their audiences, and they warned against the dangerous ideas of pacifists who opposed the war, castigating them as naive and misguided, or, worse, "dupes" of the enemy.

Women donated volunteer labour to registration campaigns, promoted Victory Bonds and food programs, set up hospitality

saw the first troops going away," she wrote in her wartime book, *The Next of Kin*, "I wondered how mothers let them go . . . It was the *Lusitania* that brought me to see the whole truth. Then I saw that we were waging war

Top left: Annie Rogers, right, and her daughter, Amelia, await word of the well-being of Annie's sons in this photo circa spring 1917. The Welland, Ontario, woman's worst fears were realized when both sons, Ernest and Richard, were killed in action between April and May 1917. In a sad twist, it was Richard, in waist-deep mud, who helped carry the stretcher that bore his dying brother from the battlefield. (Submitted by Wes Murray. Annie was his great-grandmother. Ernest and Richard were his great-uncles.)

Top middle: Mary Macfie knits for her sons, who are serving overseas, circa 1916. On her wool bag is stitched a patriotic message: "Knit and do your bit." Macfie, of Dunchurch, Ontario, had three sons who served in the 1st Canadian Battalion. Roy and Arthur survived, but the youngest, John, was killed in action in May 1917. (Submitted by John Macfie. Roy Macfie was his father, Mary was his grandmother, and Gladys was his aunt.)

Top right: Mary Macfie's daughter, Gladys Macfie, left, and friend Velma Whitmell collected money for the Red Cross in 1918. They raised nearly sixty dollars while canvassing their neighbourhood. (Submitted by John Macfie.)

houses near military bases, and were active in the Canadian Patriotic Fund, which provided charity to the wives of soldiers. In this philanthropic work, the conflicts of class became visible. Well-meaning upper- and middle-class women visited working-class women who were recipients of the fund to check on their spending and social habits.

But working-class women were offended by the notion that they needed moral overseers to make sure they were not wasting money, or worse, "stepping out" while their husbands were away. A labour paper lashed out against such indignities, cautioning soldiers' wives to beware of these visiting ladies who only pretended interest in the welfare of others: "These women are the wives of men making fortunes, while we suffer, scrape by, and serve overseas." They were said to be the same people "who moralistically inspect your Patriotic Fund spending, claiming [you] were not conducting yourself in a manner

becoming a lady," daring to "go out to the movies" rather than scrubbing floors.

The idea persists today that positive social change was taking place at this time because women were flooding into non-traditional jobs. The birth of this perception had much to do with the Canadian government using propaganda images of British women working in munitions plants overseas. The intent was to induce Canadian women into "men's jobs" so that more men might be pressed into service and to reassure the public that women could do these jobs.

Yet the actual placement of women in men's jobs in Canada was limited compared to Britain and primarily occurred in central Canada, where most munitions factories were located. Understandably, we often remember photographs of these women dressed in trousers and bandanas while handling machinery and making large shells. These images became seared in public memory because they were unconventional, interesting, and unusual.

Another enduring myth was the patriotic participation of affluent women in war production. A woman featured in a 1994 National Film Board documentary, *And We Knew How to Dance*, claims that society ladies drove up to work "in their limousines." Although some women may have perceived their work as patriotic, there is no evidence that those using limousines headed in any large numbers to munitions factories to make shells and bombs.

Working-class women did line up to secure these jobs. In Toronto, more than 6,000 women applied for munitions work in 1918. Only 2,000 were placed. Primarily young and single, these women were motivated by tales of fortunes to be made in munitions. Many longed to escape the perennial fallback job for women at the time: live-in domestic service. Munitions work, however arduous, was better paid and provided more opportunities to socialize with fellow workers. They were also happy to have any job at all—the war had wrenched the economy out of a recession that lingered until 1916.

When the economy began to recover, the Imperial Munitions Board (IMB) pressed manufacturers and provincial governments to facilitate the substitution of females for males in munitions work. Mark Irish, IMB chairman Joseph Flavelle's appointee in charge of labour, reassured employers that women would be a more malleable, less militant workforce and urged provincial governments to alter prohibitions on women's night work, though Quebec, less enthusiastic about the war, refused.

Above: A woman in Toronto sells flowers during the first "Alexandra Rose Day" in Canada, circa 1915. The charity drive raised money for local hospitals.

Facing page: Patriotic posters urged Canadians to contribute to the war effort.

The government's promotion of "dilution" was shaped by pragmatism and cost consciousness, though there was some concern about the morals of the "common" factory girl. The IMB's solution was to appoint two respectable female welfare supervisors, deemed of "good pedigree," to supervise the new female workforce. The board was less concerned about health and safety than it was about the possibility that women's sexual immorality would be unleashed in rough masculine workplaces.

Protection, as working-class women found, could become a form of surveillance. The supervision taking place on the factory floor paralleled new wartime laws to control prostitution and venereal disease and to address war-induced fears of family breakdown and youth delinquency. Whether through their naïveté or licentiousness, working-class women were perceived to be in danger of loosening the moral fibre of the nation. Blanche Read Johnston, a prominent leader in the Woman's Christian Temperance Union, worried that factory women would become "careless and reckless" about their virtue, losing their respect for "the sanctity of marriage."

The federal government and labour unions often labelled women's work in munitions as "diluted" labour, suggesting that skilled craft occupations were being watered down. In reality, most women flooding into munitions were simply replacing unskilled male labourers.

By war's end, a small number of women had tasted non-traditional work: they had operated elevators, milled tools, or worked as streetcar conductors. A more significant

KEEP THE HOME FIRE'S BURNING.

Top: Women in Toronto hold a bazaar to raise money for war aid, circa 1914–1916.

Bottom: Female workers gather for a photo at the British Cordite Co. munitions plant at Nobel, Parry Sound, Ontario, circa 1916.

number took over for men in clerical occupations, such as banking, where wartime labour shortages accelerated an ongoing trend toward the feminization of white-collar work. But most women remained in traditional female jobs where substantial differentials existed between women's and men's pay rates.

There was little or no change in textile and garment factories, where many women laboured long hours for lower pay. Toronto's Laura Hughes, the young, idealistic niece of Sam Hughes, the minister of militia and defence, was a rebel socialist in a family of war supporters; she went undercover as a worker at a knitting mill that supplied government war contracts. She then wrote a report for a local labour paper, criticizing, with considerable sympathy for the workers, the factory's bad ventilation, crowded rooms, and poor pay for piecework. Owners accrued profits by "taking it out of the hides of their working men and women and working girls by reducing their wages and in some instances increasing their hours of labour," she wrote.

Women workers proved to be less malleable than the government had predicted. Ignoring pleas not to interrupt war production, female munitions inspectors in Hamilton, Ontario, walked off the job in 1917. They were aggrieved about proposed wage reductions for incoming workers. The same year, a group of women factory workers approached *The Toronto Star* to publicize their grievances. "They are killing us off as fast as they are killing men at the trenches," the deputation of six women protested. They complained of twelve-hour shifts, night work, a six-day week, and difficult

working conditions. They also claimed they were told to leave after refusing to work a fourteen-hour shift.

Public interest was also focused on Ontario's Farm Service Corp, or "farmerettes," young women temporarily helping on farms. The press reproduced pictures of smiling women in trousers and rustic hats, posing beside large tractors with rakes and hoes. Still, a traditional division of labour remained intact: men usually harvested grain; women picked fruit. The actual number of farmerettes, especially among urban women, was smaller than the number of women temporarily recruited to other workplaces.

The YWCA set up supervised camps for the farmerettes, but amenities were rustic, with some camps having no running water. Wages were low in comparison to blue- and white-collar work in the city. Again, concerns surfaced about women's endangered morals: middle-class students were unhappy with the rowdy behaviour of the poor, rural women working beside them. In her report to the Ontario government, an inspector, Miss Taylor of the YWCA, described these rural women with some disdain: "The girls have rough house dances every night in the barn," and lacked feminine modesty, "doing their washing half-dressed." Their tents were described as pigsties with "half-washed underwear hanging on the trees."

Organized labour held a contradictory attitude toward newly recruited female

Above: Ontario farmerettes, circa 1916.

workers. Union leaders feared that women's "diluted labour" would lead to the deskilling of jobs and reductions in wages. Yet they also denounced the exploitation of women workers and called for new minimum-wage and equal-pay laws for female workers. Men working in one Toronto aircraft factory stated that they had "nothing against the employment of women," but they wanted returned soldiers to be first on the hiring list, and if women were to be hired, "they should be paid the same rate of wages as men."

War proved to be a catalyst for inflamed class tensions, resulting in increased unionization, radicalization, and protest. This tension came to a head in 1919, with general strikes across the country. Labour protest was fuelled in part by rampant inflation. Many workers resented the fortunes being made by those who were politically well-connected. Speculators, profiteers—the "one per cent" of the time—were the focus of immense anger in labour papers. Wartime rhetoric about sacrifice, the common good, and democracy wore thin for workers who, by 1917, were complaining about growing injustice on the home front.

In order to keep war production humming, the federal government widened the reach of existing laws concerning strikes and lockouts, encouraging employers and workers to use compulsory conciliation to settle disputes. Despite the best efforts of the press censor to suppress reporting on strikes, labour disruptions increased dramatically. Between 1917 and 1920, workers struck more frequently and in larger numbers than ever before in Canadian history. Women were now far more visible on the picket line. In Winnipeg, Woolworth's sales "girls" making six dollars a week, the very low end of the wage hierarchy, went out on strike, securing a raise. In Vancouver, striking female laundry workers climbed onto a bewildered male customer's car and told him to take his shirts elsewhere.

Many trade union men declared their loyalty to the lofty aims of the war but were critical of the way the war was being carried out. The government, meanwhile, stepped up its political policing of suspected radicals. J. H. Cahan, the federal government's security adviser, warned in late 1917 that workers were discontented and that "all their enthu-

siasm" for war was dissipating as they grew more aware of the "bloody sacrifices and irritating burdens" to be shouldered and as they increasingly felt disillusioned by the government.

Tensions existed, too, with so-called "foreign" workers, usually those of southern or eastern European backgrounds. While socialists called for solidarity across lines of race and ethnicity, some workers were influenced by political rhetoric lauding the "Anglo-Saxon race" and denigrating the "enemy alien."

The bitter election of 1917 and the conscription issue inflamed social divisions even more. Women lined up on different sides of the Union government's controversial Wartime Elections Act, which enfranchised women with relatives serving overseas. Supporters tended to be women of British descent. The Fédération nationale Saint-Jean-Baptiste, representing twenty-two francophone women's groups in Quebec, vociferously opposed the act, which was seen as politically motivated because it was designed to increase support for military conscription. Women with family members on the battlefront were much more likely to vote for conscription, for they saw it as a means of equalizing the sacrifice of Canadian families and thought it could shorten the war.

Even English-speaking suffragists were deeply divided. In Winnipeg, Nellie McClung supported conscription and the war effort generally, but fiery labour organizer Helen Armstrong and crusading women's columnist Francis Marion Beynon of the *Western Grain Growers' Guide* both denounced the Elections Act. They wanted women to have

the vote—but not this way. Beynon was an articulate, professional woman who slowly changed her ideas and her political allegiances during the war. She wrote more and more critical columns about the war, until she was forced to resign. She packed her bags and headed to New York City, never to return to Canadian journalism.

The image of the positive changes in women's status wrought by a terrible war became part of popular consciousness, perhaps because it offered comfort in the face of loss or anticipation of increasing gender equality in the future. Since the vote was secured in many provinces, there was, at least, an appearance of progress. On the other hand, women's work roles and gender ideology shifted only a little. The political tensions unleashed by the war also highlighted how acutely class, language, and ethnicity divided Canadian women.

Mary Corse, a Calgary working-class housewife, spoke with some bitterness about this divide when she testified before the federal Royal Commission on Industrial Relations in 1918: "If I go to the corner with a tin cup and beg for some bread for my children, I am arrested as a vagrant. Another woman can stand on the corner with her furs, boots, and corsage bouquet and collect nickels for the veteran . . . and she is commended."

Corse's words help to explain the tumultuous postwar history of strikes, unrest, and government retaliation in 1919.

Left: Arthur Frederick Boniface, shown here with his wife, Rose (née Rands), circa 1916, enlisted at age forty-two, despite having four daughters at home. After the war, he and Rose separated. Arthur's grandson Richard Frogge said he was told the marriage failed because of Boniface's rigid stance on women's equality. "My mother said that he could never become reconciled to the changing roles of women in society." (Submitted by Richard Frogge. Arthur and Rose were his grandparents.)

A BLOODY TRIUMPH

THE BATTLE OF VIMY RIDGE

JOEL RALPH

The victory at Vimy Ridge remains Canada's most celebrated attack of the war. On Easter Monday, 1917, the Canadian Corps captured one of the most dominating geographic features on the Western Front: the German fortress at Vimy Ridge.

Two Canadians in particular developed the plan to crack their enemy's stronghold. The first was General Arthur Currie, a real estate broker from Victoria, British Columbia, who rose from the militia to become Canada's top soldier. The second was McGill scientist and artillery officer Andrew McNaughton. McNaughton was a leader in counter-battery strategy—the art of destroying the enemies' guns—and even invented a sound-ranging device that helped pinpoint the location of enemy weapons. At Vimy, he coordinated the "creeping barrage" artillery tactic that helped propel the Canadians to victory.

The goal of the creeping barrage was to create a line of suppressive shellfire just in front of the Canadian troops that moved forward as the soldiers advanced across the battlefield. While others had attempted this tactic in earlier battles, the Canadians planned to march closer to the line of fire than had ever been done before. The plan was risky, but if it worked, the Canadians would catch the Germans before they could emerge from their fortified dugouts.

On the morning of April 9, 1917, all four Canadian divisions advanced side by side for the first time in a single attack. Hammering the Germans with artillery, the Canadians quickly advanced to capture enemy defensive lines. A final push by the 4th Canadian Division on April 12 captured the last major position, known as "The Pimple."

But victory came at a cost: April 9 was the single bloodiest day of the war for the Canadian Corps. With 10,000 soldiers already lost in the four months leading up to the attack, Canada suffered an additional 10,000 casualties in just four days of fighting at Vimy Ridge.

While the battle itself did little to change the course of the war, it did cement the Canadians' renown as fierce attackers, a reputation that they would carry forward over the remaining eighteen months of the Great War.

Canadian troops catch some rest during the Battle of Vimy Ridge.

Above: Great War veteran William Howie, left, wearing an armband, looks on during an inspection by King Edward VIII during the unveiling of the Canadian National Vimy Memorial in France on July 26, 1936. Howie and his wife were among the thousands of attendees to mark the occasion. The Royal Canadian Legion paid the fare for 8,000 veterans so that they and their families could attend the unveiling. Construction of the memorial began in 1925. More than 100,000 attended the event, and thousands more tuned in from their living room radios. Following the dedication, Howie accepted an invitation from the British government to attend a garden party at Buckingham Palace. (Submitted by Marie Kerr, William's granddaughter.)

Top right: Canadian General Arthur Currie.

Middle right: Henry Roy Halladay was killed in action on April 10, 1917, at Vimy Ridge. (Submitted by Hollis Morgan. Henry was her great-uncle.)

Bottom right: John "Jack" Earl Hayden of Huron County, Ontario, circa 1916. He was wounded at Vimy Ridge. He was also gassed during the war. (Submitted by Mary Bilstra, Jack's niece.)

Right: Canadian troops make their way across the blasted landscape at Vimy Ridge, April 9–12.

Bottom: Storm clouds gather over the Canadian National Vimy Memorial, France, in April 2012, during the 95th anniversary of the battle.

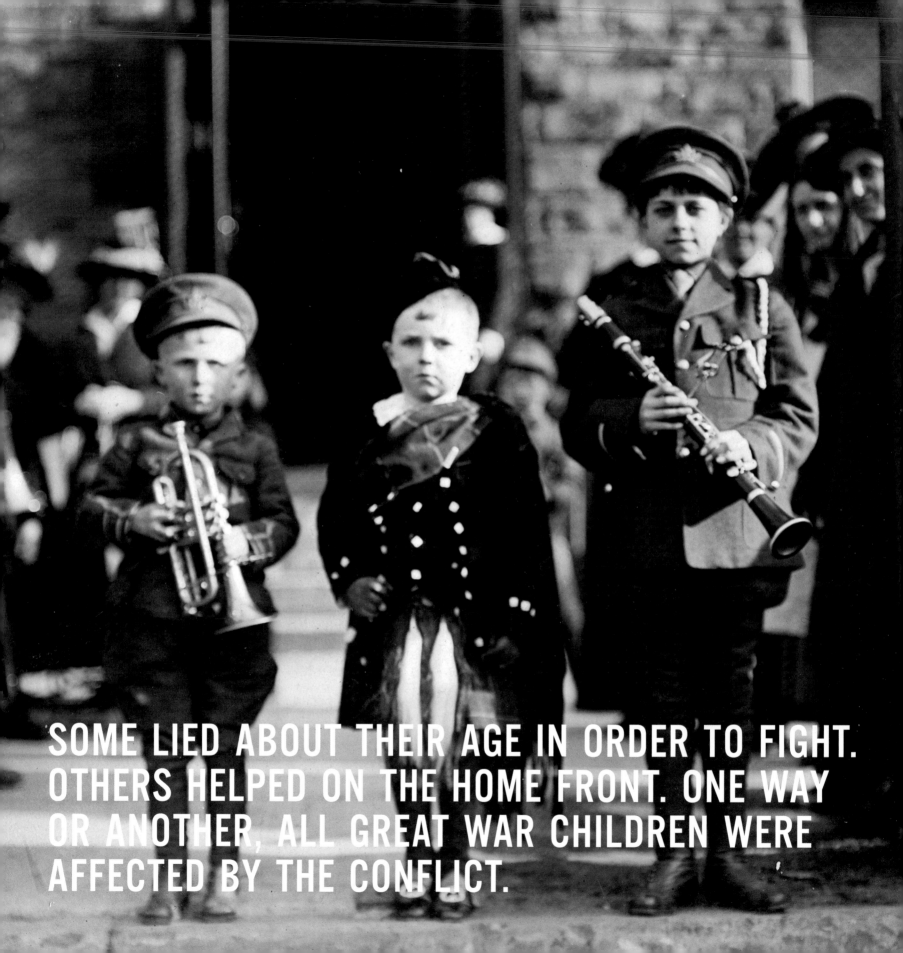

SOME LIED ABOUT THEIR AGE IN ORDER TO FIGHT. OTHERS HELPED ON THE HOME FRONT. ONE WAY OR ANOTHER, ALL GREAT WAR CHILDREN WERE AFFECTED BY THE CONFLICT.

CHAPTER TEN

Generation Lost

KRISTINE ALEXANDER

Historians have had little to say about Canadian young people's perceptions of and contributions to the Great War. Yet in many ways, children and adolescents were at the heart of the nation's war effort: as victims, volunteers, consumers, family members, and symbols of a future worth fighting for.

"I have one brother in the army. He is only fifteen, but he looks eighteen," wrote "Peggy Canuck" from British Columbia in a letter to the children's page of *The Family Herald and Weekly Star*'s September 13, 1916, edition. While most Canadian children remained far from the danger of the front lines, it is worth remembering that the war did claim the lives of several thousand youths—both civilians and combatants.

According to First World War historian Tim Cook, some 20,000 teenage boys lied about their age and enlisted in the Canadian Expeditionary Force over the course of the war. Over 2,000 of these boys were killed in action, including nearly a hundred fifteen- and sixteen-year-olds. Like the older men with whom they served, many

of the youngsters who survived the conflict returned to Canada bearing physical and psychological scars that would shape the rest of their lives.

These boy soldiers were not the only young casualties of Canada's Great War, as nearly five hundred civilian children were killed when the French munitions ship *Mont-Blanc* exploded in Halifax Harbour in December 1917. Most died instantly; other young people died in hospital, and thousands more were injured, orphaned, or left homeless. The experiences of third-grade student Millicent Upham are representative of the trauma and displacement suffered by many of the explosion's young victims: her mother and three younger siblings were killed, her family home was destroyed, and she spent weeks in hospital recovering from a series of injuries, including the loss of her left eye. Once released from hospital, Millicent, her brother Archie (who was also injured), and their father tried to start a new life, initially by lodging with nearby relatives.

Above: Toronto toddler Jose Morrel Granatstein, age three, wears a military-inspired outfit, circa 1914.

Facing page: Children dressed in military uniforms take part in a band performance in Toronto, circa 1915.

Clockwise from top left:

Howard Fielder Pledge kept this photo as a keepsake of friends lost in the Great War. Pledge, back row, third from left, wrote on the back: "Taken in France a few miles behind the lines. I remember the place but I don't know how to spell the damn name. 3 never came home." Pledge lied about his age to enlist. (Submitted by Howard Pledge, Howard's son.)

Thomas Edward Brady, a member of the 21st Battalion, poses with his sister in their hometown of Lindsay, Ontario. Brady, fifteen, enlisted in November 1914. In October 1918, he died while on leave in Scotland.

Richard Whitmore enlisted in January 1916 in Montreal. He was released from the army a year later, after it was discovered that he had lied about his age. The truth was learned only after he was sent to hospital in England after suffering shrapnel wounds. (Submitted by Ross Sherring, Richard's grandson.)

William Roy Ferguson was fourteen years old when he enlisted with the 92nd Battalion. The Manitoulin Island, Ontario, native was injured during the war and is shown here in hospital, far right, wearing a bandage on his head. (Submitted by Dora Hocken, William's niece.)

George Dudley lied about his age to enlist in September 1915, declaring he was "17 years 10 months" when he was, in fact, only fourteen and stood only four feet six inches tall. Despite this, a medical officer delared George "fit for trumpeter," and he was assigned to the 8th Canadian Field Artillery Brigade. He was sent back to Canada in May 1917 when his real age was discovered. (Submitted by Jeff Mason, George's great-nephew.)

Wilbert Lloyd Attridge was sixteen when he enlisted in the Royal Flying Corps. The Hamilton, Ontario, lad flew Sopwith Camels during the war. (Submitted by Ross Attridge, Wilbert's grandson.)

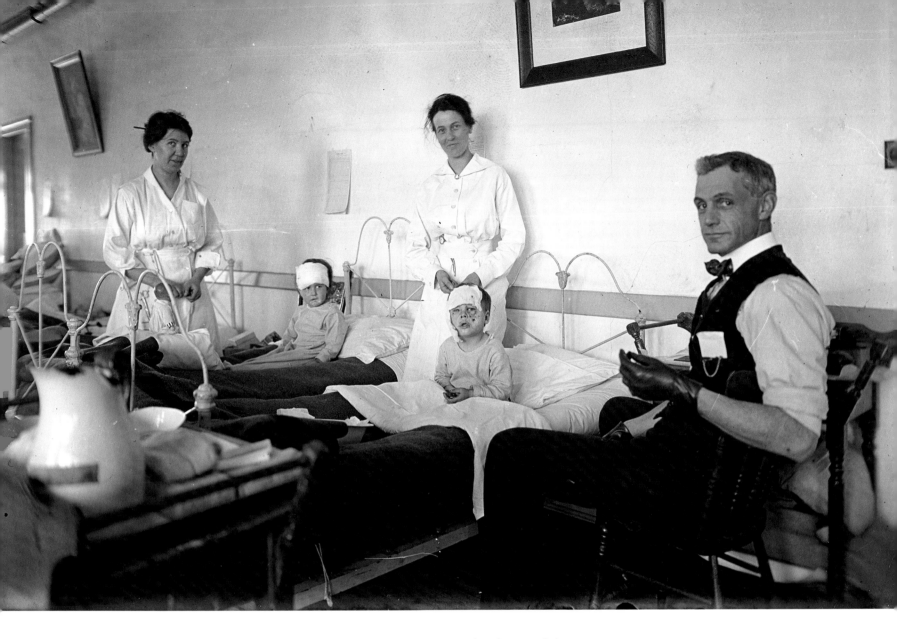

Another explosion victim, fifteen-year-old Frank Burford, was delivering a parcel when the blast hit. In an interview with historian Janet Kitz, author of *Survivors: Children of the Halifax Explosion*, Burford described the moment of the explosion: "All of a sudden there was a big bang, and I turned and I thought the sidewalk came up and hit me . . . When I woke up, I looked around. I was boxed in, lumbered in from head to foot . . . I had to drag myself out from under . . . I got my head out and then out I came. I was on a big heap of stuff, and the fires were all around me."

For most children on the home front, the war was a distant source of excitement and anxiety. They were continually reminded that the outcome of the war hinged on their willingness to sacrifice and contribute. School lessons and the mass media were especially potent sources of war-related information and pressure. As the authors of the nationally produced *Canada War Book* wrote in 1918, "BOYS AND GIRLS OF CANADA . . . You know a great deal about the world-war and you have often wished that you were old enough to go to the front as soldiers or as nurses . . . What can boys and girls do? . . . They can save food and fuel; they can save money."

Left: John Perry Murray of Toronto enlisted in March 1916 at the age of fifteen. "He lied—oh yes, he did," Murray's now eighty-year-old daughter, Diane Murray, said with a laugh. "He never said anything to his parents. He just ran away from home." Murray was discharged in December 1918 for medical reasons. For Diane, her father's fibbing about his age was typical of that generation: "They all ran off to war, all of them," she said. "That's the way they were." (Submitted by Diane Murray, John's daughter.)

Many young people enthusiastically took up this directive, but such messages must also have caused discomfort for some youngsters, particularly the children of interned "enemy aliens"—usually recent immigrants from the Austro-Hungarian Empire. Indeed, some children were themselves held in Canadian internment camps with their families. The book *In Fear of the Barbed Wire Fence*, by Lubomyr Luciuk, a professor at the Royal Military College of Canada, quotes a report by Major General Sir William Dillon Otter, who was in charge of internment operations for the Department of Justice. Otter's report mentions that, between 1914 and 1920, 8,579 enemy aliens were incarcerated, including 156 children and 81 women.

As the war progressed and young men who would normally be working on farms went off to fight, a desperate agricultural labour shortage developed. This prompted the formation of the Soldiers of the Soil (SOS) scheme in 1917. Some 25,000 boys

aged fifteen to nineteen heeded the call to "serve your country on the farm," as one government poster put it. One of them was fourteen-year-old Gerry Andrews of Winnipeg. Andrews was recruited in 1918 and went to live with the Grains, a young farm family of five, near the community of Purves, about a hundred kilometres west of Winnipeg. A city boy, Andrews quickly got used to working from dawn to dusk: "The first day or two I was nauseated by the odour of manure tracked into the house, but like the family soon got used to it," Andrews wrote later in an article for the Manitoba Historical Society.

Andrews stayed at the farm for five and a half months, earning twenty to thirty dollars per month—and a coveted bronze medal, which was later lost. "If I had it now, it would be without price, as would be the piece of paper certifying my service and good behaviour," he wrote seventy years later. Andrews went on to serve in the Second World War and attributed much of his success in later life to his experiences as a Soldier of the Soil.

Children and adolescents also helped out by growing their own produce, which they often sold, donating the proceeds to war-related charities. In Ontario, for example, the Department of Agriculture gave seed potatoes to schoolchildren, who then sold what they had grown to buy an ambulance for the Red Cross.

Children also raised significant amounts for the war effort by saving their allowances, doing extra chores, and organizing tag days, public entertainments, and bazaars. The money went to a range of war-related charities, such as the Red Cross, the Blue Cross

Fund (to assist animals affected by the war), the Belgian Relief Society, Secours National, the Duchess of Connaught's Prisoners of War Fund, convalescent hospitals and ambulances, and the Halifax Relief Fund.

At home, at school, and through voluntary groups like the Girl Guides, Boy Scouts, and Junior Red Cross, tens of thousands of youngsters knitted socks, made bandages, and sent care packages containing newspapers, candy, gum, and clothing to enlisted men and Belgian refugees. This patriotic volunteer work was seen as good for the war effort and good for young people: it supported the Allied cause, taught useful skills, and provided adult supervision for children whose fathers were away and whose mothers might be at work or busy with wartime voluntary efforts.

In letters to the children's pages of newspapers and magazines, many boys and girls explained their efforts in a variety of ways. The writer of one letter to *The Family Herald and Weekly Star* stated, "It is a terrible war and I think that it is our duty to help the poor soldiers all we can." Another wrote, "I wish I were old enough to fight . . . [and] to take care of the poor Belgian orphans."

While the archival record is dominated by accounts of the patriotic work done by Anglo-Canadian youngsters, Aboriginal youngsters also made considerable

Right: This patriotic pin was typical of those worn by children during the war.

contributions to the Canadian war effort. Much of their voluntary work was done at mission and residential schools, so it's likely that most Aboriginal children weren't given a choice about taking part in these activities. Yet some First Nations children seem to have been enthusiastic about supporting Canada's war effort—a reflection, perhaps, of their communities' high rates of enlistment. In December 1914, for example, a teacher from the mission school on the Gibson Reserve near Georgian Bay in Ontario reported that "the little Indian boys and girls of the school . . . have been working hard for the soldiers" by making handkerchiefs.

One of the students, a Mohawk boy named Alec Decaire, described his efforts in a letter that was sent overseas with his class's handiwork: "Dear Soldiers, I am a little boy from Gibson School. We made some handkerchiefs for the soldiers and we are going to send them to you . . . we hear that so many are dead and suffering, so I am very sorry for this war is going on. So I hope that the drummer-boy will get my handkerchief."

Canadian boys weren't the only ones who wanted to support their flag and country—the adventure and danger of the war also appealed to girls. While the many wartime stories aimed at girls encouraged them to serve their nation in appropriately "feminine" ways through self-sacrifice, good behaviour, and domestic work such as knitting and sewing, it is clear that many girls wanted more. One young reader wrote to the children's correspondence club run by *The Family Herald and Weekly Star*, "My earnest desire is that in the near future a girls' battalion will be made up."

Above: Toronto youngster Norman James holds the first shell manufactured in the city, circa 1914.

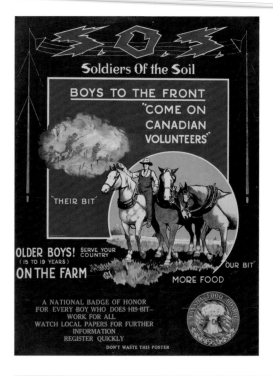

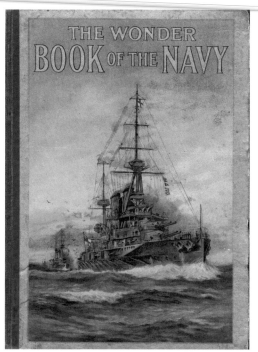

adventure and martial might were popular with young Canadians long before the war began, after 1914 there was a spike in sales of war toys and books. The 1917 T. Eaton Company catalogue, for example, included advertisements for a range of war-related toys and boy's clothing. "No boy would consider himself a soldier," the catalogue insisted, without a sixteen-inch-long toy sword and sheath. Also for sale were a toy field cannon and a "smart Khaki Drill Soldier Suit . . . of the correct military cut" for $2.75.

Children's war games reflected what they had learned in newspapers, books, and newsreels and through the increasingly militarized curricula of Canadian public and residential schools. A teacher at the Aboriginal residential school on Gordon's Reserve in Saskatchewan, for example, wrote in a letter to the *Anglican Letter Leaflet* in 1916 that "just now the boys are very fond of playing at being soldiers. They have devised for themselves a uniform, and have cultivated (with burnt cork) moustaches.

Some girls pitched in to do hard physical labour on the home front. Eleven-year-old Ellen Ada McFadden of Glenboro, Manitoba, wrote to *The King's Own* in February 1917: "I help my brother plough at summer holiday time, as men are very scarce and having three brothers in the army I have but two brothers left. I got fifty cents a day and seventy-five the last few days I ploughed. I put three dollars in the bank and gave two to the Red Cross."

The enormous financial contribution made by Canadian girls is epitomized by the number of Victory Bonds bought by two Girl Guide companies from Ontario: by 1918, members of a group from Chatham had purchased $4,300 worth of bonds, and another from Gananoque had invested $4,850.

Just as the war shaped the unpaid labour young people performed, it also shaped their play. While toy soldiers and tales of imperial

Above: The last thing Walter Hickmott, shown here, did before shipping out for service in France was to visit with his little sister. "He went to the school he had attended and said goodbye to my mother, Ada—the baby of the family," said William Siddall, Hickmott's nephew. "She was seven years old. She never saw him again, a memory she carried the rest of her life." Hickmott was killed by a sniper in April 1918. (Submitted by William Siddall, Walter's nephew and Ada's son.)

Above: Five-year-old John Edmund Stewart of Hamilton, Ontario, wears a navy-inspired outfit in June 1918. (Submitted by Nancy Stewart, John's daughter.)

Above: William Mitchell, a Boer War veteran, enlisted on April 15, 1915; two years later, he was killed in action near Vimy Ridge, leaving his wife, Ellen, to fend for the couple's four children, shown here in happier times with their parents, circa 1912. (Submitted by Dan Mitchell, William's great-grandson.)

One of them impersonates the Kaiser, and I do not know how many times they have captured and hanged him."

Canadian children and adolescents devoured war stories—many of which demonized Germany and Kaiser Wilhelm II—at school, at home, and at public libraries. Most wartime books for young people were published in the United States or Great Britain, and there is actually only one war-related adventure novel that was published in Canada during the war: Harold C. Lowrey's *Young Canada Boys with the S.O.S. on the Frontier* (1918), a tale about a group of Canadian Boy Scouts and Soldiers of the Soil who discover and stop a German plan to blow up the Welland Canal.

Many children, of course, were also affected by the absence of fathers, brothers, uncles, cousins, and neighbours serving overseas. The emotional ties between enlisted men and the children they had left behind played a big part in how many on the home front perceived the war. Melodramatic songs on this theme had titles like "I Want to Kiss My Daddy Good Night" and "Just a Baby's Prayer at Twilight (for Her Daddy Over There)." Numerous wartime postcards depicted young children writing letters while watched over by the spirit of a father in uniform.

The absence of men changed daily routines in all kinds of ways, as young people were often given new chores and encouraged to take responsibility for the emotional well-being of their mothers. The economic hardships of wartime meant that adults worried about money as well as the war—a fact that could cause upheavals and increase tensions between family members. According to an exhibit at the Canadian War Museum, women living at home on the fixed salaries of soldier-husbands overseas were faced with hard choices: lower their standard of living or enter the paid labour force while putting their children in the care of others.

For thousands of Canadian children, the war also meant grief and mourning. As Evelyn Price from Ewing, Alberta, wrote in 1918: "Our family has had pretty near its share of the war. My father was killed in action in the Passchendale [sic] Ridge Battle in November, and my uncle is in France now. There are six children in our family. Three boys and three girls. My baby brother was born two days before dad left for France and it is hard to believe he will never see him [father] again."

The First World War gallery at the Canadian War Museum contains an especially poignant reminder of the war's devastating effects on Canadian children and families: a small teddy bear that belonged to ten-year-old Aileen Rogers of Cowansville, Quebec. She gave the bear to her father, Lieutenant Lawrence Browning Rogers, when he joined the 5th Canadian Mounted Rifles in 1915. It was meant as both a good luck charm and a memento of home. The bear was in Lawrence Rogers's pocket when he was killed during the Battle of Passchendaele in October 1917. Aileen Rogers, who became a nurse and spent much of her adult life working at McGill University, left no written records about how she experienced and understood her father's death. In this respect, she resembled most of the thousands of other children whose lives were torn apart by Canada's Great War—described by historians William and Jeanette Raynsford as "silent casualties of a war fought halfway across the world."

Top left: Sisters Dora, Minnie, and Edna Harrison of Salford, Ontario, lost their older brother, Archie, back row, right, when he was killed in action in November 1917 during the Battle of Passchendaele. The siblings are shown here in an undated photo along with their parents, George and Anna, and a local boy, Fred Powell, who was adopted into the family after his parents died of pneumonia. (Submitted by Dorleen Emerick, Edna's granddaughter.)

Top right: Margaret Shortliffe is shown here as a baby circa 1917 with her parents, Ernest and Annah Aldwinckle. Ernest enlisted in October 1916 after learning that his brother had been killed during the Battle of the Somme. Ernest was himself killed during the Battle of Passchendaele in October 1917. Margaret keeps a photo of her father on her bedroom wall. "I always thought my father was something special." (Submitted by Margaret Shortliffe, daughter of Ernest and Annah.)

Above: John "Jack" Dobson poses with his wife, Annie, and children—Anne, six; John, four; and Joan, one— prior to his departure for France in 1916. He regularly wrote letters to his children; in one, he wrote: "To Miss Anne . . . You ask me if I like France. No little girl. I like home far better and I hope with God's grace to be back some day with mother and you all." Jack survived the war, but died suddenly in 1924, widowing Annie, who now, in addition to caring for five children—including infant son, Henry—was pregnant with twins. (Submitted by Henry and Barbara Dobson. Jack was Henry's father.)

Above: Songs such as "I Want to Kiss My Daddy Good Night" were popular with both soldiers and their families on the home front.

Top left: With so many families losing loved ones, it's easy to forget that there were also plenty of joyous homecomings for soldiers discharged from the war. Here, Arthur Walter Elsegood, in uniform, beams as he reunites with his wife, Edith (wearing a black dress), daughter Edna May (wearing white, in front of Arthur), and a neighbouring family that has come to join in the celebration. (Submitted by Janette Kasperski. Arthur and Edith were her grandparents.)

Bottom left: This teddy bear was found on the body of soldier Lawrence Rogers. It was a gift from his daughter Aileen.

Bottom right: Margaret Lomax lost three older brothers in the war. After the death of her mother in 1922, it fell to Margaret to stay with her father and help tend the family farm, located outside Calgary. She's shown here at age seventeen, hauling hay on the farm. This was a responsibility her brothers would have been expected to assume once they returned from the war, and the workload eventually became too much for her. "We have no idea what happened to the farm," said Ed McDonald, Margaret's son. "We suspect they just let it go." Margaret carried the sadness of the war with her the rest of her life. "When I think about it, I find it upsetting, too," McDonald added. "We might have won the war, but we lost the family." (Submitted by Ed McDonald, Margaret's son.)

TAKING THE HIGH GROUND

THE BATTLE OF HILL 70

JOEL RALPH

The success at Vimy Ridge, France, left the Canadian Corps brimming with confidence. They had become one of the best-trained and toughest attacking groups available on the Western Front.

With General Arthur Currie now in charge of all four Canadian divisions, the Corps' next mission was to capture the French city of Lens. British Field Marshall Douglas Haig hoped the Canadian attack would divert German resources away from the Allies' main summer offensive at Ypres and Passchendaele in Belgium. But Currie drew up an alternative attack—arguing that the capture of the city would be useless without control of the high ground that overlooked it, Currie proposed that the Canadian Corps be sent up Hill 70.

Haig accepted Currie's revised plan, and in the early morning of August 15, 1917, the Canadians—as they had done at Vimy Ridge—successfully attacked behind a creeping artillery barrage.

After the Corps had taken control of Hill 70, artillery observers began directing concentrated fire against German counterattacks that were moving forward throughout Lens towards the newly created Canadian lines. Over the following days, the Canadians turned back no fewer than twenty German counterattacks.

Unfortunately, the Canadians ultimately failed to capture Lens, despite suffering more than 9,000 casualties while fighting in the region. The battle also marked the first occasion that mustard gas was used against Canadian lines.

The attack was successful, though, in pulling German reserves from the Ypres Salient, and it further bolstered the troops' reputation as some the fiercest fighters at the front.

Above: Members of the 15th Battalion (48th Highlanders) fresh from battle at Hill 70 in France on August 20, 1917. Somewhere amid the marching men is forty-five-year-old James Hester of East Whitby, Ontario. Hester enlisted in June 1915, lying about his age out of fear he would be rejected as too old. He claimed he was five years younger. (Submitted by David Vesey and Kerry Hester. James was David's grandfather and Kerry's great-uncle.)

Left: A Canadian soldier inspects the remains of a German pillbox near Lens, France, circa December 1917. A few months earlier, the Canadians had defeated the Germans here in a major battle.

Winnie the Bear—the inspiration for Winnie-the-Pooh—with Canadian Harry Colebourn at Salisbury Plain, England, 1914.

WHETHER THEY WERE MASCOTS, WORKING CREATURES, OR PETS, ANIMALS BROUGHT SOLACE TO FIRST WORLD WAR SOLDIERS SERVING AT THE FRONT.

Chapter Eleven

Animal Soldiers

TIM COOK AND ANDREW IAROCCI

Above: Trooper Frederick Wood of the 10th Regiment Canadian Mounted Rifles was among the first wave of mounted troops to enter the Great War. A farmer, Wood enlisted in Saskatchewan in January 1915. (Submitted by David Wood, Frederick's grandson.)

The Great War was an industrial war, a war of machines. Yet animals of many species played a huge role. Horses and mules moved supplies. Animal mascots stoked soldiers' pride in identifying with their units. Pigeons sent vital messages when other forms of communication went down. Cats, dogs, and other pets softened the hearts of soldiers living in the maelstrom of violence. The very presence of animals was a key link with ordinary pre-war life for the soldiers of 1914 to 1918.

Of the many animals involved in the war, horses and mules were among the most essential. Part of a complex battlefield transportation system that also included human muscle, motor vehicles, and trains, their roles were crucial to the war effort. Despite all of their vulnerabilities to enemy shells, splinters, bullets, and poison gas, no mode of forward military transportation was as versatile as horses.

Within the British field armies' zones of operations—of which Canadian soldiers formed a part—animal transport units were typically concentrated near the sharp end, immediately behind the firing lines. Bulk quantities of ammunition and supplies, stockpiled at bases near the English Channel, arrived in the forward areas on broad-gauge railway lines that usually terminated about a dozen kilometres behind the front lines. From there, motor lorries carried the goods to refilling points that serviced divisions in the line. At the refilling points, horse-drawn wagons took over, hauling bullets, shells, and grenades closer to infantry and artillery units.

Looking after the horses was a daunting task. For instance, in preparation for the 1917 Battle of Arras and the assault on Vimy Ridge, watering facilities had to be provided for up to 50,000 animals in the Canadian sector. Engineers struggled to provide some 2.7 million litres of drinking water per day just to keep the animals fit. By early April, before the attack on April 9, the water supply for animals was so precarious as to permit only the most essential exertions.

Working close to the front was difficult for animals, as they scared easily under

artillery fire. "During any action," the Canadian Corps' chief engineer observed in early 1917, "the handling of mules is a difficult and dangerous problem." And because they moved at different speeds, horses and motor vehicles did not easily share roads—especially with the addition of thousands of marching men. With roads crowded with traffic, there was little space to properly exercise horses when they were not at work. There was also a shortage of clean, dry standing areas for off-duty horses. Without proper care, exercise, and a good surface for rest, the animals easily succumbed to illness.

In many cases, horses suffered abuse or neglect at the hands of soldiers who were themselves routinely overworked, exhausted, and afraid. Some transport units attempted to improve efficiency by modifying wagons and carts to carry more weight than they, or their horse teams, were intended to handle.

Adding stowage on top of the wagons made sense to sleep-deprived soldiers but exasperated the staff officers who watched in horror as draught animals struggled to pull extra weight. One officer was incredulous when he came upon some enterprising soldiers who had hitched up three or four overloaded Lewis machine gun carts in a makeshift train, with the entire assembly pulled by a single, battered draught animal.

Major D. S. Tamblyn, a Canadian veterinary officer in the 3rd Division, was appalled at the conditions endured by horses, and advocated on their behalf. Especially troubling were the instances when drivers simply abandoned broken or exhausted animals where they fell on the roadside. Tamblyn dispatched veterinary sergeants on patrols to care for the abandoned creatures. "I deem this step necessary as a number of cases have been brought to my notice of animals being

left to die on the roadside," Tamblyn wrote. "I trust this will eliminate such cruelty."

Tamblyn was not the only one deeply moved by the plight of the horses. Infantryman George Maxwell, of the 49th Battalion, wrote of a costly cavalry charge at Amiens, France, in 1918: "These unfortunate dumb animals, lying around disembowelled, with their entrails oozing out and blood flowing from their broken bodies, offended our sensibilities even more than the sight of dead and wounded soldiers."

Many horse drivers were especially caring of their animals; some even believed the animals possessed special sensitivities that humans lacked. Private James Robert Johnston, a horse driver in the transport section of the 14th Machine Gun Company, wrote, "I believe my saddle horse knew more than I did and it is one of the reasons why I lasted as long as I did. He took care of me."

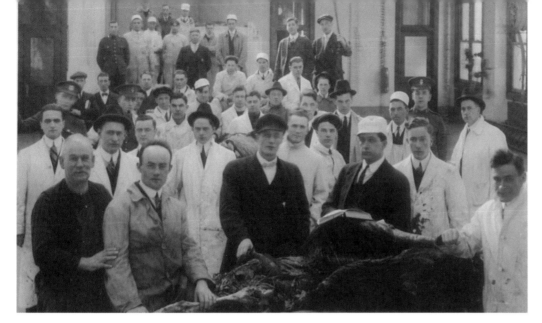

Canada's first overseas contingent embarked for the United Kingdom in the war's early months with a complement of some 7,600 horses. As the war entered its final year in 1918, the animal strength in Canada's overseas military forces approached 23,000. In comparison, the Canadians counted 1,009 motor lorries, 223 cars, 84 ambulances, and 2,327 bicycles on their transportation strength that spring—a ratio of slightly more than seventeen animals for each motor vehicle. In the final stages of a world war that was ostensibly dominated by machines, animals continued to outnumber other modes of road transportation by significant margins.

IF HORSES WERE ESSENTIAL TO MILITARY logistics, animals also buoyed the spirits of regiments and individual soldiers. Canadians often marched to war with mascots in their ranks. Animal mascots were part of the regimental tradition. They were given names and, sometimes, even a rank. Goats and dogs were popular, while black bears held pride of place with Canadian units eager to carve out unique identities within the British Expeditionary Force.

The most famous bear mascot was Winnie. Lieutenant Harry Colebourn, a veterinary officer with the Fort Garry Horse cavalry regiment, spied the black bear cub as the regiment passed through White River, Ontario, by train. The train stopped, allowing the men to get off to stretch their legs. As other soldiers bought overpriced sandwiches and alcohol, Colebourn haggled with a trapper for the bear.

Colebourn's journal entry for August 24, 1914, read, "Bought bear $20." It was a lot of money in 1914, but the bear soon proved to be a favourite among the soldiers. Colebourn named the little cub Winnipeg, after his hometown. It was soon shortened to Winnie, who was a hit at training camps in Valcartier, Quebec, and then in England. The cub was gentle and friendly to all and, to the delight of soldiers, did a number of tricks, including climbing the centre pole of the soldiers' tents.

When Colebourn was ordered to France, he needed to find a home for Winnie and made arrangements at the London Zoo. Winnie was not alone at the zoo. Between 1914 and 1917, at least a dozen black bears were presented or deposited at the London Zoo by Canadian regiments.

Goats were also popular mascots. Sergeant Harold Baldwin, of the 5th Battalion, wrote of one of his companions, Private Billy: "Billy in his early days had jumped from crag to crag of the Rocky Mountains, had been brought down to Valcartier, and, in spite of having very prominent veins on his legs, he passed the doctor, and he was the only one of our battalion who ever appeared on parade without being punished for not shaving. Billy had duly marched as was his

Top: Canadian soldiers release a messenger pigeon, May 1917.

Above: Hazen Fraser of the Royal Newfoundland Regiment with mascot Sable Chief at the 3rd London General Hospital during Newfoundland Week, September 1917. Fraser enlisted when he was only fourteen. He made it to England before his true age was discovered. He was assigned to become Sable Chief's handler. The dog died later in the war, after being struck by a truck.

wont in front of the battalion, when, to the consternation of the boys, the colonel swore, as is the divine right of a colonel, that the goat must be left behind. Here was a real difficulty. We could not part with Billy; the boys argued that we could easily get another colonel but it was too far to the Rocky Mountains to get another goat."

The *Canadian Daily Record*, a popular newspaper published for the Canadian soldiers throughout the war, featured Billy in its November 28, 1918, issue. "Sergeant Billy, the 5th Battalion mascot, enlisted at Broadview, Saskatchewan, on August 5, 1914. He has never left his unit, although he has been wounded, suffered trench feet, and had been shell-shocked." Like his comrades, Billy was known to like beer.

The 21st Battalion had Nan, a white goat. She was cared for by the transport section but was well known throughout the battalion for nuzzling men and swiping food.

On the march to the Somme in the summer of 1916, a new transport officer found the goat a burden and sold her to a French farmer for twenty francs. The battalion was outraged and staged a rescue. In a nighttime stealth operation, Nan was saved and went on to serve all the way to the Rhine River in Germany. Mascots like Nan were prized possessions for many units, building character while bringing cheer and a little pageantry to the long marches across France and Belgium.

ANIMALS ALSO CONTRIBUTED TO ANOTHER vital battlefield role: communication. Telephone lines were often cut by artillery fire, while radios were in their infancy. Human runners delivered vital messages, but they often became casualties or got lost.

Seeking a rapid and reliable means of communication, commanders turned to carrier pigeons. Messages were placed in small capsules that were attached to the pigeons' legs. Teams of pigeons were housed in mobile lofts, usually mounted on trucks or buses. As an attack was underway, soldiers at the head of the advance released pigeons to inform headquarters of their progress. Artillery support and reinforcements could then be provided as necessary.

Like most animals at the front, poison gas doomed many pigeons to a short life expectancy. There were also rumours that hungry soldiers would occasionally augment their mundane rations with pigeon pie.

Meanwhile, in the trenches, cats and dogs walked freely among the men. Many were abandoned animals found behind the lines. Soldiers soon gave them new homes.

CAPTURED AT COURCELETTE   CANADIAN OFFICIAL

Above: A postcard depicts a soldier holding a stray dog found during the 1916 Battle of Courcelette. The postcard was part of a collection belonging to Guy Elton Dingle of Brockville, Ontario. (Submitted by Ian Bartlett, Guy's grandson.)

Basil Craig wrote to his sister Grace of his unit's trench pet: "I don't know whether I told you about our famous kitten. It is called Whizz Bang. One of our men took pity on this kitten and brought it down here. It is very cute and lots of fun."

Both dogs and cats helped to control the rat population. Hal Kirkland, of the Princess Patricia's Canadian Light Infantry, wrote to his mother in April 1918: "There are numerous dogs running around the trenches and no man's land—all sizes and builds. Goodness knows where they come from. There's certainly no lack of sport for them if they like hunting rats, and some of the rats are huge enough to give a dog an exciting time."

Lieutenant Clifford Wells noted proudly that his platoon's terrier had set a record by killing forty-three rats in just a few minutes.

Yet the front was dangerous for animals and humans alike. Pools of poison gas could be active for hours, and mustard gas, introduced in the summer of 1917, persisted in mud and water for weeks. Many pets must have been lost in the toxic wasteland.

Agar Adamson wrote to his wife, Mabel, in February 1917: "My poor kitten who has not been well for some days died this morning after a fit. I am really quite upset. We had become such great friends. I and he always used to sleep in my sleeping bag. He was much more like a dog than a cat." As a long-service veteran, Adamson had seen hundreds of men killed and wounded. They too made an impression on him, but the loss of a pet could hurt in a different way. Horse drivers experienced similar emotions when their animals were killed or injured.

The keeping of trench pets revealed a deep sentimentality among the soldiers. Hardened by combat, and by the loss of their comrades, many men were moved by their animals. Small kittens could be buttoned up in a coat or battle jerkin to keep them and their owner warm. "The animals are the greatest of chums, and very popular with the soldiers," reported the *Canadian Daily Record*.

The famous poet and doctor John McCrae had a dog, as did the gruff Colonel W. E. Ironside, a legendary British soldier who was a staff officer in the Canadian 4th Division. His bulldog, Gibby, followed him everywhere, and after the war, a Canadian veteran wrote that Gibby was "badly gassed twice and came under shellfire quite often, but luckily escaped being [seriously] wounded and survived the war." Gibby returned to England with Ironside, who later became chief of the Imperial General Staff.

Perhaps the most exotic pet belonged to Andrew McNaughton. One of the Canadian Corps' most gifted artillery officers, McNaughton owned "His Highness Prince Anthony Yvon Nijinsky Boum," more commonly known as Tony the lion. Tony was born in the Paris zoo. He found a new home at the Canadian Corps Heavy Artillery headquarters, where an open-air run was constructed for him. The three-month-old Tony, in the words of one gunner, was a furry mass with large paws and an enormous head who had acquired a "reputation for unusual viciousness" and liked to claw at people who came near McNaughton. One staff officer wrote, "With us he was like a huge playful kitten," but for those who were frightened around him, he often fixed his eyes on them, opened his mouth, and crouched as if to spring.

Tony liked to lie at the feet of McNaughton, who would reach down and scratch him as he studied intelligence maps of enemy gun emplacements and planned out artillery bombardments. Visitors to McNaughton's office often missed Tony in the dim lighting—or mistook him for a rug—and he would slowly, stealthily crawl up to them and nip at their legs. Captain Lennox Napier recounted with satisfaction how one surprised Royal Air Force colonel became mute with fright upon discovering the beast and leapt back five yards. The fun did not last forever, though. Tony eventually found himself at the London Zoo, keeping company with the black bears.

WHEN THE WAR ENDED IN NOVEMBER 1918, there were about 23,000 horses and mules in Canadian service at the front. What to do with them? The London Zoo was not an option. An ocean voyage to Canada was both impractical and cruel; only a few officers' chargers went back to Canada. The Belgian government ended up purchasing Canada's war horses. The troops, some of whom had been driving the same beasts for two or three years, were heartbroken when orders came down to surrender the animals for sale. "The general feeling," according to D. E. Macintyre, a Canadian infantry officer, was that the horses deserved "as good treatment as a lot of the conscripts we have in the army."

By June 1919, virtually all of the horses had been sold to the Belgians. Postwar life for the horses included draught work on farms, delivery work in the towns, and mining work in the countryside. Some also stayed with the colours, this time with the Belgian cavalry. The last fifty horses on strength with Canadian troops in France served with burial parties, hauling decomposing corpses from temporary graves to permanent ones.

Like the horses, very few of the pets or mascots made it back to Canada. Winnie, the most famous Canadian mascot, remained at the London Zoo. A gentle bear, she enchanted visitors by allowing children to ride on her back. One of Winnie's fans was the author A. A. Milne, who took his son, Christopher, to visit the zoo. Milne was so inspired by the bear that he penned a series of stories that eventually became the beloved Winnie-the-Pooh series. On Winnie's death in 1934, several London newspapers wrote obituaries.

Nan the goat, of the 21st Battalion, was smuggled aboard ship for passage from France to England, where she narrowly escaped slaughter by order of stern members of Britain's agricultural board. The battalion refused and staged another operation to whisk her back to Canada. Nan eventually found a home at the stables of the Royal Military College in Kingston, Ontario, and lived to the ripe age of twelve.

The 5th Battalion's beer-swilling Billy returned home to Saskatchewan but died shortly after the war. Veterans had him stuffed and placed in the Great War Veterans' Association headquarters in Regina, where he undoubtedly looked on with envy as his old comrades downed their drinks. Today, his stuffed remains are proudly displayed at the Broadview Museum, in Broadview, Saskatchewan.

In 2004, a cenotaph was unveiled in London's Hyde Park to honour animals in war. A similar memorial was unveiled in 2012 in Ottawa. An inscription on the London cenotaph reads, "They Had No Choice."

The more than 60,000 Canadian dead of the First World War are commemorated as individuals, in Commonwealth War Graves cemeteries or on monuments. It is worth remembering that there are also countless mass graves, now lost to memory, for the horses and mules that served in the conflict, and many smaller unmarked graves for beloved pets and mascots who brought strength to Canada's soldiers in time of war.

Above: John McCrae, writer of "In Flanders Fields," stands beside his horse, Bonfire, and his dog, Bonneau. The dog would often accompany McCrae, a medical doctor, as he tended to wounded soldiers. (Submitted by Ian Bartlett.)

Left: Canadian soldiers play with puppies behind the line, May 1917.

INTO THE BOTTOMLESS MUD

THE BATTLE OF PASSCHENDAELE

JOEL RALPH

The Canadians didn't want to go to Passchendaele. They had been to Belgium's Ypres Salient, and they knew the near impossible task that lay ahead.

The British under General Sir Douglas Haig slogged through an offensive in the area throughout the summer of 1917. In June, they had detonated nearly 1 million tonnes of explosives buried under German lines at Messines Ridge, and on July 31, they officially launched the Third Battle of Ypres. But by August, heavy German counterattacks once again limited British success.

Throughout September and October, the British, Australians, and New Zealanders used a series of short, rapid attacks to make some gains, but their objective of capturing Passchendaele ridge—the only high ground in the region—remained elusive.

Months of battle and the onset of rain in October transformed the battlefield into a quagmire of mud and water that devoured men and matériel. Shell craters overflowed with water, and nearly every identifiable landmark that could help direct the troops had drowned into the endless mud.

The Canadians were tasked with capturing what remained of the town of Passchendaele. Their commander, General Arthur Currie, devised a series of four set-piece attacks over a two-week period that would allow them to capture the ridge.

The Canadians advanced through the wasteland towards Passchendaele, slowly clearing each German pillbox and machine gun strongpoint. In the confusing morass of mud, the attacks quickly broke down into small actions, and individual valour helped to turn the tide. The Canadians' eventual capture of Passchendaele brought an end to one of the most controversial battles of the war.

Though British commander Haig claimed victory, the human cost was once again unimaginably high. Over the course of four months of fighting, British and Commonwealth soldiers endured more than 260,000 dead and wounded, including 17,000 Canadians. Furthermore, as if to underline the futility of fighting, nearly all of the territory that the Canadians captured in 1917 was recaptured by the Germans during their spring advance of 1918.

A Canadian soldier helps two wounded Germans during the Battle of Passchendaele, circa November 1917.

Clockwise from top left:

In a letter home, Thomas Bower-Binns mentioned the joyous celebrations that accompanied the end of the war: "Nov. 11. 1918 Armstice [sic] Day. Wild times. Got good and drunk etc etc Belgium." He enlisted in 1915 and served with the 51st Howitzer Battery, 13th Brigade, Canadian Field Artillery in France and Belgium. (Submitted by Elizabeth Abel, Tommy's granddaughter, and John Bower-Binns, Tommy's son.)

Russel McBrien enlisted in June 1915 and served as a stretcher-bearer and trombone player in the 2nd Battalion. McBrien died on November 6, 1917. The cause of his death remains unknown, and his body wasn't recovered until many years later. (Submitted by Jan Rowley, Russel's niece, and Rod Heikkila, Russel's great-nephew.)

When Roy Craig returned to New Brunswick after serving with the 2nd Battalion Machine Gun Corps, his family noticed a serious change in his behaviour. After his wife, Ethel May Hanning, shown here, died of the Spanish Flu, he abandoned his children, moved, and remarried. He and his second wife, Myrtle Vail, had four more children; when Vail died, Craig sent them to an orphanage. He later married Katherine Millet-Cox and had two kids who outlived him. Patricia Lackey, Craig's granddaughter, said her father believed Craig's behaviour stemmed "from the daily horrors and dangers he saw during the First World War, which left him unable to cope with the normal problems of everyday life." (Submitted by Patricia Lackey, Roy's granddaughter.)

Kenneth Irvine Mitchell of Granby, Quebec, was seriously wounded in the elbow during the Battle of Passchendaele in October 1917. His left arm had to be amputated. He wrote many letters home during the war, describing conditions in the trenches, as well as vividly detailing some of the battles he was in as a member of the Princess Patricia's Canadian Light Infantry. Kenneth's son, Ken Mitchell, says this photo, taken sometime prior to the Battle of Passchendaele, is the only one he has that shows his father with both of his arms. In the photo, Kenneth is on the right. (Submitted by Ken Mitchell, Kenneth's son.)

Michael J. Duggan of Lloydtown, Ontario, enlisted in December 1915 at age eighteen. He joined the 92nd Highland Battalion and was wounded several times, including at the Battle of Passchendaele. Following the war, he worked at the Canadian Press. He died at the age of eighty-two in Toronto. (Submitted by Jeanne Snyder, Michael's granddaughter.)

Elias Howard Cross was the only casualty of the 15th Battalion on December 23, 1917, during fighting near Lens, France. He was shot during the relief of his battalion from the front line. Cross's parents were especially distraught at his death because they had lost their eldest son, Thomas, only a year earlier. (Submitted by Ron Cross, Elias Cross's cousin.)

Top left: Alex Mason of Ottawa, circa August 1915. The seventeen-year-old had just enlisted in the 77th Battalion. He was awarded the Military Medal at Passchendaele in 1917 for capturing a German machine gun nest. (Submitted by Jeff Mason, Alex's grandson.)

Top middle: Fred Rubidge was gassed at Passchendaele. In later years, Fred rarely spoke of the war. However, on one occasion, during a Christmas celebration with his family, he broke down in tears while listening to a radio docudrama of Dickens's *A Christmas Carol*. As the song "Silent Night" played on the radio, he told his family of how Canadian and German troops joined together one Christmas Eve to sing that song from across their trenches. "The next day they were back to killing each other," recalled R. J. Johnston, Fred's grandson. "It took some time for my grandmother and my mother to calm him down. This was the first and last time my grandfather ever spoke of the war." (Submitted by R. J. Johnston, Fred's grandson.)

Top right: John, Bertha, and Thorarinn Finnbogason circa 1916, prior to the men departing for the front. Bertha was the cousin of John and Thor of Langruth, Manitoba. The men fought at Passchendaele. Thor injured his leg during fighting at Arras, France, in 1918, and was forced to have it amputated. (Submitted by Joan Hedrick, Thor's daughter.)

Left: Stretcher-bearers carry a wounded Canadian from the battlefield during the Battle of Passchendaele circa 1917.

AS CASUALTIES ROSE, CANADA'S CONSERVATIVE PRIME MINISTER WAS DETERMINED TO IMPOSE COMPULSORY SERVICE. THIS HELPED WIN THE WAR BUT PUT THE TORIES ON THE LOSING SIDE OF GOVERNMENT FOR DECADES TO COME.

CHAPTER TWELVE

The Conscription Crisis

J. L. GRANATSTEIN

The Great War was a testing time for Canadians. Germany might have been the land of Beethoven and Goethe, but it was also seen as a nation whose leaders sought to impose their militaristic *Kultur* on Europe. Most Canadians instinctively and automatically sided with Britain and France, Canada's "mother countries," and rejected what they viewed as Kaiser Wilhelm's challenge to the peace of the world. The war that began in August 1914 mobilized millions of men and women, shifted peacetime economies into full-blast production of the munitions of war, and changed—or ended—countless lives.

For Canada, a British colony in law and in fact, there had been no choice: Canada was at war when Britain was at war. Men flocked to the colours. First in line were recent immigrants from Britain. They had come to Canada in search of a better life but retained close ties to "'ome." Slower to enlist were the Canadian-born, whatever their ethnicity, and slowest of all were French-speaking Canadians, their ties to Europe three centuries distant.

A secret British War Office study calculated at the beginning of 1917 that fewer than 10 percent of Canada's eligible men had enlisted. The researchers found that 37.5 percent of British-born Canadian men had signed up and that Canadian-born men of British extraction had enlisted at a rate of 6.1 percent. But only 1.4 percent of French-Canadian men had joined up, the study labelling this the lowest rate in the Dominions.

Québécois pointed to their early marriage age, their large families, the larger numbers living in rural areas, and their outrage at the fact that the army in Canada and overseas operated in the English language only. There was substantial truth to this. But the real truth was that in French Canada there was strong

Facing page: Harry Whitlock, third from right, and his mates, circa August 1914. The newly enlisted men are on their way to the railway station in Charlottetown and will soon head overseas. Whitlock served with the Royal Flying Corps, was shot down over France, and spent time in a German POW camp before returning to Canada. (Submitted by W. H. Soper. Whitlock was his father-in-law's brother.)

Above: This propaganda postcard purports to show German soldiers defiling a Catholic church in France or Belgium. It was created to inflame anti-German sentiment among the mostly Catholic French-Canadian population and to encourage French-Canadian men to enlist.

Methodist Church

FRIDAY EVENING June 1st

AT 8 P.M. SHARP

Captain (Mrs.) L. M. Parsons

will tell the YOUNG MEN how to

Avoid Conscription

Captain Parsons' fame as a public speaker has preceded her to Leamington and there are few who have not read of the great work she has done throughout the Dominion, and of the favorable comment her work has received from the great Canadian newspapers.

THREE SONS AT THE FRONT

Captain Parsons is not only the only woman who holds a commission in the Canadian Army, but she has three sons at the front as well, and is intimately acquainted with every phase of the great struggle.

While in this instance she does not CARRY A MESSAGE TO GARCIA, she does carry a message and a most important message for the YOUNG MEN OF LEAMINGTON who must soon decide whether they will "GO" or be "SENT FOR."

Lt.-Col. Milligan, late of the 18th Battalion, is expected to be with us and the Rev. Mr. Burrell will also give a short address.

Music by the Citizens' Band and singing by the Dunn-Trott-Beacom-Daykin "Quartette". EVERYBODY COME, as this will in all probabilty be the last meeting of this nature ever to be held in Leamington.

Rev. J. S. Leckie
Chairman

Edward Winter
Pres't of Brotherhood

Wm. T. Gregory
Chairman Rec. Com.

God Save the King and the Boys Who Wear the Khaki

P.S.—ADMISSION FREE.   **EVERYBODY COME.**

Above: Protesters opposed to conscription march along Victoria Square in Montreal, circa 1917.

Left: This notice seems to suggest that men should avoid conscription, but the organizers actually want to encourage men to voluntarily enlist—thereby avoiding the draft.

social pressure to stay at home. The Roman Catholic Church, the newspapers, and the men's families all argued against supporting what they viewed as Britain's—not Canada's—war. Abbé Lionel Groulx, the *nationaliste* historian, complained about "the wave of fanatical imperialism hanging over Canada." This was a widely held Quebec attitude.

As casualties in the trenches increased and the war hung in the balance, the demand for more men grew. By late 1916, the number of volunteers coming forward each month was far fewer than the number of killed and wounded. The answer was clear—conscription for overseas service. The impact of this issue on Canada, its politics, and its soldiers overseas proved to be profound.

No subject stirred up more emotion than conscription. Compelling Canadians to fight to defend their homes and families was one thing; obliging them to fight overseas in defence of less tangible interests was another. The British-born, those of recent British

WhEN MEN ARE BOYS   NORWOOD PLATOON

Left: A group of new recruits from Norwood, Ontario, horse around circa February 1916. Among them is Thomas Edward Cross, lying on the ground, third from the left. A married father of seven children, Cross enlisted in February 1916 with the 57th Regiment. On October 11, 1916, he wrote a letter from France to his wife, Jane, asking her to send his love to their children. "I would like to see them all for it is awful lonesome being away from you so long." On the back of the letter was a note from Cross's commanding officer: "Your husband has just received a wound and has asked me to add this to his letter. He will be all right. The wound is not very serious." Cross died five days later, his name added to the ever-mounting death toll that would eventually force the Canadian government to enact conscription. (Submitted by Ron Cross, Thomas's cousin.)

origin, and those families that had fathers, husbands, and sons at the front reacted positively to compulsory service. So too did those too old to be drafted. But for those fit men between the ages of twenty and forty-five, for French-speaking Canadians, and for many Canadians from other parts of the world, service in the Canadian Expeditionary Force had no inherent appeal; indeed, it was to be resisted.

No democratic government can easily impose a measure such as conscription without public support. But governments have many tools at their disposal, and a prime minister willing to be creative can tilt the balance in his and his party's favour. Borden, Conservative prime minister since 1911, believed fervently that the Germans must be defeated and that Canada must do its full part in the struggle. To achieve this, there was almost nothing he would not do.

Borden was no inspiring leader. He was a wooden speaker, a poor manager of his cabi-net, and faced difficulties in his caucus, not least in keeping his francophone Members of Parliament at his side. But he was determined to back up the soldiers at the front. After visiting France and England in the spring of 1917, after seeing the wounded in military hospitals, and after being persuaded that the Allies would lose the war unless more men were found for the front, he came back to Ottawa with his mind made up: conscription was essential if the Canadian Corps of four divisions was to be kept at full strength. As he wrote, he had had "the privilege of looking into the eyes of tens of thousands of men at the front who look to us for the effort which will make their sacrifice serve the great purpose for which it was intended."

The prime minister knew that this course was certain to divide the country. To forestall that, and to avoid being defeated in a future election—"Our ministers afraid of a general election think we would be beaten by French, foreigners, slackers," he wrote in his diary—Borden sought the support of all parties in Parliament. After revealing to the House of Commons on May 18, 1917, his intent to introduce conscription, he approached Wilfrid Laurier, the Liberal leader, and proposed a coalition to bring in the conscription legislation. Laurier pondered the offer and consulted his colleagues, but in the end he declined.

The Liberal leader feared that if he supported compulsory service, he would destroy his standing in Quebec and turn over power to extremist nationaliste zealots such as Henri Bourassa, the editor of Montreal's *Le Devoir*. Borden's two francophone ministers, E. L. Patenaude and P. E. Blondin, assessed the Quebec situation similarly, telling their cabinet colleagues that conscription "will kill them politically and the party [in French Canada] for twenty-five years." They were right.

With Laurier refusing to join a coalition for conscription, Borden set out to find

Top: Prime Minister Robert Borden speaks to a group of
Canadian soldiers, circa July 1918.

Bottom: Liberal leader Wilfrid Laurier.

prominent Liberals willing to come into the
government. While the Military Service Act
that sought to put 100,000 conscripts into
khaki was quickly drafted and passed in June,
his first efforts failed, as Laurier's caucus
remained loyal to the old chief. The prime
minister then decided that the government
needed political incentives in the form of two
additional measures: the Wartime Elections
Act and the Military Voters Act. The first gave
the vote to female relatives of soldiers—the
first time any women would be allowed to
cast federal ballots. The act also removed the
franchise from naturalized immigrants who
had come to Canada from enemy nations.
The second bill let all men and women in
uniform vote no matter how long they had
lived in Canada. If they could not name their
constituency, their votes would be assigned
to a riding.

The two bills shrank the ranks of
the likely anti-conscriptionist immigrants,
expanded the pro-conscription vote by adding women relatives of soldiers, and allowed
for massive manipulation of the soldier vote.
These were ruthless measures, testimony
to Borden's determination to win the war,
impose conscription, and win the election.

The two bills, when enacted, effectively
destroyed Liberal support in the West, which
was heavily dependent on immigrants who
had arrived during Laurier's period in office
from 1896 to 1911, and swung a number of

key provincial Liberals to Borden's side. By mid-October, a Union government of thirteen Conservatives and ten Liberals was in place, with three Grits coming from Laurier's caucus. Only two members of the new government were francophone Tories—Blondin and Albert Sévigny—resulting in very weak Quebec representation in a federal cabinet and a clear indication of the anti-conscriptionist sentiment in Quebec.

Farm support for the Union government was also very shaky, with agriculturists fearing that they could neither plant nor harvest their crops if their sons faced conscription. Borden threw the farmers a bone by bringing into his cabinet Thomas Crerar, president of the United Grain Growers. Then, in early December, with the general election campaign underway, the government resolved the farm problem by offering exemptions from military service to farmers. Indeed, the government's supporters knew exactly who they wanted to see drafted. As the premier of Ontario, Sir William Hearst, brutally said, he would ensure "that the people of Quebec are compelled to do their share before further sacrifices are demanded from Ontario."

The general election, the first since 1911, was one of the most vicious in Canada's history. Borden's ministers advised their leader that the Union campaign "should attack in press and on public platform the attitude of Quebec," and it did. A Union government pamphlet flatly stated that, if Laurier won, "the French-Canadians who have shirked their duty will be the dominating force in the government of the country. Are the English-speaking people prepared

Top: Ernie Barrett, second from right, poses in front of a recruiting car in Hamilton circa 1915. Barrett enlisted in September 1914 and fought at many key Canadian battles, including Vimy Ridge (where he was buried in debris for more than six hours by a shell blast). His battalion was nicknamed "The Mad 4th." At his death, Barrett had in his possession a bottle of cognac that had passed from member to member of the Mad 4th as they died, to be shared in a toast by the last surviving member. (Submitted by Al Barrett, Ernie's grandson.)

Above: In December 1917, Lieutenant Lester Harper of Edmonton wrote to his wife, Mabel, of the need for more men to join the fight. "I voted for conscription just before I came on leave," he wrote from London. "We received 250 reinforcements lately and we needed them." Harper is shown here with arms wide, hamming it up with members of the 138th Battalion at Sarcee Camp, Calgary, circa 1916. (Submitted by Barbara Dalby, daughter of Lester and Mabel Harper.)

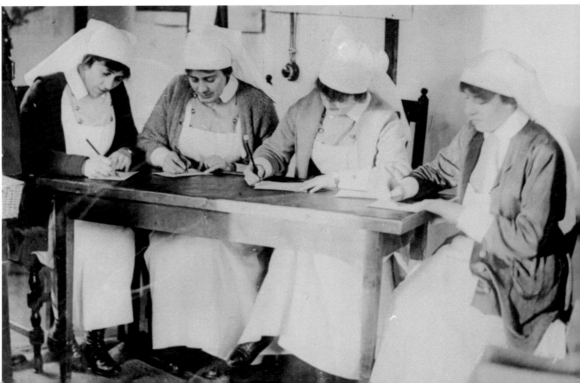

How to Vote YES

Question :

"Are you in favour of the Government having, in this grave emergency, the same Compulsory powers over citizens in regard to requiring their military service, for the term of the war, outside the Commonwealth as it now has in regard to military service within the Commonwealth?"

YES [X]

NO [ ]

IF YOU WANT TO VOTE YES
PUT YOUR CROSS IN THE TOP SQUARE

STEP INTO YOUR PLACE

PUBLISHED BY THE PARLIAMENTARY RECRUITING COMMITTEE, LONDON — POSTER Nº 104

PRINTED BY DAVID ALLEN & SONS Lᵈ. HARROW, MIDDLESEX. W. 5778. 10M. — 7/15

to stand for that?" Another pamphlet maintained that, "Laurier means to quit the war." A Unionist speaker declared shamefully, "If Laurier wins, he will win leading the cockroaches of the kitchen of Canada to victory." And Canon H. J. Cody in Toronto summed up the thrust of the Unionist campaign in his election sermon: The issue was neither grievances nor party loyalty nor the high cost of living; it was, as he put it, "Quebec *über alles*." The domination of Canada by French Canadians could not be permitted.

Spurred by the propaganda campaign, women voters mobilized for the Union. Sol-diers overseas, one government organizer wrote, were lined up by their commanding officers, who "told them plainly what they wanted them to do as a matter of duty." Overwhelmingly English-speaking (only the 22nd Battalion of the forty-eight infantry battalions in the Canadian Corps was not), the troopers did their duty, with 92 percent of the soldier vote going to Unionist candidates. This was enough to swing fourteen seats from Laurier to Borden under the particular and peculiar terms of the Military Voters Act.

Against this barrage of slander and electoral manipulation, Laurier could do little.

Above: As soldiers march, a group of civilians intending to enlist fall in behind them in this Great War recruiting poster.

Facing page, top: Canadian soldiers vote in the 1917 federal election.

Facing page, bottom left: This propaganda leaflet urges readers to vote in favour of conscription. The conscription issue dominated the December 1917 election.

Facing page, bottom right: Nurses stationed at the Canadian military hospital in Orpington, England, vote in the 1917 federal election.

His English-speaking candidates took a host of different positions, some supporting conscription, some merely supporting Laurier. One of his Quebec supporters stated his position: "Laurier is a Liberal, a Canadian patriot; above all, he is Laurier." As for the leader himself, his position on the war was clear: "I believe that our first and pressing duty is to share in the fight. I believe that it is our immediate duty to help our armies . . . [to] support them with men." But, not with conscription: "We began with the voluntary system," he said. "It is our duty to continue with it."

The results of the election on December 17, 1917, were decisive. Borden's Unionists captured 153 seats while the Liberals had 82. Ontario delivered 74 seats for the Union government, while in Quebec, Laurier took all but 3 seats. As they had predicted, ministers Sévigny and Blondin went down to defeat. The impact of the women's vote was hard to measure, but Quebec had only 20.6 percent of its total population enfranchised; Ontario, on the other hand, had 39.4 percent, an indication that soldiers' female relatives were much more numerous there. In the West, Saskatchewan, with a heavy immigrant population, had just 22.9 percent of its population with the vote, a figure that suggested that the Wartime Elections Act had had exactly the effect that its drafters wanted. At the same time, as University of Toronto historian John English has shown, 117 of the seats won by the Unionists were rurally based. The pledge not to conscript farmers' sons had also paid off.

Arthur Meighen, Borden's minister of the interior and the man who had drafted both bills, wrote to a friend that the election result showed that "French-Canadian domination in political affairs is a back number." John W. Dafoe of the *Manitoba Free Press* was equally harsh when he wrote to a Quebec friend: French Canadians were "the only known race of white men to quit" in this war. "You can do precisely as you please, and we shall do whatever may be necessary. When we demonstrate that a solid Quebec is without power, there may be a return to reason along the banks of the St. Lawrence."

As of the end of 1917, not a single man had been conscripted, though the process of calling potential draftees to report had begun in October. What was startling was that almost every man who was called up sought to be exempted from service. In Ontario, 118,000 of the 125,000 ordered to report had filed for exemption. In Quebec, the numbers were 115,000 of 117,000. Nationally, the percentage seeking exemption was 93.7. Everyone knew of the high casualties and brutal conditions at the front. Few who had not already volunteered wanted to go, no matter how they and their fathers had voted in the election. But go they would. The system was slow but sure, and local tribunals treated the appeals for exemption with dispatch.

Then, on March 21, 1918, the Germans launched a massive attack on the Western Front, smashing through Allied lines and creating near panic in London, in Paris, and soon in Ottawa. The pressure to get men into uniform quickly increased, provoking bloody riots in Quebec City and a cabinet decision to cancel all exemptions for men between

Above: A group of wounded soldiers stands in front of graffiti condemning "slackers"—able-bodied men who refuse to enlist in the war, circa 1915–1918.

twenty and twenty-two years of age. The only grounds for exemption now was the "death, disablement or service of other members of the same family while on active service." In other words, the farmers' exemptions that had helped to deliver the election victory to the Union government disappeared. The shocked outrage in the rural West and Ontario now matched that in Quebec, and the farmers' political organizing, already proceeding apace, speeded up. The Conservatives would pay a heavy price in the coming years.

But conscription did what Borden had intended. By the war's end in November 1918, 99,651 men were on strength with the Canadian Expeditionary Force. Of that number, 47,509 had proceeded overseas, and 24,132 had joined units in France. How many of those saw action is unclear, but there can be no doubt that the 100,000 conscripts could have provided the reinforcements the Canadian Corps would have needed had the war continued into 1919, as all had expected. Indeed, the 45,000 casualties the corps sustained in the Hundred Days—the brutal fighting from the start of the great Allied offensive on August 8 through to the armistice—were largely replaced by the first conscripts to reach the front.

Borden left his Conservative party in ruins, scorned in Quebec and by farmers across Canada. His legacy was the long Liberal reign that lasted from 1921 to 1957, R. B. Bennett's interregnum excepted. But he had achieved his goal of sustaining the Canadian Corps at the front and helping to win the war. To those who accused him of breaking pledges, his response was to ask if the nation had not made solemn promises to support the soldiers at the front. Did these not take precedence? Borden had been determined to do what he believed to be right and necessary. And he did.

Top left: Robert Munro of Busby, Alberta, was drafted in January 1918. In September of that year, he was killed by a burst of machine-gun fire. His death added to his family's pain and loss; two of Munro's sisters had died earlier in the year after contracting the Spanish flu. (Submitted by George Pratt. Robert was his father's cousin.)

Top right: William D. MacKenzie at Forest, Ontario, circa 1918. MacKenzie was drafted in March 1918. He served in the Royal Air Force. (Submitted by Mary Wade, William's daughter.)

Bottom left: Dewart Keir of Toronto was drafted on January 7, 1918. By mid-summer, he was dead—killed in action in France on August 8, 1918. At the time of his conscription, he had just started his first job and was engaged to be married. (Submitted by Evelyn Rose, Dewart's niece.)

Bottom right: Percy Harden of Knowlton, Quebec, enlisted in December 1916. At the time, he had been married for only a year and had a baby daughter, Ruby. Harden was killed in action in August 1917, while storming a German trench. (Submitted by Brenda Eldridge. Percy was the grandfather of her husband, Douglas Eldridge.)

6th Canadian Reserve Seaford 15/9/18. Some of the Best
Hilton Brighton

Top: Cecil Stapleton of Clarke, Ontario, was drafted in May 1918. In this photo of the 6th Canadian Reserve Unit in Seaford, England, Stapleton is front row centre. He became ill during training and didn't recover until after the armistice was declared. **(Submitted by Sharon Teves, Cecil's granddaughter.)**

Bottom: Canada barred people of Chinese descent from enlisting, but some Chinese did serve at the front in non-fighting capacities. Here, members of the Chinese Labour Corps pose for a photo at Camp Petawawa, Ontario, circa 1917. The Chinese Labour Corps was created in 1917 to play a supporting role in France. Recruited in China, roughly 50,000 men travelled by ship to British Columbia, then by rail across Canada, before crossing the Atlantic. Following the war, they returned home to China by again crossing Canada and then sailing across the Pacific. These men appear to have been put to work crushing stone during a stop at Petawawa.

GERMANY'S BLACK DAY

THE BATTLE OF AMIENS

JOEL RALPH

After the Russian Revolution in 1917, the new Bolshevik government quickly made peace with Germany. Freed from a two-front war, Germany amassed its troops on the Western Front and made a concerted effort in the spring of 1918 to break the British and French line.

Despite some significant success, they were never able to crack the Entente defences. By August 1918, the British, French, and newly arrived Americans launched their counterattack.

The Canadians, meanwhile, encamped at Vimy Ridge, avoided nearly all of the major fighting during the spring of 1918. Rested and ready, they would play a critical role during what is known today as the Hundred Days Offensive.

The first blow fell on German lines near the city of Amiens, France. After months of planning, the Canadians secretly moved into a position just beyond the city. When the Canadian artillery bombardment began on August 8, it caught the Germans completely off guard.

Despite a heavy fog blanketing the battlefield, the Canadians made good progress through the German front-line positions. Attacking side by side with the equally experienced Australian Corps, the Canadians punched a twelve-kilometre hole in the German line that changed the entire tempo of the war.

By Great War standards, it was an exceptional advance. German General Erich Ludendorff described it as "the black day of the German Army" due to the large number of soldiers who chose to surrender rather than fight to the death. Nevertheless, the Canadians still suffered 4,000 casualties.

The Battle of Amiens changed the course of the war, delivering a staggering blow from which the German army couldn't recover. For the first time, the end of the war was in sight.

Members of the 5th Battalion, Canadian Mounted Rifles celebrate
after the Battle of Amiens, circa August 1918.

Left: Seaton Graham was a lead gunner with the 31st Battalion during the war. He kept up a busy correspondence with Rebecca Wright, his wife. Graham saw action at several major battles, including Amiens and Cambrai. (Submitted by Irene Graham and Reba Scott. Seaton and Rebecca were their parents.)

Below: Laurence (Laurie) Edward Fry enlisted in 1916 and served with the 78th Battalion. He died during the Battle of Amiens in 1918. (Submitted by Laurie Jarman, Laurence's cousin.)

Facing page, top: Canadians wounded at the Battle of Amiens lie outside of the 10th Field Ambulance Dressing Station. German prisoners of war are also dispersed through the crowd. They likely carried some of the wounded back to the dressing station.

Facing page, bottom: More than thirty soldiers are needed to haul this sixty-pound gun out of the line during the Battle of Amiens circa 1918. The tremendous challenge of moving guns quickly often slowed or stalled advances at the front.

THOUSANDS OF FRENCH-CANADIANS
SERVED IN THE FIRST WORLD WAR.
SO, WHY DON'T WE KNOW THEIR STORIES?

CHAPTER THIRTEEN

Silence and Sacrifice

MICHEL LITALIEN

I am the son of a serviceman. Although I was born abroad, I grew up and have lived most of my adult life in Quebec. On the military bases of my childhood, it was perfectly natural for the school day to begin with us standing for the national anthem and morning prayers. My classmates and I stood with pride, even though, in the 1970s, this was a custom already considered outdated in Quebec.

It was the same with Remembrance Day ceremonies. I occasionally attended as a spectator and would try to catch a glimpse of my father among the many different soldiers on parade. In those days, veterans of the Second World War and the Korean War were still serving in the Canadian military. I was always impressed by the men and women wearing uniforms emblazoned with medals. And sometimes I would notice a few elderly people sitting in the front row, many in wheelchairs, proudly wearing different decorations. I was told these were veterans of the Great War. I could sense the emotion in the air during these ceremonies. For my family and my community, Armistice Day ceremo-

nies were a part of life. Despite my young age and my inability to fully understand the concept of "remembrance," I knew that it was something significant and solemn.

We moved often as a result of my father's many relocations, and I eventually came to attend an off-base public school. November 11 suddenly became a day like any other. There were no commemorative ceremonies, not even a mention in class, and there was certainly no national anthem. The Canadian history course I took in high school did cover the First World War, but it focused primarily on Quebec's objection to conscription. It was as though Quebecers had never fought in the two world wars. Remembrance Day ceremonies were televised, but because they were carried live, usually on a weekday morning, and because ordinary people did not yet own camcorders, the First World War and any remembrance thereof were gradually supplanted by my other teenage interests.

By early adulthood, I had discovered a passion for history and decided to pursue

Above: Historian Michel Litalien, at around six months of age, with his father, Fred, in Germany in 1965. Fred Litalien served in the Canadian army.

Facing page: Members of the 22nd Infantry Battalion (French Canadian) drain trenches somewhere on the Western Front, circa July 1916.

Above: Honoré-Édouard Légaré of the 22nd Battalion. The Quebec man's heroics were noted during the Battle of Courcelette in September 1916. He wrote about his war experiences in *Ce que j'ai vu . . . Ce que j'ai vécu 1914–1916*. (Submitted by Édouard Légaré, Honoré-Édouard's son.)

Above: Dr. Arthur Mignault, far right, a militia officer before the war, was one of the founders of the 22nd Battalion (French Canadian). A wealthy physician, he donated $50,000 to the federal government to raise this battalion. He did the same for the 41st Battalion (French Canadian) and for No. 4 Canadian Stationary Hospital (French Canadian). Promoted to lieutenant colonel, he took command of this medical unit.

a bachelor of arts in history at the Université de Montréal. Much to my amazement, there were no courses devoted exclusively to war or to contemporary conflicts. In the contemporary Canadian history courses, the two world wars were given little attention, with the justification being that there wasn't enough time for in-depth coverage. I, along with several of my classmates, was very disappointed not to learn more about these two wars. To rectify the lack of classroom content, students were encouraged to explore the subject more thoroughly on their own time. And that's exactly what I did.

In the early 1990s, French-language publications about Canada in the First World War were pretty rare or very hard to come by. And those that could be found tended to discuss the war in fairly general terms. There were no specifics regarding soldiers from Quebec or other parts of French Canada. Works on Quebec history tended to distill the First World War down to the issue of conscription. Some of the literature did mention that several thousand individuals (mainly conscripts, according to one popular belief) fought with the 22nd Battalion, now the Royal 22e Régiment—known in English as the "Van Doos." Not satisfied with the scant information available in French, I decided to turn to English-Canadian material. Although the literature in English was far more abundant, I encountered the same issues: the limited participation of French Canadians in the war and the conscription crisis.

In 1994, when I heard that historian Desmond Morton was coming to Montreal to teach at McGill University and that one of his courses would focus on Canada and the First World War, I decided that I had to meet him. Affable and interested, he agreed to accept me as a "special" (non-program) student. By the end of his course, I had become a true enthusiast of the history of Canada and the First World War. Among the things I had learned were that Quebecers and other French Canadians had served in units other than the 22nd Battalion, and that Quebecers were not the only people in Canada who opposed conscription.

I also found that historians tended to ignore the participation of French-speaking volunteer combatants. According to American historian Elizabeth H. Armstrong, between 32,000 and 35,000 French Canadians served under the colours during the First World War. Of these, some 15,000 fought on the front lines. I asked myself many questions: What did we know about them? What was their war experience? Was their experience any different from that of their English-speaking counterparts? There were no answers to these questions.

The silence on the subject was in part attributable to the combatants themselves. On their return from the war, most kept a low profile. Only a handful published accounts of their experiences. I turned up only five records published between the two world wars.

The lack of written accounts by francophone veterans greatly impeded the work of Canadian First World War historians. In his 1986 socio-military study, *Le 22e bataillon (canadien-français), 1914–1919: Études socio-militaire*, historian Jean-Pierre Gagnon lamented the dearth of personal recollections, which meant that certain characteristics of living conditions in the 22nd (French-Canadian) Battalion would remain in the dark. At that

time, all he had to go on were the written recollections of only four combatants.

Finding personal accounts from French Canada was a real challenge. In 2007, a colleague at the National Film Board decided to make a documentary on the First World War based on the written recollections of French-Canadian soldiers. He began by contacting government museums and archives to consult war correspondence written in French. He was told that letters in French were so rare as to be virtually non-existent. The archivists said this was because most French-Canadian soldiers were illiterate or simply didn't write. So would this mean that a farmer from Charlevoix wrote less than a farmer from Saskatchewan, or that a labourer from Montreal wrote less than a labourer from Toronto? I couldn't accept that there was any truth to this.

Top left: A long line of children in Amherst, Nova Scotia, parades past members of the 22nd Battalion, April 21, 1915, to see the men off to war in Europe.

Above: This painting of the September 1916 Battle of Courcelette was used as an educational panel for elementary-level history courses in Quebec between the 1920s and 1950s. During that time, the exploits of the 22nd Battalion, which fought at the battle, were a key part of curricula, as important as tales of New France adventurers such as Dollard des Ormeaux and Frontenac. (Painting by Desrosiers-Bertrand, 1921.)

When I started to dig deeper, I soon began unearthing previously unpublished letters, journals, and diaries written by more than one hundred First World War combatants from Quebec and other parts of French Canada. These invaluable documents were found in the homes of soldiers' descendants, in private collections, in the archives of

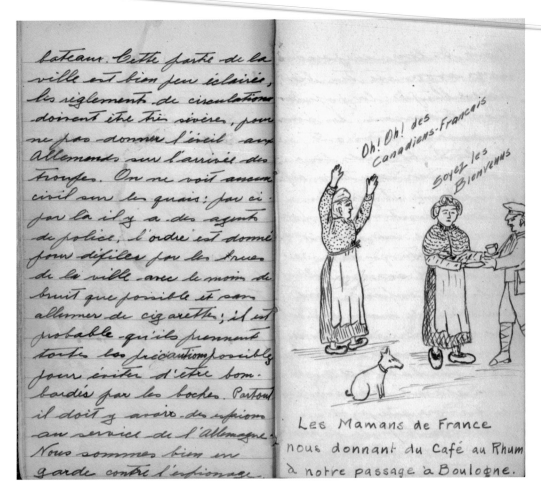

regimental museums, and in archival holdings of regional historical societies.

My search and the resultant reading fascinated me, and the accounts proved very informative. Not only did they shed light on the daily life of French-Canadian soldiers at the front, they also revealed aspects of the soldiers' social experience of the war. The war experience of French-Canadian soldiers was different from that of their English-Canadian counterparts, but not in all regards.

For example, even though the majority of francophone volunteers did not sign up "for King and country," as most of the earliest English-speaking volunteers did, the French-Canadian soldiers had much the same battlefield experience as their English-speaking counterparts. Indeed, whether they were from Newfoundland, Britain, France, or even Germany, soldiers at the front all shared much the same experience. They all, at some point, experienced the hardship of training, anxiety and nerves, the fear of their first march to the trenches, the shock of losing a brother-in-arms or of being injured, the fear of charging an enemy position or of being killed and never again seeing their loved ones.

Attributes specific to French-Canadian soldiers become evident when looking at their social experience of the war. For example, it is quite amusing to read the numerous descriptions of first meetings between French Canadians and troops from France, who were amazed by these "soldiers in English uniforms who speak French." For the French, it was something like the return of the prodigal son. One such encounter, which occurred on September 16, 1915, was described by Sergeant Édouard Légaré: "As we passed through the town of Hazebrouck in France, the battalion was singing Oh Canada [sic] and La Marseillaise. The townspeople gave each of us fruits, cakes . . . They were quite surprised to hear us singing and talking in French. We asked one, 'Sir, are we on the right road to get to Berlin?' 'Oh là, là! That's a good one,' replied the man, as he handed me a large bottle of wine. He added, 'Drink it when you get to the Kaiser's palace.' We thanked him and carried on our way . . . Much the same scene played out in almost every town we marched through."

The social experience in other countries was recorded as well. During their time in Belgium, many French-Canadian soldiers were quick to note the differences between the Dutch-speaking Flemish and the French-speaking Walloons and wrote of their impressions. Of England, they generally seemed to have fond memories, despite the language barrier. They expressed curiosity at seeing English women working in industry and other traditionally male sectors, and they wrote admiringly of the women's confidence and independence of spirit.

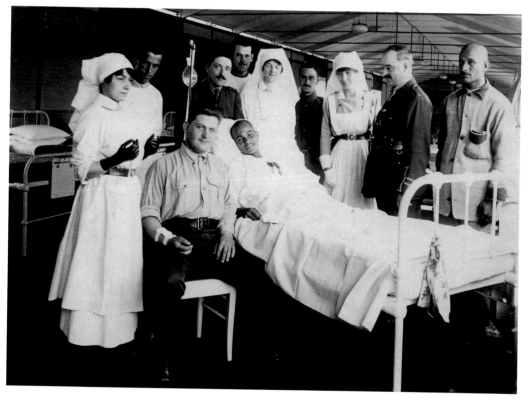

women work in all sorts of jobs. They drive trams and buses. I've seen them delivering personal belongings to homes, in cars, on bicycles or in taxis. It's quite astonishing, and it's quite surprising to see just how hard a young woman can work. They dress simply and modestly. As I observed these things, I thought of the young women in Canada, many of whom fear demeaning themselves by working. Yet the time has come, more so now than ever, for us to start thinking about the domestic economy if there is too much misplaced fear of manual work in the home or outside of it."

Pushing my quest even further, I decided to read diaries and memoirs of English-Canadian soldiers. As I went along, I noted all references to French-speaking soldiers or the 22nd Battalion. Francophones serving in English-speaking units often elicited curiosity. With a few exceptions, there was mutual respect between the soldiers of the 22nd Battalion and their comrades in other battalions of the 5th Infantry Brigade. Their battlefield exploits were recognized and saluted, but some writers wondered whether the "Van Doos" weren't a bit too nervy, even somewhat reckless. According to William Hillyer of the Borden Armoured Battery, "The French Canadian regiments are quite fearless, whether it is from them not realizing the danger or not, I don't know, but the fact remains."

Lieutenant Geoffrey Marani of the 24th Battalion (Victoria Rifles) recollected a rather unusual event: "There were strict orders when we moved into the trenches to stay low. The 22nd Battalion had been in the line just in front of Neuville Vitasse. Mercatel

Above: Private Georges Dufresne gives a blood transfusion to a Moroccan sharpshooter at No. 6 Canadian General Hospital (Laval). French-speaking personnel for this military medical hospital were supplied by Laval University in Montreal.

Left: Artilleryman Oliva Cinq-Mars, a native of Sherbrooke, Quebec, enlisted in August 1914. He served with several English-speaking units, fighting in the battles of Courcelette, Vimy, and Passchendaele. (Submitted by Michael Hall, Olivia's grandson.)

Captain Rosaire Crochetière, a chaplain with the 150th Infantry Battalion, observed: "In Europe, they're a lot more practical than we are in Canada in a wide range of things. There are a lot of aristocrats and far more wealthy families, yet there are many more people working than in Canada. You meet sons of noble families everywhere. Young

Above: In May 1916, the 163rd Battalion (French Canadian) sailed to Bermuda for garrison duty. While there, it recruited black volunteers from the British island colony, including these two men, privates Adolphus Anderson and Bernard Tucker. This apparently angered Bermuda's governor, who put a stop to the practice.

Above: The only son of lawyer and Liberal Member of Parliament Rodolphe Lemieux, a fierce opponent of conscription and the Union government, Lieutenant Louis Rodolphe Lemieux, twenty, was killed in action in France in August 1918 while fighting with the 22nd Battalion (French Canadian). A stained-glass window located in a small church in Pointe-au-Pic, Quebec, still honours his memory.

and Telegraph Hill were in the same front. They found things a little quiet around the support line, so they decided to get out and start a baseball game. There was a wonderful view because Neuville Vitasse was at quite a height. Other troops got out and became spectators until there was quite a crowd present. Then the Germans let them have it. There were lots of casualties. That was the French-Canadian nature. They were fed up with that slow-motion stuff in the trenches. Our orders were no more playing baseball."

This goes to show the importance of personal accounts in chronicling a fair and accurate history of the French-Canadian war experience. I believe that these recollections and impressions, set down by brave young combatants at the front, will appeal to and move young Quebecers. Many other character or behaviour traits of the French-Canadian soldier remain to be discovered or confirmed. For example, if a French-Canadian soldier found it easier to communicate with people who spoke the same language, he might be more tempted to go AWOL or to extend his leave without permission, as this account by P.-É. Bélanger suggests: "In this platoon was Sgt. Dufour from Hull. He was a man who feared nothing, and I never saw him drop to the ground for cover from bullets or artillery fire. He defied death. He must have served more than four years with the battalion without ever being injured. He wasn't decorated and he was always present for duty. When we were in reserve, he would say to me, 'Bélanger, take care of the platoon,' and he would disappear for a couple of days. He was never late returning to the firing line. An admirable man."

I was later able to verify this theory with records from two French-Canadian medical units. Both were located near Paris and both experienced a high number of AWOLs during the war.

In 2011, I published an essay on the personal accounts of these combatants. I continue to uncover new, unpublished written accounts on a fairly regular basis. It is my hope that these personal accounts will be widely read, so that these combatants become better known, their contributions gain greater recognition, and they never disappear from our collective memory.

There is clear evidence that, over the past twenty years or so, interest in military history, in particular the history of French Canada during the First World War, has been gaining momentum in Quebec among students as well as the general public. The proliferation of research and publications in French began in 1994, when the first entirely French symposium on military history was held at the Royal Military College Saint-Jean and the Université du Québec à Montréal. This interest had been building for some time, as can be seen from the many dissertations and theses on the subject, as well as the number, quality, and diversity of books published since that date. For example, the First World War has been examined from a variety of angles, including technology, trench diaries, diet, the home front, and remembrance. Quebec historians are making it plain that Quebec's story is about far more than conscription. Letters, journals, and diaries of French-speaking soldiers that had been languishing in attics and boxes are being dusted off and made public.

To coincide with the centenary of the Great War, a multitude of radio and television documentaries have been made on Quebecers and the First World War. There is clearly interest in the air. Let's hope these reports illuminate the sacrifices made by our soldiers and perpetuate their memory—and not only in Quebec.

Top: French-Canadian members of the 10th Canadian Reserve Battalion (Quebec) prepare a meal for the rest of the battalion, circa 1917–1918. Its primary role was to reinforce other battalions, primarily the French-speaking 22nd Battalion and the 150th Battalion.

Above Left: Onil Bessette of Marieville, Quebec, was drafted on July 20, 1918, joining the 1st Depot Battalion, 1st Quebec Regiment, based in Montreal.

Above right: J. Ernest Pagé joined the army in 1916. He was from Knowlton, Quebec. (Submitted by Louis Pagé, Ernest's son.)

ANADIANS RETURNED FROM THE FRONT AT THE DISCHARGE, DEPOT QUEBEC APRIL 6TH 1917.

Above: Joseph Walker, ninth from left, second row, poses with a group of men newly returned from the front, in April 1917. The photo was taken at the Discharge Depot at Quebec. (Submitted by J. W. Walker, Joseph's son.)

Far left: Lieutenant Archie Jenks served in France with the Royal Flying Corps. A dentistry student at McGill University, Jenks enlisted on February 18, 1915, at age twenty-five. Following the war, he set up a dental practice and married Elizabeth McKin. The couple had one child, Anson, who died at the age of two. Jenks took his own life in Montreal on July 29, 1938. (Submitted by C. Jenks, Archie's cousin.)

Left: James R. Moore, circa 1918. Moore enlisted on June 18, 1918, and trained at Camp St. Jean in Quebec. He arrived in France on October 10, a month before the armistice. (Submitted by Emy Thomas.)

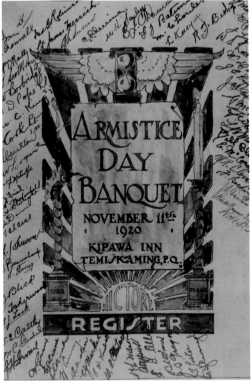

Top Left: When news broke of the death of James William Mainwaring, it devastated his family back home in Saint-Lambert, Quebec. Just seventeen years old, the youth—shown here on June 3, 1917, at Camp Petawawa, Ontario—had reportedly been driving a cart when it was struck by a German artillery shell. The entire town came out for his funeral; his brother, Joseph, who was serving overseas, was especially distraught. A few months later, Joseph got the shock of his life while on leave in London. He spotted James in a train station, apparently raised from the dead. James was quick to explain that there had been a mix-up—he had switched places with another driver shortly before the deadly blast. Needless to say, his family was elated. "There was then a huge celebration back in Canada because he was found to be alive," said James's granddaughter, Catherine Karayanis. James survived the rest of the war and settled in Bathurst, New Brunswick, where he worked for a pulp and paper company. He married Lillian Mary Nixon in 1938, and the couple had three children. A lifelong Montreal Canadiens fan, James Mainwaring died in 1981. (Submitted by Catherine Karayanis, James's granddaughter.)

Top right: Montrealer John Melody Dever enlisted in August 1916 and was assigned to C Battery of the Royal Canadian Horse Artillery. He was one of three brothers to serve in the war, after which he became a partner in a Montreal importing and exporting firm called Johnson & Dever. (Submitted by Patricia Greber, John's granddaughter.)

Left: Alphonse Leo Kelly of Alumette, Quebec, kept this menu as a war souvenir. Kelly fought at Vimy Ridge, and in a letter to home, written after the battle, he described the sumptuous meal enjoyed by the men prior to the attack. Kelly said the men feasted on bacon, butter, tea, and oranges—a nice change from the usual bland fare of bully beef and hard biscuits. "I guess the cooks opened their hearts for they knew the boys would have a hard day and it would be the last meal for quite a few of them," Kelly wrote. (Submitted by Mary Kelly, Leo's daughter-in-law.)

AN EMBOLDENED CORPS
THE LAST HUNDRED DAYS

JOEL RALPH

Having shattered the German defensive plan with their startling victory at Amiens, the Entente and Canadian forces quickly moved north to the Arras region of France to commence a final push that would lead to the end of the war.

Ahead of the Canadians lay a series of formidable defensive positions, including trenches that stretched for tens of kilometres, machine gun emplacements, masses of barbed wire, and concrete fortifications. Worse still, the Germans knew that the Canadians were coming.

To counter the lack of surprise, the Canadians opened the battle with a rare night attack on August 26, 1918. They battered their way through the German front lines, kicking off extensive fighting by all four Canadian divisions.

Within a week they had reached the Drocourt-Quéant line, one of the most daunting German defensive positions on the front. Because the Canadians had advanced so rapidly, there was little time for planning—or for the extensive artillery barrage that preceded most attacks. Nevertheless, on September 2, infantry of the 1st and 4th Canadian divisions pushed forward again, and, despite enduring heavy casualties, captured the entire German position.

Outmanoeuvred, the Germans retreated behind Canal du Nord, setting the stage for the Canadian Corps' perhaps boldest attack of the war. The deep but dry canal separating the Canadian and German lines was more than forty metres wide. The Canadian plan called for the divisions to cross a stretch of the canal only about two-and-a-half kilometres long—barely enough room for a single division to ford, let alone four at once.

The plan was dangerous, as the Canadians would be exposed to potentially decimating artillery fire over a bottlenecked area. Furthermore, the Germans maintained an extensive defensive position in Bourlon Wood, a small forested area on the canal's opposite side.

At dawn on September 27, the Canadians attacked. Nearly every lesson gained through four years of hard fighting was applied in a violent strike across the canal and through the heart of the position. The Canadians successfully captured their goal and again broke a key German line of defence.

Every square inch of ground gained came at the expense of Canadian lives. All told, the last hundred days of the war, including the Battle of Amiens, cost the Canadians more than 45,000 dead and wounded, a staggering total. Significantly, however, these soldiers' sacrifice was critical to ending the Great War.

Canadians Entering Cambrai, by Frank Brangwyn.

Top left: Findlater John Charles Crang, far left, second row, was awarded the Military Medal for leading his unit after all its officers were killed at Canal du Nord in northern France in September 1918. The twenty-nine-year-old sniper was shot in the thigh during the battle. (Submitted by Rob Crang, Findlater's grandson.)

Top right: A Japanese-Canadian volunteer shaves behind the lines near Arras, France, circa September 1918.

Left: An estimated 2,000 black Canadians managed to enlist in fighting battalions, including possibly these four unidentified men, who are in a German dugout captured during the Canadian advance east of Arras, France, in October 1918.

Facing page: Canadian soldiers haul ammunition during the Battle of the Canal du Nord, circa September 1918.

Bill Karn holds a German child while serving in the army of occupation in the Rhine region, circa 1919.

ONE ARTILLERYMAN'S MEMORY ALBUM PROVIDES A GLIMPSE INTO THE WAY MANY CANADIANS OF HIS GENERATION CHOSE TO REMEMBER THE WAR.

CHAPTER FOURTEEN

Bill Karn's War

JONATHAN F. VANCE

Sometime after he was demobilized in 1919, Bill Karn bought a photo album. It was a Strand E, made by Canadian Kodak, the largest he could find—fifty 9- by 14-inch pages. Karn expected to need them all, because he had a lot of memories to preserve—souvenirs of three years at war and anything else he might collect as he looked back on his time in the Canadian Corps.

It is difficult to know when he began to assemble the album, but he obviously took great care with it. The photographs, newspaper clippings, documents, and other keepsakes are neatly arranged, by and large in chronological order, and although few of the photos are captioned, they nevertheless tell a story. It is the story of one soldier's war—what he wanted to remember and how he wanted to remember it—but it also captures how Canada remembered the war in the decades after the armistice of 1918.

William H. Karn was a few weeks shy of his twentieth birthday when he enlisted in the 56th Battery, Canadian Field Artillery. Raised in Woodstock, Ontario, he was en-

Above: Bill Karn and a friend, possibly his sister Edith, share a laugh shortly after his enlistment in the 56th Battery, Canadian Field Artillery.

rolled at the Ontario Agricultural College in nearby Guelph when he joined other students and faculty in signing up to fight.

The first images in the album give the impression that the decision to enlist was not a particularly difficult one. Were it not for

Top left: A friend of Bill Karn tries on his hat and bandolier, likely in Guelph, Ontario.

Top right: Recruits pose on a cannon on the campus of the Ontario Agricultural College, Guelph, Ontario.

Bottom left: Bill, centre, kneeling, and pals pose for a photo in Guelph prior to departing for training at Camp Petawawa.

the uniforms, the snapshots could show any group of undergraduates from the period. They clown around on an old cannon on campus and pose on the steps of a residence hall. Young women cheekily pose in caps, tunics, and ammunition bandoliers. A line of gunners tramps along a concession road like so many boy scouts. A local factory that had been turned into a makeshift barrack looks, with its pennants and canvas cots, like a cabin at a summer camp.

A move to Petawawa, where Ontario artillery units assembled for training, brought Karn and his chums one step closer to war, but the album gives little sense of a greater intensity of purpose. There are snapshots of kit inspection and the eighteen-pounder field guns that would be their stock in trade, but

also of sharing watermelon with local girls and skinny-dipping in a nearby pond.

Even the move overseas had little effect on the tone of Karn's memory album. The battery left in railway cars gaily decorated with banners and chalked slogans, and sailed on a transport ship that offered them church services, calisthenics, and wrestling matches. On arrival in England in September 1916, the undergraduates-turned-soldiers became tourists. There are many photos that could come from any holidaymaker's album of the era: Stonehenge, canal boats, the English seaside, castles, churches, ancient cottages, and half-timbered townhouses. Clearly, the men were in training—there are pictures of gun drills, tent lines, and route marches—but Karn included nothing that betrayed the seri-

Above: Members of the 56th Battery bid their farewells as they depart by train for Camp Petawawa.

Top right: Bill Karn, second from right, and friends grab a bite to eat during training at Camp Petawawa.

Bottom right: Bill Karn, far right, and friends enjoy some watermelon during a picnic outing near Camp Petawawa.

ousness of the task that lay ahead. Even the soldiers who modelled their gas masks for the camera seemed to be doing so not to show off a lifesaver against an infernal weapon but to demonstrate a Halloween costume.

From Buckingham Palace and Westminster Abbey, the album shifts abruptly to France. It was September 1917 when Karn reached the front with his new unit, the 66th Battery, just in time to be involved in pinning down the enemy after the offensive around Hill 70 and Lens. The battery missed the last, desperate stages of the Passchendaele campaign but was in action throughout the most lethal period of the war for the Canadian Corps—the Hundred Days Offensive, the final campaign that took the corps from Amiens to Mons. It was during that offen-

sive that Karn suffered his closest brush with death. On October 9, the battery was in position near the village of Blécourt when it was attacked by a German airplane. A bomb splinter caught him right above his heart, only to embed itself in a thick packet of letters from home that he had been saving. The letters were reduced to ribbons, but Karn's life was saved.

Not surprisingly, the nature of the album changes when it covers the last fourteen months of the war. There were few restrictions on photography during training, so many soldiers could accumulate pictures of their experiences. But the use of cameras at the front was tightly controlled. Soldiers like Karn had to rely on commercial sources for photographs to use as memory aids. Some

were from French souvenir sets that he purchased during the war, and they show places he wouldn't have seen as a soldier, such as Château-Thierry, where the American Expeditionary Force fought one of its first significant battles, and the Piave river in Italy, the site of a brutal offensive in June 1918. Others are Canadian official photos printed by a Montreal studio.

For the first time, the album reveals the harsher side of the war: a ruined market square; a rubble-strewn crossroads with a sign that reads, incongruously, "This is Souchez"; a wartime newspaper article announcing the death in action of Major Victor Kent, the

Top: Members of the 56th Battery gather aboard the SS *Metagama* on September 16, 1916, to enjoy a wrestling match during the Atlantic crossing to England.

Middle: These soccer players took part in a men-versus-women match at Witley Camp, Surrey, England, circa 1916.

Bottom: A group of nursing sisters aboard the SS *Scotian*, the ship that carried Bill Karn home from the war in 1919.

officer who had signed Karn's attestation form when he first enlisted. But Karn was careful to balance the darkness with the light. There is a photo of the baseball team of the 66th Battery and an overhead view of the great Canadian Corps sports competition, held at Tincques, France, on Dominion Day 1918. Karn included official photos of Canadian soldiers with French or Belgian civilians—they show smiles all around.

After these cheery images, the album reaches the end of the war. There are snapshots of the battery crossing the Rhine into Germany and manning its field guns on the banks of the river and pictures of a couple of gunners posing beside a sign that reads, "Limits Coblenz Bridgehead area." Tucked in the spine of the album are two much later newspaper photographs showing the city of Köln in 1945, after it had been flattened by years of Allied bombing. Then, an image of field guns loaded onto railway carriages marks the beginning of the battery's long journey home.

Again, Karn gives us the same mixture of positive and negative memories. The cost of the war is evident in the rows of crosses at Vlamertinghe Military Cemetery in Belgium and, in another photo, with the grave of George Yeoman in Étaples Military Cemetery in France. This was surely taken on a pilgrimage, for Yeoman must have been a friend of Karn's; he too was from Woodstock, Ontario, and was called up in May 1918, only to die in October 1918. Views of pulverized trenches and an official photo of fly-covered corpses are interspersed with images of tennis matches, of a YMCA recreation hut, and of a group of soldiers mugging beside an enormous wrecked German tank named Herkules.

Soon, the scene shifts to the SS *Scotian* and Karn's journey home. There are snapshots taken on board the ship, an accommodation and meal ticket, a photo of a large dockside "Welcome Home" sign, and newspaper articles describing the arrival in Canada of the *Scotian* and the 66th Battery. To conclude the war section, Karn glued in his cloth divisional patch and three chevrons from the sleeve of his tunic, awarded for three years of service overseas. After the chevrons, there are a few pages of miscellaneous documents that Karn must have come across after starting his album, for they are in no particular order: his military will, a mimeographed dance card, and his discharge certificate, dated June 1919. And, with those fragments, those wisps of memory, Karn turned the page on his war.

As he chose to remember it in the first part of his album, the war was neither unremittingly gloomy nor a lark from beginning to end. He made no effort to hide the frightfulness that he surely saw, nor did he minimize the role that he, as an artilleryman, played in rearranging large parts of the landscape of France and Belgium. Looking only at such photos, one might regard Karn's war as nothing but a series of horrors: a barren and pockmarked landscape as far as the eye could see; rows of crosses stretching into the distance; towns that had been reduced to piles of shattered rubble; and artillerymen, knee-deep in mud, struggling to pull an eighteen-pounder through the ooze.

But Karn refused to let those horrors overwhelm his memory. His war was three years of light and shade, a balanced experience; there were good times as well as bad, and both occupied a place in his memory.

a moral struggle. It recalled the day when Canadian troops crossed the Rhine in 1918, reminding readers of German atrocities in France and Belgium and observing that, in contrast, Canadian soldiers in Germany acted like perfect gentlemen.

Though the war exacted a terrible toll, Canadians of Karn's generation accepted that the pain could be soothed by focusing on the lighter moments and by transforming the misery into a source of humour. To soldiers, this strategy was essential if they were to come through the war with their wits intact.

And what had worked so well for them during the war could serve the same purpose after the war. Rather than grumble about the dismal living conditions during training at Petawawa, Karn and his fellow ex-soldiers sang about them at their reunions: "Sand for breakfast, sand for dinner, / Sand for supper-time / All this God damn drilling / For a dollar and a dime." They brightened their reunion dinners by transforming the detritus of the battlefield into menu items: "Green Beans minus TNT and perfume," "18 pounder shrapnel" (olives), "Croute au Pot—ooze from Loos in mess-tins," "Celery direct from the pond, Sains-en-Gohelle." And, just as Karn and his fellow soldiers had cheerfully posed in their gas masks during training, a decade later they could still find fun in chemical warfare. At a 1926 reunion dinner, the

As the 66th Battery chronicle put it, the war experience should be recalled as a story that "we boys might read and relive with something of the passion of our youthful days: . . . the exasperating humbug of the army, the happy vicissitudes and varied experiences of the war, the barren and shell-battered wildernesses of the Front, the roar of the guns, the crump of shells, the zero hours, the gun flashes in the sky and the days and the months and the years through which we struggled as mere atoms in the great body of endless passing forms in khaki."

In the second part of his album, Karn turned to remembering the war as a whole. At this point, the personal memory intersects with the public. The keepsakes in this section are not private items, like the snapshots and badges that dominate the early pages, but public items: reunion programs, orders of service, souvenir publications. Through such keepsakes, Karn moved beyond his own personal experience to give us a picture of the First World War as Canadians wanted to remember it in the decades after it ended.

Historians have long debated the causes of the conflict. But in the minds of many Canadians of the time, it had been a just war, and the Allied nations had preserved Christianity and Western civilization from a new dark age. These messages were implicit in memorial services held in the 1920s and 1930s, including the ones Karn attended and marked in his album. The ruined villages, cemeteries, bloated bodies, and displaced civilians pictured in Karn's album were not simply the consequences of war but clear proof of Germany's guilt. Decades later, Karn added a 1942 newspaper article that confirmed this understanding of the war as entertainment included a humorous lecture on "Poisonous Gas and How to Sit on It."

At the same time, the language of war was co-opted for peaceful, pleasurable purposes. The 1926 reunion of Karn's unit was called "Return to (retro) Active Service of the 66th Battery," and the arrival of ex-soldiers for the weekend was referred to as the "Enlistment of All Ranks." One day's schedule became the "Plan of Attack," with each event numbered in good military fashion. The day began with "a little drink" and "another drink," and, by the time the veterans got to event number nine, a football game between McGill University and the University of Toronto, they had arrived at "now half-shot," soon to be followed by "DRUNK" and "paralysed!!" in the evening. With this, the forms of military routine—the "exasperating humbug of the army" that the battery history had recalled—were transformed into a schedule for merriment.

Such things offered one way to draw the sting from war; another was to find compensation in the sacrifice. For veterans like Karn, the most important legacy of service was comradeship, the bond between men who served together in times of extreme trial. The preponderance of reunion items in the album suggests that Karn attached great importance to getting together with his comrades; so too

does his tendency to have his reunion programs signed by his battery mates and his saving of newspaper articles about the postwar careers of his fellow gunners and their obituaries as the ranks of his comrades thinned, a

MENU

RHUM ISSUE

FRUIT COCKTAIL ANISETTE

CREAM OF TOMATOES, PORTUGAISE

SIRLOIN STEAK, MAITRE D'HOTEL
RISSOLEES POTATOES
GREEN BEANS AU BEURRE

APPLE PIE A LA MODE

COFFEE

TOASTS

TO THE KING

TO OUR FALLEN COMRADES

TO THOSE NOT ABLE TO BE WITH US

TO THE BATTERY

TO OUR OFFICERS

TO OUT-OF-TOWN MEMBERS
WITH US TONIGHT

66
CFA

Above: Bill Karn kept this signed reunion program as a souvenir.

fact that was wryly acknowledged by reunion name badges with phrases like, "If I fade away, ship body to _____." The 66th Battery brought together men from every province in Canada—that so many of them travelled to reunions in Montreal and Toronto (and signed Karn's programs) confirms the value all of them placed on the gift of comradeship.

Just as important as comradeship to Canada's memory of the war was the belief that a Canadian nationality had emerged from the

tragedy—all who served and died had been nation-builders, and Canada itself was born of their sacrifice. Ultimately, this was a Canadian victory, and as such the story itself had to be defended. Karn was interested in the nationalist narrative; he tucked into his album two small souvenir pamphlets that became primers of the nation-building view of the war: *The Truth about the War* and *Canada in the Great War*, both by George Drew, an artillery officer from Guelph. Drew originally put pen to paper after reading American accounts that downplayed the Empire's role in winning the war; as he put it in the introduction to *The Truth about the War*, "To the slanderous statement, often reiterated in United States publications of a certain type, that the British Empire did not bear to the full the share of the brunt of battle, this plain statement of facts furnishes an irrefutable answer."

Drew's polemic, originally published as an article in *Maclean's* and later issued as a booklet because of the huge number of requests for copies, offered a statistical refutation of the charges, arguing that the U.S. contribution was slow in coming and far from decisive when it did come. Drew presented statistics covering every aspect of the war, and Canadians clearly appreciated his analysis, if we can deduce from the pamphlet's huge sales. Indeed, it was popular

enough that, later in 1928, Drew wrote *Canada in the Great War*, "a stirring chronicle of the achievements of 450,000 Canadians who left their native land to play a heroic part in the greatest conflict in world history." While the publication's diction might have been overblown, Karn seems to have agreed with its sentiment—that, for all its horrors, the war was a positive experience, for it allowed Canadians to step onto the world stage and prove their gallantry when it mattered most.

Karn's album ends with a menu from a 1954 battery reunion in Toronto and a large photograph, presumably taken at the dinner, showing a table of older men laughing heartily at some joke. It takes little imagination to see them as the young men who, nearly four decades earlier, had clowned around on an old cannon or posed for the camera in their gas masks. Now into their sixties, perhaps they were singing an old battery song or enjoying one of the yarns that kept them in stitches while they were in the lines. Forty years after the war, Karn had no desire to cast his war memories in unnecessarily gloomy hues.

The Toronto reunion seems to have been Karn's last, for in 1957 he died. If he left no conventional record of his experiences in the Canadian Expeditionary Force, he did leave something that is rarer: an album of memories, a glimpse at how one artilleryman chose to remember his war.

- - - - - - - - - - - - - - - -

AFTER BILL KARN'S DEATH, HIS FAMILY gave his album to a comrade from the 66th Battery with whom he had attended many reunions. In 2008, it was donated to the Ley and Lois Smith War, Memory and Popular Culture Research Collection in the History Department at Western University in London, Ontario.

Above, left: A member of the 66th Battery stands to give a speech during a reunion dinner at the King Edward Hotel, Toronto, November 13, 1954.

Above, right: The cover of the program for the 66th Battery reunion, 1954.

Canadian soldiers attend to a friend's grave somewhere at the front, circa 1916–1917.

WITH THEIR LOVED ONES BURIED OVERSEAS, FAMILIES MOURNED THE FALLEN WITH HEART-RENDING EPITAPHS INSCRIBED ON GRAVESTONES MOST WOULD NEVER SEE.

CHAPTER FIFTEEN

Carved in Stone

ERIC McGEER

Canada in the years after the Great War was a country in mourning, her people proud of the achievements of the Canadian Corps but shaken at the cost in young lives. For the bereaved, already confronted by death on its harshest terms—violent, faraway, indiscriminate—the pain of a parting without farewell was compounded by the ruling of the Imperial War Graves Commission that the fallen would be buried in the lands where they had fought.

The commission compensated for this policy by allowing next of kin to have a short valediction engraved on the headstones of their loved ones. Many Canadian families took the opportunity to express their sorrow, pledge their love and remembrance, and forge a consoling link with a distant grave they would in all likelihood never see. The epitaphs on the headstones of the fallen, speaking for the parents, wives, and children who bore the burden of the war for the rest of their lives, preserve a record unique in Canadian history and central to the national memory of the Great War. Each one reveals

a depth of suffering far beyond the grim arithmetic of the casualty totals.

Could I but just have clasped his hand and whispered, my son, farewell.

At the battle of the Somme in his eighteenth year.

Somewhere in France, sleep on, dear son, our baby boy, just twenty-one.

Also his brothers David and John, killed in action June and July 1916.

Hard was the blow that compelled me to part with my loving husband, so dear to my heart.

The shell that stilled his true brave heart broke mine. Mother.

The words of the bereaved show that each death ended a part of many other lives. "The only child of aged parents"—six stark words on the headstone of a New Brunswick boy, Private Vernon Keith Merchant,

Above: Soldiers often placed rocks on the graves of fallen friends, as seen here and on the facing page.

killed in Flanders at age sixteen—capture the despair of an irreparable loss. "Death is not a barrier to love, Daddy," from Private Peter Lapointe's daughter in Trenton, Ontario, speaks for the children who yearned for fathers they could remember dimly, if at all. But those who found it hardest to accept the finality of their loss were the mothers, whose endearments, prayers, and hopes of a reunion in a life to come affirm a bond of maternal love stronger than any other. Private William Jackson, killed in 1916, was, in his mother's words, "loved beyond all human thought." The mother of a French-Canadian soldier buried in France appealed to "mothers in that far-off land" to have pity on her and offer their prayers at a grave that she herself could never hope to visit.

He fought the good fight and won the peace which passeth all understanding.

Our only boy is sleeping in Flanders fields where poppies blow.

In Flanders nobly he died by the path of duty that we might all live in freedom.

Our soldier boy endured the Cross and won the crown.

Sleep, dear son. Honour, justice, duty, all survive by your mortal fall.

In loving memory of our son who made the supreme sacrifice at Vimy Ridge.

He gave his life to end all wars between nations.

Last words to his comrade, "Go on, I'll manage."

The epitaphs also reveal the sources of consolation from which Canadians drew. The assurances of Scripture, uplifting lines from literature or hymns, and a canon of remembrance verse that included John McCrae's "In Flanders Fields" comforted the mourners and honoured the memory of the fallen. Words

like "sacrifice" and "duty" assumed new significance in the minds of a generation much more religious than our own. Many epitaphs liken the ordeal of the soldiers to the suffering and death of Christ, whose sacrifice, emulated by the Glorious Dead, had redeemed humanity. The young lives lost were not wasted if the war was cast as a crusade to create a better world and the "glorious dead" as an elect who exemplified the devotion and heroism of Canada's soldiers.

The parents of Sergeant Harold Flynn found solace in his courage: "Died for King and country while keeping the line open under shellfire." In his parents' eyes, Private George Dale had combined bravery with self-sacrifice: "Died in effort to rescue a wounded comrade." The valour and fortitude Canadian soldiers had shown in battle at Vimy, Passchendaele, and the war-winning advance of the Hundred Days set an example for the mourners to follow—to endure their sorrow in a manner worthy of the fallen. Their sacrifice imposed a duty on the survivors to uphold the ideals of freedom, justice, and a lasting peace. The world could do no other, declared the parents of twenty-year-old Private George Hargrave: "Justice owes them this, that what they died for be not overthrown."

Forth from the shadows came death with the pitiless syllable "Now."

'Tis only us who have loved and lost who realize war's bitter cost. Mother.

If death be the price of victory, O God forbid all wars.

Their words of parting have long since outlived the bereaved. Yet in their restraint and sincerity, they enlist the sympathy and the respect of later generations. The people who went through the First World War were the first to realize what kind of war fully industrialized and mobilized countries could fight, and they saw in this harrowing experience a warning to the future. The most poignant of all the inscriptions, from our vantage point a century on, are those pleading for an end to war. "Make firm, O God, the peace our dead have won," entreated the parents of nineteen-year-old Private James Sullivan, voicing a sentiment frequently encountered in Great War cemeteries.

Their plea serves as a reminder that the statesmen criticized for pursuing the policy of appeasement in the 1930s felt themselves responsible to those who, like the family of Private Robert Chalmers ("Six brothers in all answered the call. One crippled, three killed"), had lost so much and shuddered at the prospect of another war. These fears proved all too well founded. On the grave of Private Samuel Melling, killed in May 1918, is a promise of lasting love and remembrance from his wife and three little boys back home in Toronto. The youngest of them was to be killed in Holland in October of 1944. Like his father before him, Private Gordon Melling lies far from home, beneath a headstone inscribed with a similar promise from his own wife and infant daughter.

Above: The gravestone of G. F. S. Hayden bears an inscription alluding to his hometown: "A Toronto boy, Our only son, He loved peace, For Canada he served."

Top left: "In Flanders nobly he died by the path of duty that we might all live in freedom."

Middle left: "A lonely grave, somewhere in France, a lonely mother somewhere else." Thus read the June 5, 1917, obituary of twenty-year-old Thomas Arthur Metheral, an aerial gunner killed in action in Belgium. Metheral enlisted in September 1916 and was shot down just six days after reaching the front. His parents died believing their son never received a proper burial. Actually, Thomas's body had been buried among German war dead in a Belgian cemetery. In 2000, the federal government informed the family that his body had been located. "The sister and family members were surprised and delighted to know that his body had been found," said Ron Metheral, Thomas's cousin. "What a shame that his mother never knew." (Submitted by Ron Metheral, Thomas's cousin.)

Bottom left: Mary Waller visits her brother Harry Waller's gravestone in this photo likely taken in the 1960s. Mary also lost another brother, Arthur, during the Great War. (Submitted by Susan Hemmings. Mary was her great-aunt.)

454695 PRIVATE
ARNOLD LEONARD DAVIDSON
2ND BN. CANADIAN INF.
11TH SEPTEMBER 1916

THEY LOVED NOT THEIR LIVES
UNTO THE DEATH
REV. 12.11.

Right: Arnold Davidson of Beachburg, Ontario, was eighteen when he enlisted in July 1915. Critically wounded just a week after arriving at the front, Davidson died on September 11, 1916. His obituary in the *Renfrew Mercury* said: "Just entering manhood, a splendid specimen of physical strength . . . he has gone down with the many others in defence of his country and of the right principles for which she stands in this tremendous struggle." Arnold Davidson is buried in Boulogne Eastern Cemetery, France. On his gravestone, the inscription reads: "They loved not their lives unto the death, Rev. 12:11." (Submitted by Lisa Emberson, Arnold's great-niece.)

Left: George Stevens attempted to enlist in November 1915 at age sixteen, after learning his father had been killed in action at the front. A recruiter at first turned Stevens away, but the youth persisted, saying, "I'm all that's left of my small family." The recruiter relented and changed Stevens's age on his attestation papers to eighteen, enabling him to join the 87th Battalion. Stevens was killed in action on September 2, 1918. His family requested a photograph of the grave marker to help ease the pain of his death. (Submitted by Vivian Sewell Wylie. George was her father's cousin.)

THE PAINTINGS OF THE FIRST WORLD WAR HELP
CANADIANS UNDERSTAND THE COURAGE AND
SUFFERING OF THEIR FOREBEARS IN WAYS THAT
PHOTOGRAPHS ALONE DO NOT

Canadian Observation Post, by Colin Gill

CHAPTER SIXTEEN

The Art of War

LAURA BRANDON

There is a painting in the Canadian War Museum called *Canadian Observation Post* or *The Widow's House*. Painted in 1919 by British artist Colin Gill (1892–1940), it shows a distressed young man sitting on a wooden kitchen chair, his back turned to us. His hands are over his ears, his helmet is missing, and he is completely oblivious—both to the soldiers around him who are carrying rails and sandbags back and forth across the ruined remains of the widow's house, and the dead men half-buried in it.

The painting illustrates shell shock—a medical condition that was not acknowledged by wartime Canadian military authorities. "Shell shock is a manifestation of childishness and femininity. Against such there is no remedy," wrote Sir Andrew Macphail as late as 1925 in *The Medical Services*, volume 1 of the *Official History of the Canadian Forces in the Great War, 1914–1919*.

The young man reminds me of my great-uncle Robert Turnbull, who was badly shell-shocked during the war. I have a small photograph of him in uniform, which prob-

Above: Robert Turnbull, Laura Brandon's great-uncle, in England, training for service at the front. Turnbull was badly shell-shocked as a result of serving in the Great War.

ably originally belonged to my great-grandmother. It's an informal shot that shows him in cap, puttees, and greatcoat, standing in a field in front of a leafless hedge and some kind of small, tarpaulin-covered shed. A tracery of bare trees, far behind him in the distance, bisects the image. It is winter, and

he is in England, training. He is smiling, and a breeze jauntily lifts the front of his coat. That's likely how his mother would have wanted to remember her eldest son—as a strong, happy bull of a man. She would not have wanted to remember him as the damaged but deeply loved child whose postwar social life consisted of taking his young niece—my mother—to the local ice cream parlour. With attitudes such as Macphail's, his family was all he had for support.

It is paintings like *The Widow's House* that bring the much-lauded and nationally respected official war art collection into our personal worlds. The Canadian War Museum's First World War art collection does more than illustrate a conflict replete with successes that engendered enormous national pride, such as the 1917 Battle of Vimy Ridge. It is also a source of personal memories. Through its art, we can reconstruct in our imaginations the sacrifice and service of our courageous forebears who volunteered to serve overseas, and whom most of us never knew. For this gift, we must thank the first Lord Beaverbrook, William Maxwell Aitken.

Born in Ontario in 1879 and raised in New Brunswick, this slight, energetic, and charismatic man made an early fortune in Canada, although his aggressive business methods earned him accolades and suspicion in nearly equal measure. After relocating to Britain, the millionaire moved easily into its highest aristocratic and political circles. In 1911, he became financially involved with the *Daily Express* newspaper, and he bought it outright five years later, using the respected paper to expand his influence. Always a Canadian at heart, Beaverbrook's genuine nationalist fervour contributed to his decision in 1916 to initiate and take personal responsibility for a project to record the war from Canada's point of view.

Beaverbrook's media interests made him ideally suited to the task of leaving a record of the war through film, photograph, and text. But a single event turned him in another direction—documenting the war in art. The catalyst was the horrific German gas attack on the Canadians at the Second Battle of Ypres in April and May of 1915. For a variety of reasons, the event was not photographed, so in November 1916 Beaverbrook commissioned a massive 3.7- by 6-metre painting from the British artist and illustrator Richard Jack (1866–1952) through his new organization, the Canadian War Memorials Fund. Jack's realistic painting resonated with the public and the success of this venture contributed to Beaverbrook's decision to commission more artists to record Canada's war experiences. In the end, some 116 artists found employment. Beaverbrook hired some of the same artists

Second Battle of Ypres, 22 April to 25 May 1915, by Richard Jack.

to produce propaganda images for his various publications, including *Canada in Khaki*, which also made use of photography. He viewed the war memorials, however, as art of a higher order and part of a grand historic military tradition.

Beaverbrook initially thought that the oversize works, mostly commissioned from British artists, might contribute to the decoration of the new Houses of Parliament in Ottawa, the original buildings having been largely destroyed by fire in 1916. But he was also responsive to the idea that artists should spend time on the battlefield, making sketches of documentary value. Under pressure from National Gallery of Canada officials, Canadian artists were increasingly employed to fulfill this part of the mandate. When applying for charitable status for his new endeavour, Beaverbrook wrote with genuine feeling that his overarching goal was to provide "suitable Memorials in the form of Tablets, Oil Paintings, etc. to the Canadian Heroes and Heroines of the War." A hundred years later, Canadians may view many of these works as condemnations of war, but this is a response that has evolved over time. Contemporary reviews by and

Top right: Max Aitken, Lord Beaverbrook, left, circa 1916–1918.

Bottom right: John and Lucy Greey, the author's great-grandparents, and their children in Toronto, prior to the Great War, circa 1911–1914. Standing, from left, are Douglas, Allan, and John, Jr. Seated, middle row, are Paul, Lucy, Stephen, and John, Sr. Philip sits on the floor in the front row. Three of Lucy and John's sons would serve in the Great War. A fourth would be white-feathered for failing to enlist.

large aligned themselves with Beaverbrook's sentiments.

Many Canadians can point to family members with First World War experiences. My own is no exception. Five of my seven great-uncles served in the Canadian Expeditionary Force. I have worked with the war art collection for more than twenty years, and it has been good to discover how well my great-uncles' contributions are represented. My grandfather John Greey—who did not serve in the war—is also represented, but in a different way, so I shall begin with him. He probably would not have been a hero in Beaverbrook's eyes or in the eyes of his contemporaries.

A pre-war militia officer in the 48th Highlanders, he was also, at the outbreak of the war, the manager of the family's manufacturing company. He was the eldest son and the only one then with children. According to my mother, he was forbidden by his father from enlisting. The bitter and humiliating consequence for him was a practice known as "white-feathering." This dubious practice was designed to shame men into enlisting by having women present them with a white feather if they were not in uniform. I cannot imagine what it was like for my grandfather to see his closest friends and relatives enlist, serve, and die while he worked in a downtown Toronto office. Surrounded by raucous military parades and colourful admonitory recruitment and fundraising posters, he could not

Above: Propaganda posters such as this were designed to shame men into volunteering for service.

participate. He became a heavy smoker and drinker. Eight years after the war ended, on the tenth anniversary of the first day of the Battle of Vimy Ridge—April 9, 1927—John Greey died of throat cancer. He was forty-four.

Although it lacks images of white-feathering, the war art collection contains a number of First World War recruitment posters exhorting Canadians to rally to the British flag to save the Empire. Some posters are

Canadian, but many are British. At the time, Canada was part of the British Empire, so British propaganda was common. The collection includes several designs that decry those who did not enlist. Did my grandfather see the one entitled *Daddy, what did YOU do in the Great War?*, where a little girl with a big bow in her hair looks questioningly at her father? He miserably stares away from her toward us. The man looks a bit like my grandfather, and the little girl could easily stand in for my mother.

My grandfather experienced the war not only through such humiliation but also through the service of his three brothers and his two brothers-in-law. I shall begin with his brothers-in-law. Thanks to the First World War archival records held by Library and Archives Canada, it is easy to find out that a not yet shell-shocked Robert Turnbull enlisted in the Central Ontario Regiment (19th Battalion, Canadian Expeditionary Force) on February 23, 1915, at age twenty-five. Severe shell shock suffered at the disastrous Battle of St. Eloi in April 1916 so terribly affected him that he was discharged from the Canadian army shortly afterwards. On February 21, 1917, aged twenty-seven, he left Liverpool for Canada on the SS *Orduna*. Family recollections tell me that he killed himself on September 7, 1933. He was forty-three. By then, both his parents were dead. Unemployable because of shell shock and lacking the emotional and practical support his parents provided, my great-uncle did not long survive them.

The terrible sights Turnbull saw at St. Eloi are not part of the war art collection. Artists lacked the stomach for depictions of dismembered, bleeding bodies. In Canada's entire war art collection of 13,000 works, fewer than seventy show the dead. Only a few more evoke the smell of rotting flesh borne by the wind, the terrible sounds of excruciating pain, and the frightening feel of mud-soaked broken wood, compacted sand, bloated body parts, and bloodied, torn fabric. This is because, during the war, many artists developed a symbolic visual language to record such scenes, which is not always as meaningful to today's audiences. Viewers brought up in a less secular era readily understood depictions of destroyed trees and ruins as emblematic of death and bodily harm.

Consequently, the ruined abbey of Mont St. Eloi clearly epitomized for many who had fought there the horror they had been through and the staunchness of their desire to survive—battered, bruised, but not entirely broken. The fragmented religious structure, visible from all directions of the battlefield, features prominently in art related to the battle.

Robert's younger brother Alan enlisted in the Canadian Expeditionary Force on April 20, 1915, aged twenty-three. A lieutenant in the 48th Highlanders (15th Battalion), he ended up a major by war's end. Alan was wounded in November 1916 during the Battle of the Ancre Heights, part of the Somme offensive in France, and was subsequently awarded the Military Cross for

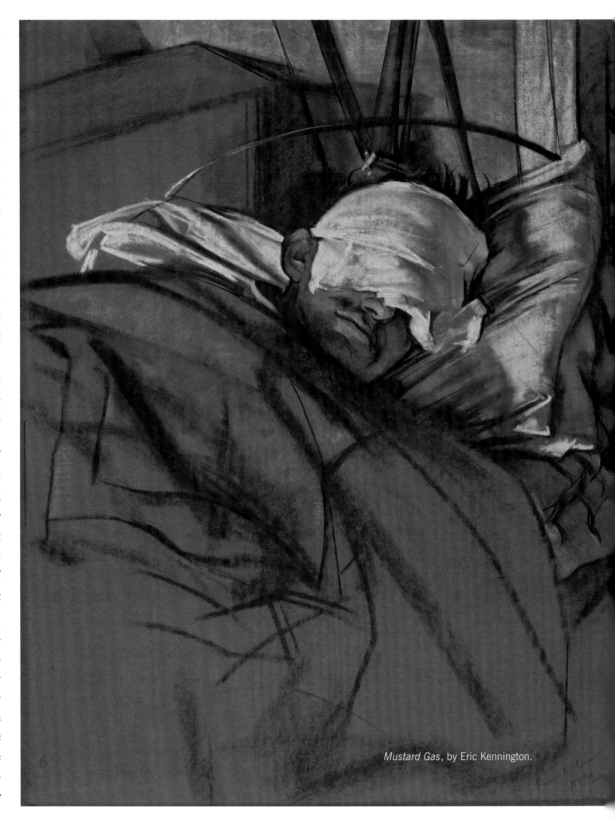

Mustard Gas, by Eric Kennington.

"an act of exemplary gallantry." He was wounded again in August 1918 during the Battle of Amiens. He was gassed on several occasions, notably at Ypres, which my mother always believed led to his early death on June 22, 1933, less than three months after his brother's. He was forty-one.

The war art collection includes a searing image of a mustard gas victim, by the British artist Eric Kennington. *Mustard Gas* is a study in brown and white, with jagged black chalk lines outlining a bandaged soldier's head lying on a pillow, the sheets drawn up to his chin. You cannot see the damage to the patient's eyes, but you know from the sight of his ears, nose, and mouth that his other senses, seemingly untouched, bore witness to what his eyes eventually could no longer see. British writer and nurse Vera Brittain wrote in her autobiography, *Testament of Youth*, published the year the Turnbull boys died (1933), of the "poor things burnt and blistered all over with great mustard-coloured suppurating blisters, with blind eyes . . . all sticky and stuck together, and always fighting for breath, with voices a mere whisper, saying that their throats are closing and they know they will choke." Mustard gas killed, and usually it was a four- to five-week lingering death. It took Alan Turnbull fifteen years to die.

Three of John Greey's brothers also enlisted, and survived, but I believe they were all scarred by the war. Allan Greey, aged twenty-seven, enlisted in the Mississauga Horse, his pre-war militia regiment, on February 24, 1916. He ended up in the 20th Battalion and saw a lot of action. He was at Passchendaele, Belgium, in October

to November 1917 for that long, drawn-out, mud-drenched, inconclusive battle, where people died as much from drowning as they did from shellfire. It was Field Marshal Sir Douglas Haig who said in the immediate aftermath of the battle, "Good God, did we really send men to fight in that?"

One painting in the art collection, *Mud Road to Passchendaele* (1917), by Douglas Culham, captures the battle's challenging reality as Allan might have experienced it. Culham served in the 3rd Canadian Division Ammunition Column, which brought shells nightly to eighteen-pounder batteries in the field. In this painting, a dark and foreboding sky forms the backdrop to a smoke- and fire-laden landscape over which tired men and

horses trudge. Half-swimming through the mud, weighed down with equipment, Allan must have wondered if he would survive. But he did. On December 2, 1918, he was awarded the Military Cross "for conspicuous gallantry and initiative during an attack."

A second brother, Paul, enlisted in the 69th Battery, Canadian Field Artillery, on November 1, 1917. As I look at the date, it is hard not to imagine that knowledge of Allan's recent experiences at Passchendaele had some effect on his decision. Besides his mother—and, perhaps significantly, not his father—only Allan is listed as his next of kin in his enlistment papers. Perhaps the untold story lies in the fact that he was now twenty-one, of age, and able to face a strong-

Mud Road to Passchendaele, by Douglas W. Culham.

Ancre Valley, by Adrian Hill.

willed father who had already determined that his eldest son should not fight, and who might indeed have prevented Paul from enlisting earlier.

A third brother, Douglas, aged twenty-two, had graduated in 1914 from the Royal Military College alongside the future air ace Billy Bishop. He enlisted in the 4th Brigade, Canadian Field Artillery, on March 18, 1915. A little over a year later, he was badly wounded by fragments from a high explosive shell that blew up near him during the 1916 Battle of the Ancre Heights, the same battle in which Alan Turnbull was wounded.

The strategically insignificant victory at Ancre Heights is represented in the war art collection by a quite wonderful small wash drawing made a few months after the battle. *Ancre Valley* shows the devastated landscape of the Ancre valley in northern France, a scene of churned-up earth, splintered trees, and smoke. Completed on the spot by the British official war artist Adrian Hill (1897–1977), it is devoid of human figures or any symbolic content. It is a simple, clear-eyed, unsentimental, and unsanitized view of the appalling physical devastation caused by war. Looking at it today through my art-historian eyes, I wonder how Alan and Douglas would have related to it.

Sometimes I think my great-grandmother Lucy Greey was another family victim of the Great War. She died in 1919 at the age of sixty. Having three enlisted sons must have stressed her deeply, but I also wonder whether, weakened by worry, she fell victim to the Spanish flu that swept across Canada that year. I have a pre-war photograph showing her at the centre of a family group with her husband and six sons. They all look like fine boys. Douglas is wearing his Royal Military College cadet uniform, and her youngest son, Philip, aged about eight then, is wearing a sailor suit. She looks old already and is a bit crippled; she suffered from arthritis. But with all the war talk she must have heard in the months and years preceding the outbreak of the war, and with sons active in Canada's militia, did she in some way already know what was coming, and did it age her?

I like to remember her in the context of one massive painting that hangs in the Canadian War Museum: *Sacrifice* by Charles Sims (1873–1928). This vast painting is split in half by a crucifix on which, seen from behind, hangs the dead body of Christ overlooking the corpses, the dying, and the wounded half-buried in the mud and swamp that constituted the Western Front. Below the cross, mourners in the form of mothers, children, and the elderly both grieve and continue their work. When I look at the elderly woman on the lower right who is numbly staring out of the picture, I think of my great-grandmother, who, in the family photograph, looks somewhat like her. In the painting, the woman sits beside her husband, who holds a telegram telling them that their son is dead. For me, this sad woman is an important figure in Lord Beaverbrook's panoply of heroes and heroines. She is also a tribute to the success of his innovative First World War art endeavour—an endeavour that, for Canadian families, remains a personal site of memory as well as a national legacy.

The link between Canada's war art and its people is brought home to me most strongly when, at different times of the day, I pass through the Canadian War Museum's lobby. Here, I pass a wall of male and female portraits. Surrounded by the museum's dramatic angular concrete walls, its undulating green slate floor, and a multiplicity of angled reflecting glass surfaces, I almost invariably

see visitors standing in rapt concentration in front of an artwork. They're lost to time and the here and now. The war art has given them entry into the past, perhaps their own. I walk quietly by. I do not want to disturb them. This matters.

Above: *Sacrifice*, by Charles Sims.

Children in June 1918 lay flowers on the graves of Canadian soldiers buried at Shorncliffe, Kent, England. Shorncliffe was the site of a major Canadian training camp.

WILL FUTURE GENERATIONS RECALL—AND LEARN FROM—THE WAR THAT WAS SUPPOSED TO END ALL WAR?

CHAPTER SEVENTEEN

We Remember

PETER MANSBRIDGE

The First World War was so horrible, so appallingly savage, so vast and terrible, that it amounted to more than four years of ghastly indifference to human dignity. The numbers challenge our imaginations to comprehend: Worldwide, an estimated 8.5 million soldiers died. Two hundred and twenty-eight soldiers were killed every hour. Four every minute. One every fifteen seconds. That is slaughter on a scale that seems impossible. And that does not include the civilians who died.

None of us alive today was a personal witness to the battlefield conditions of the Great War. Most of our population was born at least fifty years after the war ended. That may not be a long time in history, but it's a long time for any individual. I was born less than fifty years after the Boer War, in which 7,000 Canadians served and 244 were killed. That conflict seems like ancient history to me, no more memorable or concrete than Marathon or Waterloo.

So how can we properly remember what we don't know in the first place? And why should we remember? The history books tell us we should be proud of Canada's contribution to the war effort. We punched above our weight. We fought like tigers. Our men came together for the first time as a true Canadian

Above: Canadian graves near Vimy Ridge, France, are easily discernible by the distinctive maple leaf.

FREDDIE HUNT ON SKYE BLUE - CALGARY STAMPEDE   OLIVER © 314

Clockwise from top left:

George Brockie Bannerman and his wife, Margaret Jean Milne, in 1962. Bannerman trained as a medic and served as a stretcher-bearer in France. In August 1917, he earned the Military Medal for gallantry during the Battle of Hill 70 in France. (Submitted by Gordon Bannerman, George's son.)

Veteran Stanley Thomas Sellick attends a Remembrance Day ceremony in 1975. Sellick enlisted in Winnipeg in November 1915 and fought with the 8th Battalion. Sellick's brother David and brother-in-law Sydney Stibbard were both killed in action. (Submitted by Scott, Todd, and Miriam Sellick, Stanley's grandchildren, and Burton Sellick, Stanley's son.)

Great War veteran Fred Hunt rides Skye Blue at the Calgary Stampede sometime in the 1930s. A rodeo cowboy, Hunt served with a British cavalry regiment on the Egypt-Gaza front. He emigrated to Manitoba following the war. (Submitted by Neil Hill, Fred's great-nephew.)

contingent, freed from British commanders. In 1917, we won a bloody victory at Vimy Ridge, a place where the Germans had thrown back British and French attacks time and time again. It is said that Canada came of age during the war. No one dared to deny us a place at the 1919 peace treaty negotiations in Versailles, France.

We should know all that. But there will come a time—inevitably—when our grandchildren and our great-grandchildren will be so far removed from the war that it is probably expecting too much to hope that they will recall much more. History tends to tell big stories: who won, who lost. It concentrates on government leaders and commanding generals. It looks for heroes and analyzes blunders.

But if we are careful now to capture a vivid picture of what happened during the First World War, how it was unlike anything that had come before, then maybe future generations will appreciate more than the bare-bones facts. Maybe they will under-

stand, even remember, the everyday citizens of a young country who answered when they were called and whose lives were snuffed out in a relentless series of frontal assaults that usually changed nothing.

We've had a fairly recent experience with war. Think of how the country reacted to each death the Canadian Forces absorbed in Afghanistan: solemn repatriation ceremonies; citizens gathered at highway overpasses as the bodies were transported to the coroner's office; nationally televised funerals.

Canadians suffered 158 fatalities over ten years. We probably lost that many at Vimy Ridge in ten minutes. But we feel deeply about the 158 in Afghanistan because we were each part of the story. These casualties aren't history, they're news. No one has to remind us to remember these poor souls.

It shouldn't be very difficult, then, to imagine the grief that shrouded Canada from 1914 to 1918. Death wasn't a distant phenomenon you read about in the newspapers.

Top left: Four generations of Kilburns gather at veteran Percy Kilburn's house in Oshawa, Ontario, circa 1962. Percy is on the far right. Next to him is his son, Cyril Kilburn; grandson John Franklin Kilburn; and great-grandson, Robert Jay Kilburn. Percy enlisted in 1914, but was honourably discharged after injuring his foot. (Submitted by Robert J. Kilburn, Percy's great-grandson.)

Top right: Veteran Alexander Grant MacLachlan of Kingston, Ontario, visits the grave of a fallen comrade sometime after the end of the war. (Submitted by Tim Soper, Alexander's grandson.)

It wasn't in another province or another city. It was down the road, around the corner, across the street, and even at your very door. That's the sobering reality that should infuse every telling of those years.

The Great War tortured Canada. We were a country of about 8 million people—and more than 66,000 young lives were stolen from us. That's the pity. Some 66,000 people who might have contributed mightily to our nation. We'll never know.

When the war broke out, the Canadian government called for 20,000 volunteers. In less than a month, 40,000 had signed up. Eventually, 600,000 men and women enlisted.

What made them do it? For some, it was undoubtedly the money. Here was a chance to secure a steady income. For others, it was a matter of succumbing to pressure, not wanting to feel embarrassed at being able-bodied and not part of the war effort. One poster of the day asked, "Do you feel happy as you walk along the streets and see other men wearing the King's uniform?"

But, for a great many, volunteering to serve was simply a patriotic reflex. That seems hopelessly naive, but it was a different age. When your country went to war, you signed up. No questions asked.

I was once preparing for a CBC Remembrance Day broadcast by talking to a veteran of the Second World War.

I said to him, "Do you think young people today, seventeen, eighteen, nineteen years old, would volunteer for duty in wartime as quickly as you did?"

"No," he said. "They're too smart today."

But it's not that Canadians weren't bright enough a hundred years ago to dodge the war. It's that it just didn't occur to most of them. They really didn't know what they were in for. War was portrayed as a gallant undertaking, a noble cause, even an exciting adventure from which you were sure to return with stories of derring-do that would serve you well into old age. The filth, the muck, the rats, the fearsome noise, the barbarity they would eventually encounter never entered the equation. Who would have

thought that four out of ten who enlisted would be casualties?

It's a measure of the brutal nature of the war that almost 20,000 Canadians who were killed have no known burial site. That is a polite way of saying they were torn into so many pieces that it was impossible to figure out who they were.

If you visit the cemeteries of France and Belgium where Canadians are buried, you're confronted by rows of gleaming white headstones. They are arranged beautifully. Visitors are appropriately quiet. They whisper as they walk. The peacefulness is in complete contrast to the way these men lived and died during the war. The cemeteries have the power to overwhelm our emotions. They bring us closer to those who were killed. But it's only when you start reading the individual inscriptions on the tombstones that you understand the intimacy of the loss. Suddenly, the dead aren't just soldiers. They're sons, brothers, fathers, husbands. And they're so young. Some are teenagers. It's rare to find someone as old as thirty-five or forty.

There's a maple leaf on every Canadian headstone. So, no matter what else they were, these dead were part of us. The men who wore the Canadian uniform from 1914 to 1918 deserve to be remembered because, for whatever reason, they did what their country asked of them.

They became ensnared in a war that turned its back on any concept of civility or decency, or even common sense. It was years of fighting and suffering and dying for nondescript patches of land.

In the first major conflict after Confederation, they sacrificed their lives. They for-

feited love, children, walking in the park, seeing a hockey game, reading books, suppers around the kitchen table, playing charades in the parlour.

We can't possibly make sense of, or even properly remember, the more than 66,000 war dead. Our brains don't like big numbers. Our hearts can't bear the burden. But we can certainly try to understand those terrible years and that piercing pain. We can begin, I think, by remembering that those who were killed called themselves "Canadians." In that respect, they were family.

Above: The Great War veterans may be gone, but their families keep their memories alive in myriad ways. Evelyn Dreiling honoured the memory of her father-in-law, Curtis Frederick Robarts, by drawing his portrait. (Submitted by Evelyn Dreiling, Curtis's daughter-in-law.)

Left: Alfred Prescott of Port Perry, Ontario, front row centre, poses with his cousin Charles, front row right, and friends during training circa 1916. Prescott got the surprise of his life in March 1919 when he returned home from the war. "He found out his girlfriend was married," said Alfred's son, Herb, "but eventually he met and married my mother." (Submitted by Herb Prescott, Alfred's son.)

Bottom left: Alfred James Cook circa 1915–1918 with his wife, Jennie Stokes, seated, daughter Myrtle, and son Edward. Myrtle today is celebrated for being a member of the "Matchless Six"—a group of athletes who, in 1928, became the first Canadian women to compete in the Olympic Games. (Submitted by Don McGowan, Cook's grandson.)

Bottom right: George and Catherine Scherer (née Crawford), date unknown. George Scherer enlisted in January 1916 in Toronto. He received the Military Medal at Hill 70 for staying in the fight despite suffering a serious wound and being ordered to the dressing station. He added a bar to the medal in August 1918 at Amiens. After the war, he married Catherine and the couple had two daughters. (Submitted by Norman MacInnes. George and Catherine were his grandparents.)

Top right: Family legend holds that Robert Frederic Hawke, far left, back row, was so eager to fight overseas that he forged his transfer papers to get reassigned from the secretarial pool to the artillery. A trained stenographer, Fred enlisted at Quebec City in November 1915. He fought in Belgium and France. During the Second World War, he served as a range officer, training new recruits. (Submitted by Julie Hawke, Fred's granddaughter.)

Bottom left: Two men in this photo would not survive the Great War. One would go on to become prime minister of Canada. Taken in late 1916, it shows, from left, Jon Einarsson, Allan MacMillan and John Diefenbaker in England. The men were all articling law students from the 196th (Western Universities) Battalion. Diefenbaker was invalided home in late 1916. MacMillan was killed at Vimy Ridge on April 9, 1917. Einarsson was killed on October 25, 1917, at Passchendaele. Many decades later, Diefenbaker sent this photograph to Jon Einarsson's youngest brother, who was his mailman in Prince Albert, Saskatchewan. (Submitted by Joe Martin, nephew of Jon Einarsson.)

Bottom right: Great War veteran Austin Cook of Zephyr, Ontario, toured the battlefields of France and Belgium in September 1990. He was ninety-three years old at the time. During the trip, two Belgians asked to shake his hand—simply because he was a Canadian veteran and they both wanted to personally thank him for helping save their country from the Germans. (Submitted by Eldred Cook, Austin's daughter.)

"The Fighting Sixth Battery." Annual Reunion. —1937—

Above: Planes fly overhead as the Canadian National Vimy Memorial is unveiled in 1936.

Left: At the end of the war, members of the 4th Platoon, 19th Battalion bought a bottle of fine whisky and pledged to meet each year in reunion in Toronto. They agreed the last two men standing would open the bottle and toast their fallen comrades. Harry George James, left, second row, never got to taste that whisky. He died in 1978 at the age of eighty-eight. (Submitted by Dorothy Witzke, Harry's daughter.)

Top left: In a letter home to his girlfriend, May (later his wife), James Herbert (Herb) Gibson described the horror of seeing the grave of his best friend, Tom Butler. "Perhaps you can imagine my feelings, May, as I looked upon the grass-covered mound and wooden cross," Gibson wrote. "Here, standing in a foreign land, beside the grave of my chum, neighbor and finally comrade in arms, my thoughts flashed back to the quiet peaceful homes from whence we came, on an errand the full consequences of which we did not realize then." Gibson returned to Canada in 1919 after serving with the 75th Battalion. (Submitted by Evelyn Gibson Walters, Herb's daughter.)

Top right: Francis Xavier Cahill was born February 8, 1889, and served with the Divisional Engineers, 11th Field Company. He died November 11, 1916. He has no known grave, and his name is listed on the Canadian National Vimy Memorial. (Submitted by John Kennedy. Francis is the brother of Kennedy's mother-in-law.)

Bottom: William Norman Johnston Campbell enlisted on May 14, 1915, but didn't tell his widow mother, Eleanor, shown here, until the day he was leaving. "He would have been her pride and joy and [she] cannot have been too happy to say goodbye to her only child," said Brenda Spilker, Campbell's granddaughter. He survived the war and later asked that his boots be put on his feet when he died, a request that was carried out in 1978. "This was dutifully done," Spilker said, "so that the old soldier could die the soldier." (Submitted by Brenda Spilker, William's granddaughter.)

Vimy Day, Tuesday, April 9

Dear Comrade:

A small group of exsoldiers are arranging for the Annual Vimy Day Banquet to be held at Dunn's Restaurant, Alliston, on the evening of

TUESDAY, APRIL 9, AT 6.30 p.m.

There has been no program arranged as yet but it is expected that some worth while talent will be secured.

Mainly, it will be a get together and a perpetuation of that memorable event.

We will likely make up our program as we go along and possibly after the meal we may repair to Hunter's Hall.

Mrs. Dunn will be anxious to know how many will be present and it is important that you let us know if you will be present in order that sufficient, yet not too much, may be provided.

Please notify Cecil Scott, E. Skelton or H. Falkner at once if you will be present.

The cost will be 65c per plate. This will barely cover the charges for the meal and a few incidentals which will be explained at the meal table.

Secure your tickets from one of the above named or advise them that you will be there.

MARSHALL DOWNEY, Chairman of Committee.

Left: William Marshall Downey of Alliston, Ontario, enlisted in October 1915. After the war, he chaired a veterans' committee that threw an annual banquet to commemorate those who had fought at Vimy Ridge in 1917. This undated invitation was sent to Downey's fellow Vimy veterans. (Submitted by Roseanne Beyers, Downey's daughter.)

Above: Queen Mary visits nurses and patients at the No. 3 Canadian General Hospital (McGill unit) with Sir A. T. Sloggett, left, and commanding officer of the hospital, Colonel H. S. Birkett, right. Nursing sister Kate McLatchy, behind the queen, was a matron at the hospital and wrote about the visit on July 3, 1917. "The [nurse] sisters said I was very cool and did not show any signs of nervousness. It was a trying ordeal but all said everything went all right." After the war, McLatchy lived in Grand Pré, Nova Scotia, with her sister. (Submitted by Sheila Davenport, Kate's niece.)

Above: Charles Irish of Toronto was drafted in January 1918 and fought with the 54th Battalion. He was wounded but he survived and upon returning to Canada worked as a carpenter in Toronto. In 1923 he married Mary Hemphill. In later years, he told his family that during the Hundred Days Offensive he had lost many friends at Bourlon Wood, and for all his life, he kept a series of glass negatives and photographs depicting the place—including pictures of soldiers' graves. (Submitted by Isabel Irish Wessell, Charles's daughter.)

Top right: Samuel Scott of Caron, Saskatchewan, enlisted in February 1915, joining the 46th Battalion. At the time, the twenty-one-year-old was engaged to Annie Gertrude Rowe. Sadly, Scott was killed in action on September 5, 1916. His body was never recovered, and his name is etched into the Vimy Monument in France. Rowe later married Louis Rutherford and the couple had two children, Helen and Shirley. (Submitted by Shirley Tucker, née Rutherford. Shirley's mother, Annie, was engaged to Samuel.)

Middle right: Charles Trendell of Toronto enlisted in February 1916 and served overseas with the 38th Battalion. He kept a detailed war diary that described, among other things, the Battle of Vimy Ridge. He also served in the Second World War. (Submitted by Ruth Warburton, Charles's daughter.)

Bottom right: Alex Woodworth of Ancaster, Ontario, was killed in action in June 1916. He was twenty-two. Woodworth, a member of the Canadian Mounted Rifles, was wounded three times while manning a machine gun during a battle at Hill 62 in Belgium. In a letter to Woodworth's mother, Private Ellis Scott described how his friend Alex "stopped hundreds of the advancing enemy" before his death: "With the gun boldly mounted on the parapet and his finger pressing the trigger, this brave son of yours and true friend of mine died with a bullet through his heart." Woodworth's name is inscribed on the Menin Gate at Ypres, Belgium. (Submitted by Reg Woodworth, Alex's nephew.)

Top left: William Edmund Sterling, back right, and friends pose for a photo postcard during the Christmas season of 1916. Sterling was likely on leave at the time. In the corner, he's written, "If we don't move soon, I will be an old man." Sterling lived in Westboro, Ontario, at the time of his enlistment in January 1916. He sent this postcard to his cousin, William Sterling Lamb, an elementary school teacher in Quebec City. The pair had gone to school together in Valleyfield, Quebec. (Submitted by M. Anne Sterling, Edmund's granddaughter.)

Top right: John Leonard Carr of Woodstock, Ontario, shortly after enlisting in September 1915. (Submitted by Mike Spence, Leonard's grandson.)

Bottom: Clair Addison Clendening, in the middle of the second row, and fellow members of the 222nd Battalion at Boissevain, Manitoba, on April 12, 1916. Clendening was a gas officer in the Battle of Arras. (Submitted by Ann Bates, née Clendening.)

Top left: In letters home to his sister, Charles Sedore spoke often about his living conditions, but seemed cheerful despite having so little. "We are in a cellar, the only room in the house. We each have a blanket so that is not too bad," Sedore wrote to his sister in October 1916. "They feed us good and give us tobacco cigarettes and rum. We have lots of rats and lice but they are good company." He served as a private in the 19th Battalion and saw front-line action in Belgium and France, including at Passchendaele, Ypres, and Vimy. (Submitted by Evelyn Rose, Charles Sedore's daughter.)

Top middle: Russel Sage Falconer, right, from Sombra Township in Ontario, was a private in the 33rd Battalion. He died in 1962. (Submitted by Caroline Brant, Russel's great-niece.)

Top right: Gilbert Ryckman, right, was a private in the 97th Battalion when he was shot and sent to a hospital in England. Once recovered, he attended a dance where he met his future wife, Mary Louise Judge. Judge became a war bride, returning to Alberta with Ryckman in 1919. (Submitted by Meloney Patterson, Gilbert's granddaughter, and Mary Louise Williams, Gilbert's daughter.)

Left: Dennis Joseph Sampson served as a gunner in the 2nd Canadian Heavy Battery. He spent nineteen months in the trenches and described the shelling in a letter to his niece: "When there is shelling from the big guns it is an awful sight. The high explosive shells strike the earth and throw up huge columns of black smoke, and one has to duck his head quickly, for the splinters of shell fly with a sound like the hiss of Grandma Sampson's angry old gander when Mama and I used to tease him when we were little like you and he would chase us all over the field." (Submitted by Marie Ford, Dennis's great-niece.)

THE SEA BAG

VANCOUVER NAVAL VETERANS ASSOCIATION
VOL. V NUMBER. VII SEPTEMBER 11TH 1991.

Consider the Passing Years...

...do a little mental arithmetic. How many years have passed since 1915? Seventy-six, to be exact. So it's 76 years since Gordon Brett joined the R.C.N. (Official Number: 48V).

That's Gordon in the photo at right, leaning against the conning tower of C.C.1, one of the two subs purchased by then-B. C. Premier Sir Richard McBride and presented to the infant Canadian Navy. The other photo, equally faded and yellowing, shows C.C.1 in company with HMCS NIOBE, another ship on which Gordon served.

The two subs, in company with mother ship HMCS SHEARWATER, were the first to negotiate the Panama Canal under the White Ensign.

Mr. Brett served aboard both subs, as well as HMCS NIOBE, RAINBOW and ARMENTIERS.

He arrived in Halifax on Dec. 7th, 1917 --

the day after the munitions ship MONT BLANC exploded, destroying much of the harbour. Later, while aboard NIOBE on wups in Jamaica, he was so badly injured in an explosion that he spent two years recovering in a hospital in Port Royal.

Back for more in WW II, Mr. Brett served for five years in the RCAF.

This man -- history personified -- will be the VNVA's special guest at Make'n'Mend 1991's Reunion Banquet. Gordon Brett, now 93, of Ashcroft, will be accompanied by his son, Gordon Jr., and daughter in law, Joan, of Walhachin, and his daughter, Marlene Hood, of Delta.

Meet him on September 21st. His kind do not pass this way often. Consider the passing years...

New Members

Five new members were initiated at the Sept. 8th meeting: Brian Prentice, Eric Bearpark, Cy Keighley, Lloyd Cunningham, and Neil McLeod.

Two others were accepted for membership: Mo Sabourin, who lives in Regina, Sask., and Bob Crawshaw, who was unable to attend due to injuries received in an auto accident last week. An eighth recruit, Ted Eggert, was a guest and will be initiated in October. Pictures will be in the October SEA BAG, along with service details. We've neither space nor time, this month.

Sick bay

Pat Webb is being treated in Surrey Memorial. Howard Williams of North Van is at home following cataract surgery. Bill Beaton, in Victoria, is at home after his latest bout under the knife. And Len Olson is taking things very easy out in Coquitlam while await-ing a bed for a needed bypass operation. Keep us posted, Shipmates. Our thoughts are with you.

NEXT REGULAR MEETING: SUNDAY
October ·6

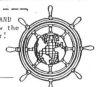

MOVING? O.K., we'll make it easy for you! IF YOU MOVE, CLIP AND MAIL IN THIS SLIP. Make it easy for US! Let us know the effective date of your change, too...and phone number!

OLD ADDRESS   NEW ADDRESS (please print)

PLACE LABEL HERE _____

Postal Code: _____

Above: Gordon Brett was the focus of a special article in this 1991 edition of *The Sea Bag*, a publication for navy veterans. Brett joined the Royal Canadian Navy in January 1915 and served on submarines and aboard the ships HMCS *Niobe*, HMCS *Rainbow*, and HMCS *Armentières*. He was discharged in February 1919 and later lived in British Columbia, where he died in 1993 at the age of ninety-six. (Submitted by Marlene Hood, Gordon's daughter.)

Top right: Leon C. Eckenfelder was one of three partners in St. Anne Ranch Trading Company, which evolved into the town of Trochu, Alberta. He returned to fight for his native France in the First World War, but considered himself Canadian. Postwar, he worked for the Alberta government in Edmonton until his death in 1923. (Submitted by Trochu and District Museum.)

Bottom right: William Alexander Allen was well liked for the short time he served as a lieutenant in the 58th Battalion. "Everybody liked him, but he wasn't the outgoing, bubbly kind of person," says Allen Anderson about his great-uncle. Allen was killed while on his way to his billet in April 1917. (Submitted by Allen Anderson, William's great-nephew.)

Five months after this photo of Freddie Redfern was taken, he died from the Spanish flu. Here, Redfern is fishing on the banks of the Grand River outside of Paris, Ontario, in May 1918, at his uncle's house. He loved fishing and would take pride in his very small catches, which he placed in his mother's rose bushes. His parents were devastated to lose their first son only a few days after he fell ill with what they thought was a common cold. In October 1918 the flu was at its peak in Paris and claimed twenty-six victims there, including Redfern. (Submitted by James Frederick Hopper, Freddie's nephew.)

AM/1.

IMPERIAL WAR GRAVES COMMISSION.

Any further communication on this subject should be addressed to—

"THE SECRETARY,"

and the following number quoted :—

CCM/79534.

82, BAKER STREET,
LONDON, W.1.

11th February 1924.

Madam,

       I am directed to inform you that it has been found necessary to exhume the bodies of the British Soldiers buried inOignies Communal Cemetery German Extension, and to re-inter them in order to secure the reverent maintenance of the graves in perpetuity.   The body of Private T.A.H. Williston   has accordingly been removed and re-buried in Plot 7, Row "J", Grave 13, Cabaret Rouge British Cemetery.

       The new grave has been registered in this office.   The re-burial has been carefully and reverently carried out.

       I am to add the numbering of the grave must for the present be regarded as provisional and liable to alteration.

       I am, Madam,
         Your obedient Servant.

T.J. Blake

for PRINCIPAL ASSISTANT SECRETARY.

Mrs. Williston,
   Bay Side P.O.,
     Northumberland,
       New Brunswick,
         Canada.

Afterword

DEBORAH MORRISON Former President and CEO, Canada's History Society

An estimated one in six Canadian households were affected by the First World War, as more than 13 percent of the male population served during the war. With statistics like those, it is easy to accept the claim that no family in Canada was left untouched. My family was no exception.

On my grandfather's side, the family operated a fire hydrant foundry that, like many other factories, was converted to manufacture military supplies as part of the war effort. On my grandmother's side, my great-great-uncle Richard Kenny enlisted as a doctor early in 1915 and was awarded the Military Cross for his service. He left his wife and two young toddlers at home. Luckily, Uncle Dick returned home, and they had another child before he died quite young in 1945. I don't know very much about him or his family; that branch of the family tree is rather sparse. None of his children ever married and two of the three siblings died before the age of forty-five. I cannot help but wonder now how the Great War affected them, and if their experiences contributed in some way to this branch of our family withering away.

Canada's Great War Album has captured the interest of everyone here at the History Society. Since many of us are too young to have had any direct contact with the Great War generation, this book has restored a vital, personal connection to this seminal moment in our history. It's been a privilege to have been invited to look through family photographs, and to hear more about the men and women who shaped Canada's Great War contribution.

Our mission at Canada's History Society is to promote greater popular interest in Canadian history. Indeed, we've been telling Canada's stories for ninety-four years, through the pages of our flagship magazine, *Canada's History*, and our ten-year-old magazine, *Kayak: Canada's History for Kids*, through books such as *100 Photos That Changed Canada* and *100 Days That Changed Canada*, as well as online at CanadasHistory.ca. We also aim to encourage the efforts of others through the Governor General's History Awards, the Heritage Fairs program, and other history programs that support educational and community networks in Canada.

Increasingly, our projects seek to involve more Canadians directly in the telling of our history. Through projects such as *Canada's Great War Album*, the History Society encourages Canadians to share their stories with a wider history audience.

With this in mind, Canada's History has created an extensive online archive at CanadasHistory.ca/GreatWarAlbum, where readers can explore more of the stories and collections we've gathered for the project, and where they can upload their own family photos and remembrances.

For most Canadians, our country's involvement in the First World War stands out as a particularly defining moment—one that brought us together as a people and shaped us as a nation. We hope this book will help us all to better understand the extent of the war's impact on our country, our society, our families, and ourselves.

In this striking nighttime photograph taken behind Canadian lines at Vimy Ridge, a British naval gun fires in support of the Canadian attack. Approximately 1,000 Allied guns and mortars pounded the ridge prior to the assault, a period the German defenders called the "week of suffering."

O.1321

ACKNOWLEDGEMENTS

Words cannot express the gratitude that Canada's History Society feels towards the hundreds of Canadians who shared their family photos, artifacts, and memories with us throughout this project.

When we issued the call for submissions in late 2012, we hoped for some response but never anticipated the emotional outpouring we received from our readers. We did our best to include as many of your stories and images as possible, but, as with any finite medium, not all could be included. To those whose submissions made our book—and to those whose submissions are not included here but will be featured in our special online collection at CanadasHistory.ca/GreatWarAlbum—we humbly offer our deepest thanks. Your collective determination to share and preserve the stories of the Great War generation will help to ensure that future generations never forget the veterans and their families.

Canada's History is grateful to the historians and authors who contributed chapters to this book. Their poignant, thoughtful essays give us the context and perspective we need to fully appreciate the sacrifices of the Great War generation.

Special thanks to *Canada's History* magazine editors Nelle Oosterom and Phil Koch and Danelle Cloutier and Jessica Knapp for their help in copy-editing *Canada's Great War Album* and to art director James Gillespie for ordering the archival photos in this book.

Thanks as well to the entire team at Canada's History Society who—in addition to their day jobs of producing and promoting both of our magazines, *Canada's History* and *Kayak: Canada's History for Kids*, our website, CanadasHistory.ca, and our amazing educational programs—have also lent their time and expertise to ensure the success of this book: Danielle Chartier, Joanna Dawson, Patricia Gerow, Tanja Hütter, Maria Cristina Laureano, Deborah Morrison, Mary Murphy, Nancy Payne, Joel Ralph, Jen Sguigna, Beverley Tallon, Janet Walker, Melony Ward, Andrew Workman, P. J. Brown, Scott Bullock, Leigh McKenzie, and Nicole Harris, as well as the members of our Board of Directors and Advisory Council.

During the creation of the book, Canada's History Society benefitted from the research and writing services of several talented interns. Special thanks—and congratulations—to Hayley Caldwell, Danelle Cloutier, Steve Ducharme, Elizabeth Fraser, Kristy Hoffman, Jessica Knapp, and Mark Schram.

Canada's History Society extends its thanks to the team at HarperCollins who helped us turn the vision for this book into reality. We are also grateful to Andrew Johnson, Sarah Jane Flynn, and the team at History Television and Shaw Media for helping to bring our veterans' stories to life in a series of Great War television interstitials.

Canada's History received assistance and advice from a host of archives and museums. Our thanks go out to the Canadian Letters and Images Project at Vancouver Island University, the Canadian War Museum, the Canadian Museum of History, Library and Archives Canada, the Laurier Centre for Military Strategic and Disarmament Studies at Wilfrid Laurier University, the Toronto City Archives, the Provincial Archives of Newfoundland and Labrador, the Rooms Museum in St. John's, Calgary's Glenbow Museum, the Edmonton Archives, the Archives of Manitoba, and the Royal Newfoundland Regiment Archival Collection, among others.

Contributors

KRISTINE ALEXANDER is Canada Research Chair in Child and Youth Studies and an assistant professor of history at the University of Lethbridge. She received her PhD from York University in 2010. Her current research focuses on Canadian children, families, and letter-writing during the First World War.

LAURA BRANDON is the author of the award-winning biography *Pegi by Herself, Art or Memorial?*, and the internationally respected *Art and War*, a survey of Western war art. She has curated close to forty exhibitions, including, in 2014, two innovative travelling First World War art exhibitions for the Canadian War Museum.

TIM COOK is the First World War historian at the Canadian War Museum and a former director of Canada's History Society. He has published six books, including the two-volume history of Canadians fighting in the Great War, *At the Sharp End*, which won the 2007 J. W. Dafoe Prize and 2008 Ottawa Book Award, and *Shock Troops*, which won the 2009 Charles Taylor Prize for literary non-fiction. In 2013, he was awarded the Governor General's History Award for Popular Media: The Pierre Berton Award.

SUZANNE EVANS is an Ottawa-based writer and former research fellow at the Canadian War Museum. Her works, including her book, *Mothers of Heroes, Mothers of Martyrs*, focus on Canadian women and war.

J. L. GRANATSTEIN taught history for thirty years, is a Fellow of the Canadian Defence and Foreign Affairs Institute, was director and CEO of the Canadian War Museum, and writes on Canadian history, foreign policy and defence, and politics. Among his publications are *Broken Promises* and *The Greatest Victory*.

CHARLOTTE GRAY is one of Canada's best-known writers, and the author of nine non-fiction bestsellers. Her most recent book is *The Massey Murder*. Her previous books include *Gold Diggers*, *Reluctant Genius*, and *Sisters in the Wilderness*. Charlotte lives in Ottawa, and is former chair of the board of Canada's History Society, a member of the Order of Canada, and a Fellow of the Royal Society of Canada.

NATHAN M. GREENFIELD is the author of *Baptism of Fire*, *The Damned*, *The Forgotten*, and *The Battle of the St. Lawrence*. He has also written a world-history textbook used in Ontario.

ANDREW IAROCCI teaches history at Western University, and was a research fellow at the Canadian War Museum from 2007 to 2010. His publications include *Shoestring Soldiers* and *Vimy Ridge*. He is now working on *Chariots of Mars*, a study of transportation and mechanization in the Canadian and British forces during the First World War. Iarocci was the director for the 2013 Canadian Battlefields Foundation Study Tour in France.

MICHEL LITALIEN is the program manager, Canadian Forces Museums and Historical Collections at the Directorate of History and Heritage of the Department of National Defence, which is mandated to preserve and communicate Canada's military history. He is the author of several books on military history, including *Dans la Tourmente* and *Écrire sa guerre*. He was a member of the Canadian Forces from 1982 to 2009.

PETER MANSBRIDGE is the chief correspondent of CBC News. In more than forty years with the CBC, Mansbridge has provided coverage of the most significant stories in Canada and around the world. He has received thirteen industry awards for broadcast excellence and has been awarded ten honorary degrees from universities across the country. He has also been recognized by leading universities in the United States and the United Kingdom. In 2008, Mansbridge was made an Officer of the Order of Canada. Born in London, England, in 1948, Mansbridge was educated in Ottawa and served in the Royal Canadian Navy in 1966 and 1967.

ERIC McGEER is a teacher and writer living in Toronto. He is the author of *Words of Valediction and Remembrance: Canadian Epitaphs of the Second World War* and is preparing a companion volume on Canadian epitaphs from the Great War.

CHRISTOPHER MOORE is a Toronto-based writer, historian, and blogger, and a long-time columnist on history and historians for *Canada's History* magazine. He has twice won Governor General's Literary Awards, most recently in 2011 for his book *From Then to Now*. His grandfather served in the British Army's artillery corps and participated in the Somme offensive and other campaigns.

DEAN F. OLIVER is the director of research at the Canadian Museum of History and, formerly, the director of research and exhibitions at the Canadian War Museum. In 2010, Queen Beatrix of The Netherlands made him a Knight in the Order of Orange-Nassau. He co-authored *The Oxford Companion to Canadian Military History*, which won the C. P. Stacey Prize.

JOEL RALPH is the director of programs for Canada's History Society and a graduate of the Masters in Public History Program at Western University. As a student at the International Study Centre in England, he explored Canadian battlefields, including Vimy Ridge.

WAYNE RALPH was born in Newfoundland and has had a flying career with the Royal Canadian Air Force and in commercial aviation. His biography, *William Barker VC*, received the McWilliams Medal of the Manitoba Historical Society. His second book, *Aces, Warriors & Wingmen*, is available as an e-book.

JOAN SANGSTER is a specialist in gender and working-class history who teaches in the Department of Gender and Women's Studies at Trent University. She has written articles and monographs on working women, the history of the labour movement and the Left, the criminalization of women and girls, and Aboriginal women and the law. Her most recent book is *Transforming Labour*. She is a Fellow of the Royal Society of Canada.

ROGER SARTY is a professor of history at Wilfrid Laurier University. While at the Department of National Defence from 1981 to 1998, he contributed to the official history of the Royal Canadian Air Force and was a senior author of the new official history of the Royal Canadian Navy. He later moved to the Canadian War Museum, where he headed exhibition development for the new museum building that opened in 2005.

JONATHAN F. VANCE is a professor of history at Western University in London, Ontario, where he holds the J. B. Smallman Chair. His books include *Maple Leaf Empire*, *Unlikely Soldiers*, and *Death So Noble*, which won the Sir John A. Macdonald Prize, the C. P. Stacey Prize, and the Dafoe Book Prize. Vance is a frequent contributor to *Canada's History* magazine.

PHOTO CREDITS

The author would like to thank the following for permission to reproduce images in this book:

B=bottom; BL=bottom left; BM=bottom middle; BR=bottom right; T=top; TL=top left; TM=top middle; TR=top right

IV   Canadian War Museum 19710261-0090

VI   Prince Edward Island Archives and Records Office

X   Goodspeed, D. J., The Armed Forces of Canada, Directorate of History, Canadian Forces Headquarters, Ottawa, 1967

XIBL   Canada Dept. of National Defence/Library and Archives Canada

XIBR   Canada Dept. of National Defence/Library and Archives Canada

XIIT   Canadian War Museum 19800618-014

XIIIBR   Canadian War Museum 20070132-003

XVI   Library and Archives Canada/C-008482

3T   Edmonton Archives EA-159-5

4TL   Canada Dept. of National Defence/Library and Archives Canada

4TR   Library and Archives Canada/C-033428

6TL   Library and Archives Canada/PA-034015

7   Glenbow Archives NA-769-8

10TL   Canada Dept. of National Defence/Library and Archives Canada

14   The Ley and Lois Smith War, Memory and Popular Culture Research Collection, Department of History, Western University

17   Canada Dept. of National Defence/Library and Archives Canada

18   Canada Dept. of National Defence/Library and Archives Canada

20   Canada Dept. of National Defence/Library and Archives Canada

29TL   Library and Archives Canada/C81374

29BL   Archives of Alberta A4837

31   Prince Edward Island Archives and Records Office

32   Canadian War Museum 19920085-540/George Metcalf Archival Collection

34   Canada Dept. of National Defence/Library and Archives Canada

35   Glenbow PO-WW1-2-8

36BR   Canadian Letters and Images Project

36TL   Canadian Letters and Images Project

36TR   Canadian Letters and Images Project

40T   Library and Archives Canada/PA-149311

40B   Canadian Letters and Images Project

42TR   Canadian Letters and Images Project

49   Library and Archives Canada, Acc. No. 1983-28-819

50–51   Canada Dept. of National Defence/Library and Archives Canada

52   Canada Dept. of National Defence/Library and Archives Canada

54   Canada Dept. of National Defence/Library and Archives Canada

63   Canadian War Museum 19890086-534

64TL   Maritime Command Museum, HS030966r03

64TR   Maritime Command Museum, HS030966r28

65B   Russells & Sons/Library and Archives Canada/C-063513

66TL   Maritime Command Museum CN 3266

66TR   Maritime Command Museum CN 3265

66BL   Maritime Command Museum HS 8933

67TL   Queen University Archives 5072-Box68, File 32, No.3-1913-1953

67BR   Maritime Command Museum NS 22624(2)

67TR   *The Imperial Oil Review* 11, no. 9 (September, 1918)

69TL   The Canadian Letters and Images Project

71   The Canadian Letters and Images Project

72   The Canadian Letters and Images Project

75TL   Canada Dept. of National Defence/Library and Archives Canada

75B   Canadian War Museum/Courtesy Tim Cook

76T   Canadian War Museum/Courtesy Tim Cook

76BR   Canada Dept. of National Defence/Library and Archives Canada

76BL   Canada Dept. of National Defence/Library and Archives Canada

77TR   Canada Dept. of National Defence/Library and Archives Canada

79   Canada Dept. of National Defence/Library and Archives Canada

80   The Rooms Provincial Archives Division, B 24-1

81   Canadian War Museum 198 20340-010/George Metcalf Archival Collection

82   The Rooms Provincial Archives Division, A 8-91

82BR   The Royal Newfoundland Regiment Historical Collection

82BL   The Rooms Provincial Archives Division, B 3-10

83   The Royal Newfoundland Regiment Historical Collection

84TL   The Rooms Provincial Archives Division, B 3-12

84TR   The Rooms Provincial Archives Division, VA 37-17.4

85TL The Royal Newfoundland Regiment Historical Collection

85TM Royal Newfoundland Regiment Advisory Council Museum/Ken Forbes-Robertson Collection

85TR The Rooms Provincial Archives Division, A 11-165

86 The Royal Newfoundland Regiment Historical Collection

87T The Rooms Provincial Archives Division, B 5-173

87B The Rooms Provincial Archives Division, NA 11029/R. T. Parsons

89T Canadian War Museum 19700140-077

92 Canadian War Museum 19740049-001

93TL Archives of Ontario/F1374

93TR Library and Archives Canada

94 Library and Archives Canada E010767801

94BL Toronto City Archives, Fonds 1244, item 900

96BL Canadian Letters and Images Project

97BL Canadian War Museum 20020150-001

98T Canadian War Museum 2000105-043

100BL Library and Archives Canada

100BR Library and Archives Canada

102 Toronto City Archives, Fonds 1244, 2278

103 Canadian Letters and Images Project

104 Library and Archives Canada MUSCAN-a-230-8

106 Canadian War Museum 19890086-530

107 Toronto City Archives, Fonds 1244; item 886

108T Toronto City Archives, Fonds 1244, item 872

108B Toronto City Archives, Fonds 1244, item 1389

109 Toronto City Archives, Fonds 1244, item 640

113 Canada Dept. of National Defence/Library and Archives Canada

115T Library and Archives Canada

115B Mark Collin Reid

116 Toronto City Archives, Fonds 1244, item 846

117 Toronto City Archives, Fonds 1244, item 844

118TR Canadian Letters and Images Project

119 Toronto City Archives, Fonds 1244, item 1782

120B Canadian War Museum 20030334-006

121 Toronto City Archives, Fonds 1244, item 852

122TL Canadian War Museum 19890086-885

122BR Canadian War Museum 20030334-020

122TR Canadian War Museum/Hartland-Molson Library Collection VA 454 W6 [1919]

122BL Canadian War Museum 19860157-008

124BR Canadian War Museum 19850374-010

125BL Canadian War Museum 20040015-001

127B Canada Dept. of National Defence/Library and Archives Canada

128 Manitoba Archives, N 10467

131B Canadian War Museum 19810917-001

133 Library and Archives Canada/PA-002552/James Gillespie detail

134T Library and Archives Canada/PA-001378

137B Library and Archives Canada/PA-001201

139 Canada Dept. of National Defence/Library and Archives Canada

141B Library and Archives Canada

143 Musée régimentaire Les Voltigeurs de Québec/Michel Litalien

144L Canadian War Museum 19860131-08/George Metcalf Archival Collection

144T Library and Archives Canada/C-006859

146T Canada Dept. of National Defence/Library and Archives Canada

146B Canadian War Museum 19930003-534/George Metcalf Archival Collection

148BR Canada Dept. of National Defence/Library and Archives Canada

148T Canada Dept. of National Defence/Library and Archives Canada

148BL Canadian War Museum 20020045-1509/George Metcalf Archival Collection

149 Glenbow Archives, Poster-91

150 Library and Archives Canada, Acc. No. 1983-28-726

151 Toronto City Archives, Fonds 1244, item 726

153B C. P. Meredith/Library and Archives Canada/C-068867

155 Canada Dept. of National Defence/Library and Archives Canada

156T Canada Dept. of National Defence/Library and Archives Canada

156B Canadian War Museum 19930012-427/George Metcalf Archival Collection

158 Canada Dept. of National Defence/Library and Archives Canada/PA-000396

160TR Michael Litalien Collection

161TR Michael Litalien Collection

161TL Jonathan F. Vance Collection

162 Le Musée Royale 22e Réegiment/Michael Litalien Collection

163T Michael Litalien Collection

164TL Michael Litalien Collection

164TM Michael Litalien Collection

164TR Michael Litalien Collection

165T Jonathan F. Vance Collection

165BL Jonathan F. Vance Collection

169 Artist Frank Brangwyn, Canadian War Museum 19710261-0978

170BL Canada Dept. of National Defence/Library and Archives Canada

170TR Canada Dept. of National Defence/Library and Archives Canada

171 Canada Dept. of National Defence/Library and Archives Canada

172 The Ley and Lois Smith War, Memory and Popular Culture Research Collection, Department of History, Western University

173 The Ley and Lois Smith War, Memory and Popular Culture Research Collection, Department of History, Western University

174TL The Ley and Lois Smith War, Memory and Popular Culture Research Collection, Department of History, Western University

174TR The Ley and Lois Smith War, Memory and Popular Culture Research Collection, Department of History, Western University

174BL The Ley and Lois Smith War, Memory and Popular Culture Research Collection, Department of History, Western University

175TL The Ley and Lois Smith War, Memory and Popular Culture Research Collection, Department of History, Western University

175TR The Ley and Lois Smith War, Memory and Popular Culture Research Collection, Department of History, Western University

175BR The Ley and Lois Smith War, Memory and Popular Culture Research Collection, Department of History, Western University

176T The Ley and Lois Smith War, Memory and Popular Culture Research Collection, Department of History, Western University

176M The Ley and Lois Smith War, Memory and Popular Culture Research Collection, Department of History, Western University

176B The Ley and Lois Smith War, Memory and Popular Culture Research Collection, Department of History, Western University

177 The Ley and Lois Smith War, Memory and Popular Culture Research Collection, Department of History, Western University

178 The Ley and Lois Smith War, Memory and Popular Culture Research Collection, Department of History, Western University

179R The Ley and Lois Smith War, Memory and Popular Culture Research Collection, Department of History, Western University

179L The Ley and Lois Smith War, Memory and Popular Culture Research Collection, Department of History, Western University

180 W. I. Castle / Canada Dept. of National Defence / Library and Archives Canada / PA-000969

181 Canada Dept. of National Defence / Library and Archives Canada

183TL Eric McGeer

183TR Eric McGeer

186 Artist Colin Gill, Canada War Museum 19880266-003

187 Courtesy Laura Brandon

189 Artist Richard Jack, Beaverbrook Collection of War Art, Canadian War Museum / 19710261-0161

190T Canada Dept. of National Defence / Library and Archives Canada / PA-022988

190B Courtesy Laura Brandon

191 Canadian War Museum 1972008-007

192 Artist Eric Kennington, Canadian War Museum 19710261-0332

193 Artist Douglas W. Culham, Canadian War Museum 19890222-001

194 Artist Adrian Hill, Canadian War Museum 19710261-2447

195 Artist Charles Sims, Canadian War Museum 19710261-0662

196 Canada Dept. of National Defence / Library and Archives Canada

197 Eric McGeer

203T Library and Archives Canada

214 Canada Dept. of National Defence / Library and Archives Canada

All other photographs, as noted, were generously submitted by readers.

FRONT OF JACKET
(left to right, top to bottom)

First row: Queen's University Archives 5072, Box 68, File 32, No. 3-1913-1953; submitted by Jane Dimock-Mahoney; submitted by Judy Modray; Canada Dept. of National Defence / Library and Archives Canada; submitted by Tim Soper; C. P. Meredith / Library and Archives Canada / C-068867

Second row: submitted by Christine Willis; submitted by Scott, Todd, and Miriam Sellick; Canada Dept. of National Defence / Library and Archives Canada; submitted by Frances McColl; submitted by Ruth Borthwick

Third row: submitted by Sherill Zellis; submitted by George Pratt; submitted by Michael Snell; submitted by Lt(N) Robert J. Rogers, UE, RCN (retired); submitted by Barbara Dobson

Fourth row: submitted by Robert Sutherland; submitted by Barbara Dalby; The Canadian Letters and Images Project; The Canadian Letters and Images Project; The Canadian Letters and Images Project

FRONT OF CASE
Canada Dept. of National Defence / Library and Archives Canada

Canada Remembers

Photographs, documents, and personal stories in *Canada's Great War Album*, generously provided by family and friends to Canada's History Society, feature the following individuals:

A full listing of the men and women who gave their lives for Canada in the First World War can be found in the seven Books of Remembrance, housed in the Memorial Chamber in the Peace Tower on Parliament Hill, Ottawa. For more information on the Books of Remembrance, visit: veterans.gc.ca.